D1263447

To Apply The Gospel

To Apply The Gospel

SELECTIONS FROM THE WRITINGS OF HENRY VENN

Edited with an Introduction

by

MAX WARREN

WILLIAM B. EERDMANS PUBLISHING COMPANY
Grand Rapids, Michican

To
the Members
of the
Church Missionary Society
and all who are
"not ashamed of the Gospel"

EDITORIAL FOREWORD

Henry Venn is a legendary figure in Protestant missions. He exerted a powerful influence in shaping the common pattern of the missionary enterprise through the nineteenth century, an influence that continued in a considerable measure right down to the middle of the twentieth century. Venn and his contemporary American counterpart, Rufus Anderson, together gave the Protestant mission throughout the world its general orientation and the principles by which it operated, since Anglo-American agencies predominated and they generally followed Venn and Anderson, although the policies of some of them differed in details. A generation later Gustav Warneck put his stamp on German and Scandinavian overseas missions, but because of the language barrier and other factors he had relatively little effect on Anglo-American theory and practice. He did not present a challenge to the Venn-Anderson tradition. British missions have been diffused throughout the world and established in independent lands and in the colonies of other European powers, but were, quite naturally, especially and intimately involved in the development of the British empire. Consequently Henry Venn played a role in imperial and colonial affairs far more influential and important than Rufus Anderson's part in the foreign affairs of the United States. Venn touched colonial policy at many points, but his participation appears most effective and important with respect to West Africa. Venn is as important for the understanding of the history of West Africa as for the history of Protestant missions. This man should be rescued from status as a "legend" and be known and understood as the theoretician and practical administrator who was the foremost mission statesman of his time and who still has much to say to us regarding the world mission of the church.

The first resource needed for understanding Henry Venn is a collection of his own writings which sets forth his views, convictions, and theories about mission. He never systematized his principles in a book or even a long article, and his small publications, mostly printed for distribution among the members of the Church Missionary Society, are not generally available today outside London. Canon Max Warren, former General Secretary of the Church Missionary Society and widely acknowledged authority on missiology, has with great labor and excellent judgment selected material from Venn's voluminous writings and made this book. The selections have been so arranged and so clarified by introductory sections that Venn's thought can be easily mastered by the reader.

We take pride in the publication of *To Apply the Gospel* in *Christian World Mission Books* in the series comprising anthologies, sourcebooks, and reprints of historical material. A biographical-missiological study of Henry Venn is also being prepared for *Christian World Mission Books* by Canon John V. Taylor, present General Secretary of the Church Missionary Society.

R. PIERCE BEAVER
Editor

TABLE OF CONTENTS

FOREWORD   11

BIOGRAPHICAL DETAILS   13

INTRODUCTION
Henry Venn, The Man, His Thought and His Practice – An Interpretation   15

BIBLIOGRAPHY   35

I. The Coming into Being of a Church   51

II. The Calling and Work of a Missionary   85

III. The Principles and Working of a Missionary Society   105

IV. 4 Voluntary Society and Its Relations with Ecclesiastical Authority   143

V. Towards Ecumenicity   175

VI. The Role of a Missionary Society in Promoting Welfare and Education   183

VII. Missions and Governments   207

INDEX   237

FOREWORD

All who are concerned with the Christian mission must be grateful to the William B. Eerdmans Publishing Company for their bold design of making available a number of volumes that will introduce readers and students to the thinking of great leaders in the Christian missionary enterprise.

An invaluable volume, edited by Dr. Pierce Beaver, on the thinking of Rufus Anderson of the American Board of Commissioners for Foreign Missions has already been published. In more senses than one this is a companion volume, dealing as it does with the thinking of Henry Venn of the Church Missionary Society of London. Both men were born in the same year, 1796. Both occupied key positions in their respective societies during approximately the same years. Both confronted very similar problems as they sought, each with single-eyed devotion, to advance the gospel. To a remarkable degree the judgments of both coincided on many subjects. Yet, although they were in touch through correspondence and had one memorable meeting, it would appear that they were essentially independent thinkers. What is certain is that both were creative in their influence on missionary thinking and practice. For all that they were men of their own time and age, they were so well grounded in fundamental principles that they have still much to say to their successors a hundred years later.

No biography of Henry Venn has been published since the *Memoir* by William Knight, published in 1880 (2nd edition, 1881). There are, of course, innumerable references to him in Stock's great four-volume history of the Church Missionary Society. He is frequently referred to, in passing, in books on missions and in the biographies of missionaries. Not infrequently some of his statements, such as the one about "the euthanasia of the Mission" are quoted out of context and in almost the opposite sense to that which Venn intended. But serious study of his thought there has been none. Interestingly enough there is today an increasing study of the "colonial" era in British history, more particularly of the nineteenth century. Historians, among them a growing number of Africans, are exploring the archives of the missionary

11

societies. As a result Henry Venn is coming to be recognized as the far-seeing statesman that he was. Notable among recent studies is *Christian Missions in Nigeria, 1841-1891 — The Making of a New Elite,* by Professor J. F. A. Ajayi of Ibadan University, Nigeria. Dr. Ajayi provides ample evidence of Venn's creative influence in laying the foundations of some of the independent African nations in what was formerly British West Africa.

The student of Venn's writings is faced with a vast mass of correspondence covering every aspect of the Society's work. The labor of producing a complete bibliography, noting all his letters, as well as printed pamphlets and circulars, has been begun but will not be completed for some years. The bibliography in this volume covers all the printed material so far discovered. The letters quoted can safely be described as typical, although many others still remain to be studied.

One peculiarity of many of the papers and letters should be noted. Often these were signed by Henry Venn and by other Secretaries of the Society. Internal evidence, however, can determine with virtual certainty which were actually written by Venn. His style is quite distinctive. All the material in this volume can with confidence be attributed to Venn himself.

The archives of the Church Missionary Society are, for the most part, in good order. They offer a remarkable field for research, of which an increasing number of students from all over the world are taking advantage.

The preparation of this volume has involved a great deal of painstaking copying of documents, and their arrangement, and the checking of references, for most of which I have depended on the patience and skill of my wife. For the typing and retyping of all the material prepared for the printer I have to thank my secretary, Anne Dickinson. But there is another debt of gratitude I must pay, and that is to the C.M.S. Archivist, Rosemary Keen. Always ready to help, to answer questions, to make suggestions, and to fetch documents, her quiet efficiency makes working at the Archives a pleasure where it might be a drudgery. And in thanking her I do not forget the librarian, Jean Woods, whose more important occupations I have so often interrupted, and though her patience must often have been tried I have never found it exhausted.

The punctuation, spelling, and the use of capital letters in Henry Venn's correspondence have, except in a few instances, been retained as in the original.

M.W.

BIOGRAPHICAL DETAILS

1796   Feb. 10. Born at Clapham, the son of John Venn, Rector of Clapham
Privately educated at home

1812   Living with Professor Farish at Cambridge

1814   Entered Cambridge University as an undergraduate at Queens' College

1818   B.A. degree (19th Wrangler)
Stayed part of the summer with William Wilberforce at Rydal

1819   Elected to a Fellowship at Queens' College, Cambridge

1819   Ordained deacon by the Bishop of Ely

1821   Ordained priest by the Bishop of Norwich

1822-1826   Assistant curate of St. Dunstan's-in-the-West, London

1822   Became a member of the Committee of the Church Missionary
Society

1824   Returned to Cambridge as Tutor at Queens' College

1827   Vicar of Drypool in Yorkshire
Appointed by Charles Simeon on the recommendation of Wilberforce

1829   Married Martha Sykes

1834-1846   Vicar of St. John's Church, Holloway
Rejoined C.M.S. Committee

1838   Serious heart trouble prevented him preaching for eighteen months

1840   Death of his wife

1841   Appointed as Hon. Secretary of the C.M.S.

1846   Resigned the living of St. John's Holloway
Appointed a Prebendary of St. Paul's Cathedral

1868 (Dec.)-1872 (Nov.) Editor of the *Christian Observer*

1872   Resigned from C.M.S.

1873   Jan. 13. Died.

INTRODUCTION

Henry Venn
A Man Called to Apply the Gospel

A modern American social-anthropologist and historian, himself by no means over-sympathetic to the missionary enterprise, Paul Bohanan, has recently gone on record as saying:

> The great debt that Africa owes to missionaries is that in a situation in which the forces of trade, colonial government and the missions themselves were creating cultural havoc, it was only the missions that began to rebuild, and gave them a chance to rebuild. Whatever any individual Westerner may think of the missionary edifice, every African knows that it is to missionaries that they owe the beginning of the African educational system.[1]

In fairness it should be added that in the twentieth century, at any rate, colonial governments also made a significant contribution to the rebuilding of Africa, and the forces of trade helped to shape that rebuilding in many ways that most Africans would recognize today as a positive contribution to the new Africa. That said, what Paul Bohanan has stated is substantially true of the nineteenth century. This volume may, in part, serve as a commentary on that statement, a commentary that may perhaps convince the reader not only that Paul Bohanan is not overstating the case, but that a fair claim can be made for the fact that one of the greatest of all the "re-builders" of Africa was Henry Venn.

Support for such a view is to be found in an unpublished essay that was presented to a postgraduate seminar in the Institute of Commonwealth Studies in London University in 1956. The author was an African, J. F. A. Ajayi, now a professor in Ibadan University and a distinguished historian. He

15

entitled his essay "Henry Venn and the Policy of Development." His opening paragraph ran as follows:

> The history of British Administration in Tropical Africa has revolved largely round what is comprehensively referred to as the "Native Question". There are broadly two things Europeans can do with the "native": they can either attempt to develop − and spoil − him, or try to preserve − and stultify − him. The case for the Preservatives, both the distinguished theorists and the less perceiving practitioners, has been often put, but the Developers who were first in the field have been more often damned as "the missionaries" than studied. I wish to suggest that Henry Venn deserves more notice than this.

The whole essay is a fascinating one for any student of the missionary scene in the nineteenth century. The argument of the essay, which is an outline of Henry Venn's contribution to the development of West Africa, has been more fully expressed in a wider context in Dr. Ajayi's book already referred to in the Foreword. But one further quotation from Dr. Ajayi's essay is relevant here:

> Missionaries who set out to change a people's religion and beliefs are, by definition, reformers and must be regarded as Developers. On the other hand, there were many missionaries who denied that they had any business promoting civilization in other countries. The idea of the Developers was in fact not so much missionary as mid-Victorian, arising out of the influence the Abolitionists exerted upon people's thinking towards Africans, as well as the confidence of the Victorians in their progress and the assurance that others would approximate to their civilization in so far as those others progressed. Henry Venn, however, brought to bear on the pre-conceived idea of his age a fresh vigorous mind reacting on the events and personalities of West Africa, India, Ceylon, etc., whose affairs he followed closely for so long. He accepted the programme of the Abolitionists, as he did those of the Evangelicals; but his ideas were more than just a reflection of the wishes of the Church or the prejudices of his age. His primary work was to evolve a policy for the organization of native churches to fit into the humanitarian programme and to outline what Government and private individuals could do to carry out the rest of the programme.[2]

Who was the man of whom an African historian one hundred years later could write in such terms? What were the inner springs of action that made of Henry Venn such a master of applied Christianity that it can be said of him that he was indeed one of those of whom the prophet speaks: "They shall build the old wastes, they shall raise up the former desolations of many generations" (Isa. 61:4, KJV)? Venn would have recognized the appositeness of the quotation from Isaiah as a fair description of the essence of the missionary task as he was called to undertake it. Who was this Henry Venn?

On another page (p. 13) a calendar is set out presenting the bare facts of his life. But something must be said of his heredity, of that background of family and social conditioning which plays so decisively upon circumstance and so deeply influences a man's response to all the unpredictable eventualities of life.

Henry Venn came of a clerical family with what must surely be a unique record. The family can be traced back to the sixteenth century, if not further. What is on record is that in 1595 William Venn was ordained by the Bishop of Exeter and in 1599 was instituted as Vicar of Otterton in Devon. His son, Richard Venn, was instituted to the same parish in 1625. In 1645 he was dispossessed because of his vigorous convictions about "Church and King." Restored to his parish in 1660, he died in 1662. His son Dennis was ordained in 1670 and died in 1694. Richard Venn, the eldest son of Dennis, was ordained in 1716. It is also recorded of Richard that he was an intimate friend of Henry Temple, the first Lord Palmerston, whose great-grandson was twice Prime Minister and with whom Richard's great-grandson was to have so many dealings, more particularly in regard to Britain's policies in West Africa. Richard's son Henry was ordained in 1747.

Hitherto this family of clergymen was formed in a firmly traditional mold of high churchmanship. Of Richard, ordained in 1716, it is recorded that:

> Though he would not go so far as to assert that salvation was only to be obtained within the pale of the episcopal church, yet he would say that Dissenters had nothing to trust to but the uncovenanted mercy of God.[3]

It is also on record that he was the first clergyman in London to refuse his pulpit to Mr. Whitefield. His son Henry, who was ordained in 1747, was likely to have followed the same tradition. From his father he imbibed a most fierce dislike of all Dissenters. But a great change was to come soon after his ordination. He was a great reader of books, and for a time was profoundly influenced by the writings of William Law, the Non-Juror, best known for his *Serious Call to a Devout and Holy Life*. Venn was eagerly looking forward to a new book by Law, only to be profoundly disconcerted when, in it, he came to a passage,

> wherein Mr. Law seemed to represent the blood of Chirst as of no more avail in procuring our salvation than the excellency of his moral character. "What", he exclaimed, "does he thus degrade the death of Christ, which the Apostles represent as a sacrifice for sins, and to which they ascribe the highest efficacy in procuring our salvation? Then farewell such a guide! Henceforth I will call no man master!"[4]

This, as the author of the *Annals of a Clerical Family* put it, "was the turning point in his religious life, and marked his departure from the old type of Churchmanship which he had inherited, to that now familiar as Evangelicalism."

This spiritual change was not achieved without much inward struggle. But essentially it was the fruit of a deep and continuous study of the Scriptures. It was not a sequel to any contact with others who were experiencing a new birth of evangelical religion. It is perhaps possible to see in the very individuality of his spiritual development a characteristic that he inherited from the vigorous individual character of his forebears, a characteristic that his grandson, the subject of this study, so precisely reproduced.

Between the two Henrys came that gentler but no less devoted character, John Venn, who, as Rector of Clapham, was to be the spiritual guide and friend of that remarkable group of distinguished laymen which included William Wilberforce, Henry Thornton, and Charles Grant, to mention only three. When, on April 12, 1799, the Church Missionary Society was officially formed at a public meeting John Venn was in the Chair. And it was John Venn who later was to draw up a paper entitled "An Account of a Society for Missions to Africa and the East," which laid down the principles and regulations that guided the development of the Society.[5]

Henry Venn, who from 1841 to 1872 was to be the chief Secretary of the Church Missionary Society, was heir to the family tradition that has here been briefly recorded. He possessed the same firmness of character as that which inspired his royalist ancestor. His intense devotion to the Church of England was hardly second even to his Evangelicalism. In a tract that he wrote for the Jubilee of the Society he endeavored, as he said in a letter to the Bishop of Calcutta,

> to state the facts of the case in a fair though plain way. I trust that may not be without benefit both as a guide to the Committee in the maintenance of a large and candid and moderate Churchmanship — and as a fresh incentive to prayer.[6]

There is an eighteenth-century flavor about the words "a large and candid and moderate Churchmanship," which are revealing of one side of Venn's personality. He was essentially a "moderate" man. After his death a contribution to the *Church Missionary Record* spoke of his "tact and skill, almost diplomatic, combined with remarkable wisdom and prudence in conducting public affairs."[7] This essential moderation of mind and temper of soul enabled him to thread his way through the incessant and vociferous appeals of rival enthusiasms, to plot the course of the Society in the face of continuous misrepresentation and suspicion, and to win the respect and confidence of men immersed in politics and business.

But for all his moderation there was a fire burning in his bones. And that fire was an inheritance through his father back to his grandfather whose name he bore. It was the fire of the gospel as a personal possession that had to be shared. There is no understanding of Henry Venn that underestimates his utter dependence upon and his complete commitment to the gospel of the grace of God. How to apply this gospel to himself and how to apply it in his life and how to make others aware of their need for the same application was the guiding star of all his thinking and of all his actions. His consuming passion, like that of St. Paul, that he might "by all means save some," is the key to any serious evaluation of his thinking and of his practical statesmanship.

Henry Venn wrote so voluminously in memoranda, in committee minutes, and above all in correspondence that it is extremely difficult to give a clear picture that does justice to the man. It would be easy to collect a number of isolated passages from his writings that would present the portrait of one who was a mass of unresolved contradictions. He could certainly be tortuous in argument. In defending some cherished principle he could outlawyer the most legally minded of that profession. Yet, for all the truth in such judgments, they present only a caricature of the man. His contemporaries knew that he was a man who could not be trifled with when it came to matters of principle. But they also knew him as a man with a largeness of heart, a sweetness of temper, and a most gentle spirit toward others. Perhaps it would be true to say that the sheer force of his character and his singleness of mind were somewhat intimidating to lesser men. His prodigious energy was startling enough. His capacity for mastering detail without ever losing sight of the main ends to which some policy was directed made the position he occupied in the Society so dominating that his colleagues must have been men of rare spiritual stature if they were never nicely balanced between exasperation and paralysis! Yet his humanity breathes through so many passages in his correspondence that one must believe that he was able to inspire affection even when it was most often mixed with awe. One small token of his care for people and his very special concern for the young is mirrored in a note he sent to a man who was considering missionary service. To him Venn wrote:

> should you be sufficiently prepared to offer yourself to the work and with that in view to visit London allow me to propose that you should make my home at Highgate your headquarters during your stay.[8]

This was no isolated instance. To another potential missionary, who was later to give long and devoted service in India, he wrote:

> I shall most probably leave home on the 14th July for three or four weeks but my house and servants will be at your service as soon as you can make use of them if it suits your convenience.[9]

Venn was given to hospitality. This was one of the ways in which, on true New Testament principles, he applied the gospel.

Complementary to his other qualities there was in Venn a trait that can, not unfairly, be described as God-intoxicated opportunism. Such a man, undisciplined by guiding principles, could be a menace to society. Venn's opportunism was tempered by some of those very limitations which later generations found it hard to understand. One such check on his opportunism was his deeply felt devotion to the church Establishment. While it is true that the mid-nineteenth-century attempts to export the religious Establishment of Britain provided him with many opportunities, which he gladly seized, of prosecuting the missionary task of the Society, yet he watched the extension of the Episcopate overseas with a jealous eye lest, in enthusiasm for that extension, the proper constitutional checks on prelacy were lost to view. Chapter 4 and the long closing extract to Chapter 7 afford ample evidence of how his opportunism was tempered with vigilance.

But his opportunism had plenty of scope outside the ecclesiastical field. Opportunism was in the very air men breathed in the middle of the nineteenth century. It was one of the great ages of exploration, particularly in Africa. It was an age in which the initiative in regard to the industrial revolution that was held by Britain led to an immense commercial expansion and, with the expansion, the extension of British political influence. For Venn, as for so many of his generation, and not least the philanthropists among them, the extension of the British empire was part of the providential ordering of history. While keeping spiritual ends always in view Venn was practically minded enough to see that the West African squadron of the British Navy must not be withdrawn lest more important things than British commerce should suffer loss (see Chapter 7, pp. 208-212). In like fashion he could view the military conquest of the Punjab as a providential means of opening up a new area of India to missionary work. As he wrote in a letter on June 10, 1846.

> We desire to urge the consideration of the great mercy vouchsafed to us in the late victories as a motive to enlarged exertions on behalf of Indian Missions generally.[10]

The idea of the providence of God active in the events of history was one of Venn's cardinal convictions. The sense of a divine overruling of all human affairs was for him a compulsion that he pressed upon the committees of the Society and upon the missionaries, as innumerable memoranda and correspondence make clear. Others could not always follow Venn's interpretation of providential actions. He himself was no slave to consistency in this respect. But the tenacity of his grip on this conviction underlay all his thinking and practice. In this, as in a number of other respects, his missionary methods were contemporary adaptations of those of St. Paul. But they were adaptations. The precise methods of one age cannot serve as detailed models for very different ages.

In one respect, in particular, Venn's God-intoxicated opportunism may have something to say to us one hundred years later. The world that was opening up to the Victorians was a very exciting one, though often viewed by many of them with some alarm. It was in many respects a new age in which industrialization and exploration were opening up new vistas to the human mind. Our own generation might substitute technology and our explorations into space and the human psyche, and so find a parallel with the spring and early summer of the Victorian age. What is much less certain is whether we can match anything like the confidence in the gospel, anything like the single-minded determination to apply it, that inspired Venn and so many of his contemporaries. A certain dedicated opportunism in our missionary endeavors today is perhaps one element necessary to our recovery of a missionary commitment. Here, and by no means only here, Venn "being dead yet speaketh."

Before turning to consider the material here provided from Venn's own writings, one important point calls for notice if we are to see Venn both in context and in perspective. He was, indeed, a man of the mid-Victorian period. A recent historian has described the years 1852-1867 as "The Age of Equipoise."[11] The dictionary defines "equipoise" as a "condition of perfect balance or equilibrium." No doubt, for certain purposes and viewed through a telescope from the nineteen-sixties, some justification for the title might be found. But for those living at the time, and especially for those engaged in the great debates in the national life and in the life of the church, and especially for those concerned with the missionary enterprise, the term is a misnomer. The Crimean War, the Indian Mutiny, British policy in West Africa, the American Civil War, were hardly expressions of equilibrium. Palmerston, who died in 1865 and believed in "gun-boat" diplomacy, was then active, a reliable source of international disturbance. Nobody could credit Palmerston with contributing to equipoise! A letter of Venn's written in 1851 expresses a view of the situation in the Church of England that mirrored the anxieties of many. He wrote:

> The affairs of our Church at home are full of apprehension. The Tractarian movement has created in the minds of the laity a degree of distrust and suspicion towards the clergy which alarms me greatly. At present the great body of the laity stand with the Evangelical clergy. But it is not as formerly. A notion is springing up that the bishops have so failed in their duties that there must be a reconstruction of the Church. I tremble at the sentiments I now hear from many quarters.[12]

Venn's reference to the failure of the bishops as causing alarm is obscure. Most probably he was thinking of the Tractarian reaction to many of the episcopal appointments at this time. Certainly it would have been from that direction that proposals for the "reconstruction of the Church" would have come.

But there can be little doubt as to the real cause of Venn's anxiety. It was not primarily doctrinal. It was not even, at bottom, a fear that Tractarian ideas might prevail. What worried him was that the very foundations of the constitutional position of the Church of England were under attack. Not only his heredity, but his whole reading of history made him a strong upholder of the Church of England as by law established. For him the church Establishment was a safeguard of spiritual liberty, and by spiritual liberty he had in mind liberty for different opinions to be held within the church, and in particular for evangelical opinions. And his concern for evangelical opinions was no narrow, party preoccupation. He was essentially concerned for the freedom of the gospel. No doubt he did too narrowly identify the gospel with an exclusively evangelical interpretation both of its meaning and the way in which to apply it. But it was a passionate conviction about the gospel that dominated his thought and determined his action. This was the source of his anxiety.

For all these reasons Venn would have described the years 1852-1867 as an age of dangerous unrest, not of equipoise. Yet when all this is said, and it is important that due note should be taken of the situation in England as Venn saw it, his main preoccupation was always with the "regions beyond." Constraint was ever upon him to secure for the gospel an extension of its influence. Domestic issues were always subordinated to this grand objective. A man may have strong views on many different subjects. In estimating the significance of these views and their influence upon actions it is important that a right conclusion be reached as to which of the views was dominant and had a controlling influence on practice. For Venn it cannot be disputed that what he was really committed to with every fiber of his being was the proclamation of the gospel to the whole world. This was central. All else was peripheral.

But there is another sense in which Venn was a man of his own age, though in this respect he achieved a distinction shared by few. To a remarkable degree the two great streams of humanitarianism and Evangelicalism found in him a unity of expression hardly to be discovered in such depth in anyone else. William Wilberforce, Lord Shaftesbury, and David Livingstone are the only other names in nineteenth-century Britain that can be considered as offering a comparable synthesis.

In our more cynical age it is not easy to accept as genuine the rhetoric of public speakers who identified Christianity and civilization, and who indubitably identified civilization with the English way of life. But historical judgment demands that we try imaginatively to put ourselves back into the age of the Great Exhibition of 1851, to "feel" what it meant to be members of the world's leading commercial and industrial nation, and to sense the penetrating influence of the revival of religious concern that, in varying degrees, affected all sections of Society.[13] To feel and sense this may be difficult for us living in so different a political and religious climate; but unless we can so exercise our imaginations we will not be able to understand the age we are studying or appreciate that many-sided representative of the age, Henry Venn.

A glimpse of how Venn saw things in this context is illuminated by a letter he wrote to his great friend Daniel Wilson, Bishop of Calcutta.

> ... Since last I wrote I have spent two months in a tour in France and Switzerland and have returned more than ever impressed with the responsibility of England as having immensely larger opportunities and means of evangelizing the world than all the Protestant states of Europe if combined together. I had long thought that Germany would furnish a larger proportion of men. But even in this respect I think the prospect is much in favour of England.[14]

When Venn speaks of the "responsibility of England" and its "opportunities and means of evangelizing the world," he is thinking of the opportunities provided by its commercial and industrial pre-eminence. He shared the vision of Livingstone that Christianity and civilization would march together with the opening of Africa. With Buxton he was ever ready to collaborate in insuring that "the Bible and the plough" went together. What made Venn so important a figure in the contemporary marriage of humanitarianism and Evangelicalism was that through his long tenure of office as chief Secretary of the Church Missionary Society he was able to exercise a direct influence on so many of those who were actually taking the opportunities for evangelizing the world. A continuity of influence from 1841 to 1872 that, while being exercised in Britain itself, was extended to Africa, India, Ceylon, and China, to the Middle East, as well as to Australia, New Zealand, and Canada; and, through correspondence with Rufus Anderson, also to the U.S.A. — such continuity had an importance for the missionary movement that can hardly be exaggerated.

What has so far been attempted, in this Introduction, is no more than a sketch of Venn seen against the background of his time and in some measure in the light of those deep spiritual convictions which shaped his thought. It is to be hoped that this volume will tempt some to a curiosity about this man that will lead them to explore the large range of sources that exist. It is likely that such curiosity, perseveringly indulged, will yield an interpretation of the man, his thought and practice that will complement what is here attempted. Such a complement is much to be desired. In a sense not so very different from what Dr. Ajayi was earlier quoted as saying, "Henry Venn deserves more notice than this! "

Explanation must now be given to justify the order of subjects into which this study of the writings of Henry Venn has been divided. The complexities of his task as chief Secretary of the C.M.S. for thirty-one years make any neat division of his labors impossible. It baffles the imagination to contemplate the variety of matters for which he carried the responsibility.

In all ecclesiastical matters it fell to Venn to take charge of the correspondence. Only rarely was this of a routine nature. Often he was involved in controversial matters of church order that called for patience, courtesy, and firm determination, together with a readiness to find a ground of compromise rather than to force issues to a climax. Notable in this respect are his dealing with the issue of the extension of the Episcopate to India (pp. 163-167); his reasoned defense of the Society's proper independence as against proposals for uniting all the missionary agencies (pp. 132-134); and his insistence on the right of a voluntary Society to seek support in parishes irrespective of whether the incumbent approved of the Society or not (pp. 131-132). In the archives will be found a long correspondence with the Bishop of Madras over the decision of the Society to withdraw its support from a missionary on the ground of his theological views. This difficult issue came to the Archbishop of Canterbury for arbitration. Venn's moderation and capacity for finding a just compromise is well illustrated in this instance, though the material does not lend itself to reproduction in this volume. (See the case of the Rev. W. J. Humphrey, G/ACI/3, 4 and 5.)

But besides correspondence with ecclesiastical authorities Venn had to answer endless queries from supporters, many of whom had zeal unmixed with discretion and untempered by any knowledge of what might be possible in the situation overseas in which they happened to have discovered an interest. He was also intimately concerned with the recruitment of missionaries. Besides all this he had the care of all the churches overseas with which the Society was connected, a care that a man less generously constituted with physical energy and largeness of heart would have found intolerable. The student who reads through the letter books that contain his correspondence with missionaries will be filled with astonishment that any man could have carried so vast a commitment of detail, and could have handled it with so much sympathy and spiritual insight.

And all the while we have to see Venn carrying the main responsibility for drafting the committee minutes and the memoranda upon which the Society's policy was determined. That for the first six years of his secretariat he was at the same time incumbent of a London church and did not neglect his parochial duties, lifts his achievement into the realm of the miraculous. That is not hyperbole but a statement that no student of Venn's writings or reader of his diaries will wish to dispute.

Perhaps the above paragraphs will serve to explain why it has not been easy to determine why many of the extracts quoted should appear in one chapter rather than another. It is of the very nature of the work of a chief Secretary of a missionary society that the range of his correspondence will make any tidy arrangement impossible, a fact that has been the despair of successive generations of filing clerks, and creates insuperable problems for those concerned with the Society's archives. Students of the missionary enterprise have not always understood this aspect of the material which they seek to explore. For this reason alone, a man like Henry Venn deserves the attention of a great many different scholars who, between them, may be able to arrive at a just estimate of the man and his achievement.

Nevertheless the order of the chapters has a sequence that, it may be hoped, Henry Venn would himself have approved. The first chapter is entitled "The Coming into Being of a Church." Venn had very clear ideas about how this could best happen. He saw the church coming into being as a result of the faithful preaching of the gospel. The agent of the preaching was a missionary. The missionary might be a foreigner, and often was, but there was in Venn's thinking no necessity for this. He saw the gospel being preached in a great variety of ways, from any one of which a body of believers might be formed. For their instruction, where a missionary was not available, a lay catechist would be provided. The organization of a native church should according to Venn's thinking grow from the bottom up. The bishop, and Venn always envisaged the due appointment of a bishop, would be the crown of a development and not its foundation.

Because this theory and practice was rejected by other Anglican societies and has been criticized as inconsistent with church principles, some further observations may be appropriate. In practice the evidence would seem to justify the claim that Venn's policy has proved every whit as successful in bringing churches into existence as has been the other method by which a mission was launched with a bishop as its head. The considerable churches of Sierra Leone, Nigeria, Uganda, Kenya, and much of the subcontinent of India/Pakistan, in so far as they have been Anglican, came into being on the principles advocated by Venn. This is not to claim that such churches are in any way better than churches whose founders were bishops, but simply to state that God appears to have honored both methods.

Venn, we must remember, was deeply committed to the goal of a genuinely native church. His great ambition was to see a native church become self-governing under a native bishop. This, so it seemed to him, was much more likely to happen if the church grew naturally with only a very simple organization to begin with than if there was foisted upon it from the start the complex structure that in Venn's time seemed likely to be necessary, once a foreigner was appointed as a bishop.

It remains to be observed that Venn, from the very nature of his strong views about the merits of the ecclesiastical Establishment in England, was reluctant to see bishops appointed abroad without any constitutional checks upon their authority. (See Chapter 4, pp. 163-164.)

Too much, however, can be made of this aspect of Venn's views. He had his vision of what he felt to be the ideal, but he was far too practical a man, and far too deeply convinced of the importance of episcopacy as a principle of order, to follow any line of rigid consistency. In Rupert's Land, in Sierra Leone, and in Hong Kong, he pressed for the appointment of a bishop. In none of these instances could the appointment of a bishop be described as the crown of that development which he felt to be ideal.

The key to all Venn's policy in regard to the native church was his concern that always it should be potentially a church of the country, a church that could become self-governing, self-supporting, and self-extending. This was his guiding light. In pursuit of that end he was never concerned to make a virtue of consistency. He was essentially a pragmatist when it came to applying his principles, but he always had principles that he sought to apply. Chapter 1 contains a number of illustrations of how he saw a native church coming into being. As such it deservedly comes before the reader for a first consideration. Let Venn speak for himself. There is more than a little of his cardinal thinking in the following brief extract that he wrote to the C.M.S. Secretary in Madras in 1860:

> . . . it must ever be borne in mind that Ordained Native Ministers, acting as the agents of a foreign Mission Society are not in their true position in relation to the Native Church. They are in danger of being trained up as exotics, and of becoming unfitted for holding the right position in the Church of their nation to which their first duty attaches them.[15]

There is expressed in that quotation a far-ranging vision. Venn shared to the full the paternalism of his contemporaries. But of him it can surely be said that he was totally devoid of any kind of spiritual imperialism. A native church tied to a Western pattern would be from his point of view a tragedy. By all means allow the missionary to exercise control at the beginning; what Venn was never tired of insisting was that unless the foreigner made himself unnecessary he was frustrating the purpose of God. One hundred years later we are learning in many painful ways to recognize how profoundly true was Venn's vision, to acknowledge sadly how few were the missionaries who shared it.

There is an intriguing incident, which has been preserved in one notice that appeared after his death, which shows Venn's empirical approach to the practical application of his principles. A native merchant from Sierra Leone was one day taking tea with Venn in his London home. The merchant had been telling of his travels when Venn interrupted,

> Now, if you can afford to spend this money on travelling for your pleasure, why don't you contribute something to the support of your own clergy, instead of leaving it all to us in England?

The merchant replied:

> Mr. Venn, treat us like men, and we will behave like men; but so long as you treat us as children, we shall behave like children. Let us manage our own Church affairs, and we shall pay our own clergy.[16]

The hint was followed up and in 1853 a plan for regulating the affairs of the local church was drawn up so that it might be independent of the Missionary Society. That this was no decision unrelated to any principle can be seen from the extract on p. 60, which was one of the earliest statements of Venn's opinion. Not for the first or last time a good idea had failed of immediate application. But it does not call for much imagination to picture Venn's delight at having provoked that merchant's reply. The merchant had put into a sentence what Venn was forever trying to get missionaries to understand.

Nevertheless missionaries were the only instruments Venn possessed for translating his ideas into practice, for applying the gospel as well as preaching it. Chapter 2 begins with four extracts from his voluminous correspondence with missionaries, four extracts that reveal Venn's sense of priorities. No missionary theories, however sound, would achieve anything unless the missionary in his own life demonstrated the gospel and applied it in his relationships. The Apostle Paul saw this as crucial to his own missionary labors. Francis Xavier, as Venn makes clear on p. 180, was forever stressing the paramount necessity for "love of the brethren." Failure at this point has perhaps done more to retard the progress of the gospel than any other factor, including persecution. Venn agonized over his missionaries. But he did not only exhort. He knew also how to advise. Several extracts are printed here showing him as a shrewd advisor, though some of the most interesting extracts will be found in other chapters.

In one particular Venn was always most insistent. If the supporters of the missionary at home were his partners in God's work abroad, no less certainly was the missionary a partner with the supporters at home. As Venn saw it the Society was essentially a partnership in the gospel. This meant in very practical terms that the missionary had a duty to keep the partners at home informed as to how the work abroad was progressing, recording its encouragements and disappointments. Missionaries have not always found this aspect of their responsibilities congenial. As the Letter of Instructions (pp. 98-103) makes clear, Venn knew how to lay this particular burden and privilege on the shoulders of every missionary. And he based his appeal on scriptural principles, as valid today as when Venn quoted them.

Chapter 3 sets before us Venn's understanding of a voluntary missionary society. He was deeply convinced that his views were those upon which the Church Missionary Society had been founded. But it fell to him to give expression to those views which had hitherto been largely unformulated.

During the early years of the Society's existence everything had been tentative. There were few precedents, if any, for what the Society was attempting. For it has to be remembered that it was a voluntary society whose members were members of the established church. But the authorities of that church had not given any official recognition to the Society. Venn was the statesman who saw that if the Society were to influence the church at home as well as to preach the gospel abroad, it was necessary so to state its principles as to win the approval of the church's leaders. This is the very great importance of the document that finds its place in Chapter 4 (pp. 152-158). This masterly statement secured the adhesion to the ranks of the Society of the Archbishop of Canterbury and the Bishop of London. It comes properly in Chapter 4. But behind that document lies the driving conviction of Venn that the Church Missionary Society as a voluntary Society had a life of its own, independent of whether it won the approbation of ecclesiastical authority or not. Its life depended on the fact that it was a voluntary association of persons who not only shared a deep common belief about the gospel, but were also of one mind as to how the gospel was to be applied, and in particular how its good news was to be communicated to the heathen world. Venn, in common with the other members of the Society, gladly recognized the efforts of others organized in other ways who were yet concerned with propagating the gospel. What Venn and his companions insisted upon was their freedom of association, and, within the broad limits of church order, their freedom of action. It fell to Venn to define this freedom and also the limits within which it could be exercised. So well did he do his work that one hundred years later the Society he led is still able to enjoy this freedom of association and to exercise a like freedom of action.

The extracts in this chapter show Venn working out those principles by which the Society has continued to live and work.

Reference may perhaps be made appropriately at this point to a curious misunderstanding of one of Venn's statements to which considerable currency has been given in this century. Writing of his vision of a native church he said:

> Regarding the ultimate object of a Mission, viewed under its ecclesiastical result, to be the settlement of a Native Church under Native Pastors upon a self-supporting system, it should be borne in mind that the progress of a Mission depends upon the training up and the location of Native Pastors; and that, as it has been happily expressed the "*euthanasia* of a Mission" takes place when a missionary, surrounded by well-trained Native congregations under Native Pastors, is able to resign all pastoral work into their hands, and gradually relax his superintendence over the pastors themselves, till it insensibly ceases; and so the Mission passes into a settled Christian community. Then the Missionary and all Missionary agencies should be transferred to the "regions beyond".[17]

Venn saw as wholly desirable the "euthanasia" of a passing phase of the missionary enterprise, the phase in which a foreigner exercised authority over a native church. He is misquoted as meaning the "euthanasia" of the missionary society. Nothing was further from his mind as the last sentence makes clear. Venn believed that there was an abiding value in the principle of a voluntary missionary society whatever the nature of the "regions beyond."

Enough has been said in this Introduction and in the preparatory note to Chapter 4 to make clear what were the principles that guided Venn in his thinking about the relations of the Society with episcopal authority and with the extension of the Episcopate overseas.

Two further matters call for notice. There is a curious illusion which some ecclesiastical historians have conspired to foster that evangelicals in the Church of England take a "low" view of the church. It is commonly assumed by the same writers that to take a "high" view of the church involves taking a "high" view of the Episcopate. Henry Venn as an outspoken evangelical confuted both propositions. Precisely because he was an evangelical he took a "high" view of the church as the "people of God." He refused, in his thinking, to promote the Episcopate above the people. For the Episcopate, in its proper relation to the people of God, Venn had the most profound respect. Few men have done more to promote episcopacy as a form of church government all over the world, but as his writings make clear, it was a constitutional episcopacy with which he was concerned. Of any other kind of episcopacy he took a very "low" view indeed.

The last paragraph is no mere play on words, but is rather a necessary correction to a fashionable misrepresentation of Venn himself and of the evangelical tradition of which he was so distinguished a representative. In this respect, as well as in others, Venn is coming into his own today.

There is, however, in Chapter 4, an omission that would seem to call for notice. Nothing in any part of this volume takes up the remarkable story of Venn's long friendship with Samuel Crowther, his encouragement of him in the inauguration of the mission on the Niger and his influence in securing his consecration as a bishop – the first African to be raised to the Episcopate in modern times. Justice, however, cannot be done to the story in the brief compass that is available here. Extracts would be misleading. Full-scale research is needed into Venn's policy in regard to the mission on the Niger. Heavy mortality among Europeans in previous attempts to explore the Niger certainly pointed to the need for African leadership if a mission was to be attempted. Venn in choosing Crowther chose wisely. But was it as wise to press for his consecration as a bishop? It was not as though such an appointment accorded with Venn's own declared policy for the development of a native church. There was no native church in that area that was remotely within sight of producing its own native ministry, let alone a native bishop.

For many years such African clergy as Crowther had at his disposal were as much foreigners to the region as Crowther himself, or as any white bishop would have been.

Again we must ask why Venn vacillated over the area of Crowther's jurisdiction, why he allowed the disapproval by the missionaries of Crowther's appointment to sway his judgment. There were strong arguments to justify Crowther being appointed as bishop in the Yoruba country, for he was himself a Yoruba. Yet Venn never pressed such an appointment, though it could have had a fair measure of justification on his own principles. Why again did he appear to give such relatively lukewarm support to Crowther once he had taken up his episcopal duties? Surely the magnitude and difficulty of his task, well known to Venn, should have dictated a concentration of resources that was never made. How much of the sad history of Crowther's later years and the unhappy controversy between the local African leadership and the C.M.S. could have been avoided had Venn insisted on giving Crowther greater assistance? These are questions of very great importance. They bear not only on Venn's own record, but on the subsequent history of the church in Nigeria, on the growth of African independent churches, and on the development of African nationalism.[18] Part, but only part, of this research has been undertaken so far! Much remains to be explored if justice is to be done to Crowther as well as to Venn. One guess may be hazarded. Venn never had the opportunity to visit the West African missions. There were no airplanes or facilities for rapid travel in his day. His policies had to be thought out at long range. Others had to apply them. Venn, as a result, often made miscalculations. Evidence may well prove that Crowther was the victim of just such a miscalculation. What is certain is that whatever strictures such evidence may prove to be legitimate in the case of Venn will be likely to enhance Crowther's own reputation as a man of rare spiritual stature and of very great ability. Venn was right in his recognition of these qualities in Crowther. His failure, in so far as it was failure, lay in the very circumstances of his work. What seemed so obvious in Salisbury Square, London, might well appear very obscure in Lagos; perhaps even more so in Calcutta! Venn's vision and his attempts to pursue it were always at hazard. In assessing his achievement this needs to be remembered.

The fifth chapter has for its title "Towards Ecumenicity." The ecumenical movement as we know it today has a range beyond anything that Venn or his contemporaries could have imagined. But they were engaged in laying its foundations. The missionary movement was part of that foundation, as the extracts that form this chapter make clear. Equally important was the movement for united prayer. This is well documented in Rouse and Neill's *History of the Ecumenical Movement*.[19] This movement was becoming a great spiritual force during the years of Venn's secretariat. His letters contain frequent references to the subject. On pages 86 and 87 there are brief illustrations. Their brevity should be interpreted as an indication of something thought to be so obvious as hardly to need argument. Again, the regular meeting of the secretaries of the various missionary societies, at which "prayer was wont to be made," was one of Venn's most cherished activities.

Another, and in some ways an intriguing illustration of Venn's ecumenicity is to be found in an incident in his relationship with the Bible Society, the interdenominational aspect of which found in him an eager supporter. In the eighteen-twenties there was some controversy among supporters of the Bible Society as to whether or not the Apocrypha should be printed with the rest of the Bible, with particular reference to its circulation on the Continent. In 1825, Venn, at that time a Tutor at Queens' College, Cambridge, drew up a lengthy memorandum advocating the inclusion of the Apocrypha.[20] This memorandum was signed by a number of senior members of the University and sent to the Bible Society. Venn's argument was that the Apocrypha ought to be included if only as a means of insuring the circulation of the Scriptures in places where they would not otherwise be allowed to circulate. The document is well worth study as an illustration of Venn's statesmanship. Statesmanship, no less than enthusiasm, has contributed to the growth of an ecumenical spirit. And Venn was nothing if not a statesman.

The division of the material from Venn's writings has been necessarily arbitrary. This is clearly seen in the last two chapters, one dealing with his concern for social welfare, the other showing something of the way in which the working of a missionary society involved frequent and delicate relations with governments. Pious declarations about the separation of church and state commonly obscure the fact that such separation can never be absolute. Venn went very much further and welcomed the relationship. In this again he was a faithful follower of the Apostle Paul! Some explanation of Venn's policy in regard to the state, which for him in practice meant the government of Britain, is called for. The extracts quoted in this volume make clear that for Venn there was never any question of an uncritical subservience to the state. If ever a man was a "protestant" in regard to the state it was Venn. He was never tired of protesting the right understanding by the state of its proper responsibilities. In doing so he was always vigorous in protesting the independence of the church.

His belief in the "nation under God" and therefore of the true "moral personality" of the state was no mere erastianism.[21] Venn's childhood had been spent in Clapham among a group of Christian laymen who were influencing the whole character of public life. William Wilberforce was one of his heroes. But Wilberforce did not stand alone. In the British Parliament he was the leader of a group of men who revolutionized parliamentary manners. Howse, in his important book *Saints in Politics,* says of these men that

The whole group presented to the House of Commons of their day the impressive spectacle of men who put principle before party or profit.

He adds then a quotation from G. O. Trevelyan's *Life of Lord Macaulay* to the effect that these were men

who looked to the facts of the case and not to the wishes of the minister, and who before going into the lobby required to be obliged with a reason instead of with a job.[22]

The forces of redemption at work in British political life in the first half of the nineteenth century go far to explain Venn's political opportunism, and, indeed, his political optimism which found a virtue in the extension of British political influence around the world. The reader who would understand Venn in this context will be well advised to read the volume by Howse that so faithfully and graphically describes that social and political environment in which he felt himself to be so much at home.

These two closing chapters show Venn active in applying the gospel to the way in which men have to live. His "Suggestions for the Improvement of the Social and Intellectual Condition of the Native Africans of Sierra Leone" (pp. 186-189), his letters to Africans like Mr. Johnson (pp. 189-190), and his sharp comments on the neglect by the colonial governments to develop the natural resources of Africa (pp. 194-195) show how practical Venn could be in his applied Christianity. No detail was too small for his attention, whether it was encouraging the growth of cotton, securing opportunities for Africans to be trained in commercial or other skills, or spending some part of his holidays experimenting with aneroid barometers, prismatic compasses, sextants and telescopes, and thereby qualifying himself to encourage missionaries in geographical researches as well as in their specifically missionary labors. The last two extracts in Chapter 6 deal with the importance of reducing African languages to writing. They dramatically illustrate the immense range of vision and practicality that were combined in Venn as in so many of the great Victorians. Crowther was not exaggerating when in regard to Venn's editorial work on orthography he wrote:

you have done more, sir, today for Christianity in Africa than you ever did before; for now we can write down our own languages without fear of being misunderstood.[23]

This study of Henry Venn, and the particular selection made from his writings, have posed a difficult problem in the choice of a general title. *To Apply' the Gospel* has been decided upon for several reasons. Primarily it refers to the closing verses of the twelfth chapter of St. Paul's first letter to the Christians in Corinth. In the teamwork of spreading the gospel St. Paul lists a number of different categories of workers. In this list come "administrators" (v. 28, RSV). Venn was essentially an administrator of missions.

Never a missionary himself, he devoted all his energies to making it possible for the gospel he loved to be communicated all over the world. That was his single aim. But to have described him as administering the gospel would have suggested something impersonal, wholly foreign to his character and manner of working. The Shorter Oxford Dictionary came to the rescue. To "administer," it says, is to "manage as a steward," to "apply." Venn, in very great humility, would have assented to the claim that it was his life's work to "apply the gospel."

Notes

1   Paul Bohanan, *African Outline – A General Introduction* (N.Y.: Doubleday, 1964; Penguin African Library, 1966), p. 216.
2   University of London Library, TD/56/2.
3   John Venn, *Annals of a Clerical Family* (London: Macmillan, 1904), p. 50.
4   *Ibid.*, p. 74.
5   Michael Hennell, *John Venn and the Clapham Sect* (London: Lutterworth, 1958), provides important material for an understanding of Henry Venn's family background and the formative spiritual influences that shaped his career.
6   CI.1/L3, p. 413, Sept. 19, 1848.
7   *C.M.R.*, Feb. 1873.
8   G/ACI/5, p. 69, Dec. 3, 1845.
9   G/ACI/4, pp. 425-426, July 1, 1844.
10 G/ACI/5, pp. 134-135.
11 W. L. Burn, *The Age of Equipoise – 1852-1867* (London: Allen & Unwin, 1964).
12 CI.1/L3, p. 530, April 19, 1851. Letter to the Hon. James Thomason.
13 Ernest Marshall Howse, *Saints in Politics – the "Clapham Sect" and the Growth of Freedom* (Toronto: University of Toronto Press; and London: Allen & Unwin, 1952), provides evidence and documentation for this claim.
14 CI.1/4, p. 405, Oct. 10, 1856. For the grounds of Venn's optimism with regard to the recruiting of missionaries in Britain see Max Warren, *Social History and Christian Mission*, pp. 55-56.
15 G/AZI/1, No. 113, Oct. 2, 1860.
16 *C.M.I.*, April 1873, p. 141.
17 M.P.M., Vol. 3, No. 6, *The Native Pastorate and Organization of Native Churches.* First paper 1851, second paper 1861, third paper 1866.
18 See J. F. A. Ajayi, *op. cit.*, pp. 206-269; E. A. Ayandele, *The Missionary Impact on Modern Nigeria 1842-1914 – A Political and Social Analysis* (London: Longmans, 1966); James Bertin Webster, *The African Churches Among the Yoruba 1888-1922* (Oxford: Clarendon, 1964).
19 Rouse and Neill, *A History of the Ecumenical Movement* (London: S.P.C.K., 1954), pp. 345-349.
20 *Remarks on Propriety of Applying the Funds of the British and Foreign Bible Society to circulating Scriptures and Apocrypha* (1825). B.M. T.1195(2). A second edition appeared in the same year with preface and comments by G. C. Gorham. B.M.1897. b. 38.
21 A. R. Vidler, *The Orb and the Cross* (London: S.P.C.K., 1945); see chapter 4, pp. 48-81, "Is the State a 'Moral Personality'? "

22 Ernest Marshall Howse, *Saints in Politics,* p. 173; G. O. Trevelyan, *Life of Lord Macaulay,* Vol. I, p. 70.
23 *C.M.I.,* April 1873, p. 139. Crowther is referring to *Rules for reducing unwritten languages to alphabetical writing in Roman characters with reference especially to the languages spoken in Africa* (edited by Henry Venn, Oct. 1848). A copy of this pamphlet is in the C.M.S. Library.

BIBLIOGRAPHY

ABBREVIATIONS

A.M.	Africa Miscellaneous
B.M.	British Museum
CI.	Christianity in India
C.M.I.	*Church Missionary Intelligencer*
C.M.P.	Church Missionary Pamphlets
C.M.R.	*Church Missionary Record*
C.M.S.L.	Church Missionary Society Library
C.O.P.	Circulars and Other Papers
M.P.	Miscellaneous Papers
Miss.P.	Missionary Pamphlets
M.P.M.	Missionary Publications Miscellaneous
M.R.	*Missionary Register*
P.	Pamphlets
P.A.M.C.N.Z.	Papers on Africa, Mauritius, China and New Zealand
P.M.E.	Pamphlets Missionary and Ecclesiastical
P.O.M.I.	Pamphlets on Missions, India, 1857
P.I.	Papers on India
P.I.M.	Papers on India Miscellaneous
P.M.I.	Papers Missionary India
P.P.I.	Pamphlets and Papers on India
R.L.	Reports and Letters

C.O.P. – The printed papers under this head are in the C.M.S. Archives. Otherwise than those marked B.M., all these printed sources are available to be studied in the C.M.S. Library at 157 Waterloo Road, London, S.E. 1.

N.B. Footnote references in the text not listed among the above abbreviations refer to the C.M.S. Archives.

WRITINGS BY HENRY VENN

The Missionary Life and Labours of Francis Xavier (Published, London, 1862). C.M.S.L.

A Memoir of his grandfather, the Rev. Henry Venn of Huddersfield, had been prepared but never completed by his son the Rev. John Venn, Rector of Clapham, the father of Henry Venn of the Church Missionary Society.

35

Henry Venn edited this Memoir, made substantial additions to it, and was responsible for its publication. A copy of the 6th edition, dated 1839, and published by John Hatchard & Son, London, is available in the Church Missionary Society Library.

A review of Dr. Rufus Anderson's *Foreign Missions, Their Relations and Claims. C.M.I.,* 1869, pp. 327-335.

A preface to *Memoir of the Rev. John James Weitbrecht, compiled from his Journal and Letters* by his widow (Published, London, 1854). C.M.S.L.

Printed Papers and Circulars Available Only in the British Museum Library

The Asiatic in England by J. Salter. Preface by Henry Venn (1873).
B.M.4192. bb.43

Remarks on propriety of applying the funds of the British and Foreign Bible Society to circulating Scriptures and Apocrypha (1825).
B.M. T.1195(2)

Another edition of above with preface and comments by G. C. Gorham (1825).
B.M.1897. b.38.

Colonial church legislation — A letter to Sir R. H. Inglis (1850).
B.M.4183. b.45

Memorial of the Rev. Thomas Gajetan Ragland (1859).
B.M.4193. bb.32

The responsibilities of the seniors of the university as respecting the salvation of souls. A sermon at Cambridge (1853).
B.M.4903. ccc.36(8)

Academical studies subservient to the edification of the church. A sermon at Cambridge (1828).
B.M.4475. f.54(6)

Sermon after the funeral of Baron Northbrook (1866).
B.M.4906. cc.51(6)

Sermon on the occasion of the death of Mrs. Wilson (1863).
B.M. 4920. d.53(18)

Sermons

A sermon on the occasion of the death of Josiah Pratt, Oct. 20, 1844.
> *1 Peter 4:10-11*
> C.M.P., No. 3
> M.P.M., Vol. VI, No. 8

A sermon on the occasion of the consecration of the Rt. Rev. George Smith to be Bishop of Victoria (Hong Kong), and the Rt. Rev. D. Anderson to be Bishop of Rupert's Land, May 29, 1849.
> *Acts 11:22*
> P.M.E., No. 2

A sermon on the occasion of the consecration of the Hon. and Rt. Rev. John Thomas Pelham to be Bishop of Norwich, June 11, 1857.
> *2 Cor. 4:7*
> P.M.E., No. 5
> M.P.M., Vol. VII, No. 10
>> To which is appended an historical sketch of the revival of evangelical preaching in the Church of England.

A sermon on the occasion of the death of the Rt. Rev. Daniel Wilson, Bishop of Calcutta and Metropolitan of India, Feb. 14, 1858.
> *Acts 20:24*
> P.M.E., No. 6 (pp. 53-65)

Printed Pamphlets

(1) Madras and South India Mission — Papers relative to the education of the natives of India, through the medium of the English language, Sept. 1845.
> C.M.P., No. 7.

(2) The founders of the Church Missionary Society and the first five years.
> C.M.S. Jubilee Pamphlet No. 5, Sept. 1848.
> M.P., Vol. II, No. 4.

(3) Rules for reducing unwritten languages to alphabetical writing in Roman characters with reference especially to the languages spoken in Africa.
> Editor, Henry Venn, Oct. 1848.
> C.M.S. Library.

(4) Letter to the Principal of the Church Missionary Institution (Islington) re marriage regulations, June 11, 1849. Letter is contained in appendix to the report of a sub-committee on marriage regulations.
> M.P., Vol. II, No. 13.

(5) The Missionaries' Children's Home — a statement of intention, Oct. 30, 1849.
> M.P., Vol. I, No. 54.
> C.O.P. (G/AZI/1), No. 49.

(6) Petition of Church Missionary Society to the House of Commons

deprecating diminishing or removal of the West African squadron, March 18, 1850. See duplicate in C.O.P. (G/AZI/1), Nos. 55 and 56.
C.M.I. (1850), pp. 267-269.
M.P., Vol. I, No. 9.

(7) The case of Archdeacon Henry Williams, in reply to a statement by the Rev. E. G. Marsh, Oct. 13, 1851.
P.A.M.C.N.Z., No. 53.

(8) Some account of the efforts made by the African Native Agency Committee to promote the growth of cotton and of other exportable produce by means of native African agency itself. Henry Venn, a member of this committee.

See also p. 29, Oct. 22, 1853. Letter from Henry Venn to Mr. Henry Johnson re agricultural developments in Sierra Leone and the cultivation of new plants.
A.M., Vol. III, Nos. 5 & 10.

(9) Instructions of committee to missionaries proceeding to various stations, June 16, 1854. This contains an important statement on annual letters.
M.P., Vol. II, No. 14.

(10) Circular to the Society's missionaries in India re government plans for education, June 27, 1854.
M.P., Vol. I, No. 27.
C.O.P. (G/AZI/1), No. 80.

(11) Minute re scruples of certain missionaries in Bengal in respect of government grants-in-aid, Dec. 4, 1855.
M.P., Vol. I, No. 25.
C.O.P. (G/AZI/1), No. 89.

(12) Letter to the Bishop of Melbourne on the employment of unpaid lay preachers, Jan. 1, 1856. N.B. Henry Venn was one of the Bishop's commissaries.
P.M.E., No. 3.

(13) Colonial church legislation — an enquiry into the ecclesiastical law of the colonies and dependencies of Great Britain; and into the best means of remedying its defects, 1856.
P.M.E., No. 4.
P.M.I., 1857, No. 15.

(14) Minute on the different departments of business connected with the Secretariat of the Church Missionary Society, July 22, 1856.
M.P., Vol. II, No. 30.

(15) Minute of the committee of the Church Missionary Society on the question of the extension of the Episcopate in India, April 14, 1856; April 13, 1857.
CI., No. 7.
C.M.I. (1858), pp. 158-167, 169-177, 177-181, 194-207.
C.O.P. (G/AZI/1), No. 92.
P.I., Vol. II, No. 1.
P.O.M.I., No. 3.
R.L., Vol. II, No. 13.

(16)Memorial to the Queen on the India crisis, Dec. 1857, reported at a Special General Meeting of the Society, Jan. 12, 1858. See No. 2, pp. 8-17.
P.I., Vol. I, Nos. 1 & 2.
P.O.M.I., No. 5.

(17)Letter to a friend on the views of the Committee of the Church Missionary Society on Extension of the Episcopate in India, April, 12, 1858.
M.P., Vol. I, No. 23.
C.O.P., No. 98.

(18)Deputation to Lord Stanley, President of the Board of Control, Aug. 7, 1858. See pp. 16-18 for remarks by Henry Venn (extract from the "Record," Aug. 9, 1858).
P.P.I., Vol. II, No. 4.

(19)Valedictory dismissal of missionaries to India, Oct. 14, 1859.
M.P., Vol. II, No. 11.

(20)A plea for an open and unfettered Bible in the government schools of India, 1859.
P.P.I., Vol. II, No. 11.

(21)Letter to Mr. Royston of the Madras Corresponding Committee about new plans for the organization of the mission in relation to the local church, Oct. 2, 1860.
M.P., Vol. I, No. 22.
C.O.P. (G/AZI/1), No. 113.
See subsequent letter to Mr. Royston on the same subject, Jan. 1867.
P.I., Vol. II, No. 42.

(22)Address to Colonel Sir Herbert B. Edwardes, K.C.B., Commissioner of the Cis-Sutlej States, Punjab, on the occasion of his return to India, with some notice of his reply, Jan. 3, 1862.
M.P.M., Vol. III, No. 1.

(23)West African Native Bishopric Fund, 1864.
M.P., Vol. I, Nos. 3 & 4.

(24)Retrospect and prospect of the operations of the Church Missionary Society, Jan. 10, 1865.
M.P., Vol. I, No. 12.
M.P.M., Vol. II, No. 9.

(25)Greetings to the Basle Missionary Society on the occasion of its Jubilee, May 8, 1865.
M.P., Vol. I, No. 47.
C.O.P. (G/AZI/1), No. 143.

(26)Obituary of the Rev. Henry Venn Elliott reprinted from the *Christian Observer*, April 1865. This contains a vigorous statement of evangelical principles.
M.P.M., Vol. VII, No. 9.

(27)West African colonies — Notices of the British colonies on the west coast of Africa. Publ., London, 1865.
A.M., Vol. III, No. 7.

(28) Letter to the Secretary of State for the Colonies on the adoption by the Synod of Ceylon of a new form of clerical declaration and subscription, Jan. 18, 1866.
R.L., Vol. II, No. 36.
C.O.P. (G/AZI/2), No. 345.

(29) Address to the Sierra Leone Church Missionary Association, Oct. 8, 1866.
P.A.M.C.N.Z., No. 16.
C.O.P. (G/AZI/1), No. 148.

(30) The native pastorate and organization of native churches.
First paper 1851 ⎫
Second paper 1861 ⎬ in one pamphlet
Third paper 1866 ⎭
M.P.M., Vol. III, No. 6.
P.I., Vol. II, No. 37.
P.I.M., Vol. IV, No. 11.

For another interpretation of this subject see *C.M.I.* (1862), pp. 121-134.

(31) Minute on the New Zealand Mission, No. 20, 1866.
P.A.M.C.N.Z., No. 50.
C.O.P. (G/AZI/1), No. 150.

(32) Letter to the Bishop of Kingston (Jamaica) on the state of the Negroes in Jamaica, Jan. 1867.
M.P., Vol. II, No. 23.
C.O.P. (G/AZI/1), No. 152.

(33) Statement, explanation and appeal re the financial position of the society, Aug. 12, 1867.
M.P., Vol. I, No. 53.
C.O.P. (G/AZI/1), No. 155.

(34) Memorial to Secretary of State for India re slavery in East Africa, Feb. 16, 1869.
R.L., Vol. II, No. 5.
C.O.P. (G/AZI/1), No. 158.

(35) Minute of the Society on the projected appointment of a missionary bishop to Madagascar, Dec. 12, 1870.
M.P., Vol. I, No. 50.
M.P.M., Vol. III, No. 10.
C.O.P. (G/AZI/1), No. 163.

(36) Correspondence respecting the Madagascar bishopric, Dec. 12, 1870; Jan. 7, 1871.
M.P.M., Vol. III, No. 9.
C.O.P. (G/AZI/2), No. 237.

(37) Memorandum to the Bishop of London re Madagascar bishopric, Feb. 10, 1871.
M.P., Vol. I, No. 51.

(38) The Church Missionary Society and the Madagascar bishopric. Letter to friends of the Society, March 21, 1871.
M.P.M., Vol. III, No. 11. *C.M.I.* (1871).

(39) Correspondence re consecration of churches in India and the liability of a missionary society for their upkeep. Letters to the Bishop of Calcutta, Jan. 10, 1872; July 19, 1872.
R.L., Vol. II, No. 26.
C.O.P. (G/AZI/2), No. 373.

(40) "Providential Antecedents of the Sierra Leone Mission," reprinted from the *Christian Observer*, No. 419, Nov. 1872. This was probably the last contribution of Henry Venn.
P., Vol. II, No. 19.

Note: "Minute of the Committee of the Church Missionary Society on the present state and future prospects of China," April 13, 1857
P.O.M.I., 2.

and:

"A Memorandum for the use of a Deputation of the Church Missionary Society appointed to wait upon Viscount Palmerston, to solicit protection for liberated Africans, being British Subjects, who have emigrated from Sierra Leone to Badagry and Abbeokuta, and for the European Missionaries who reside at those places." Undated.
P.O.M.I., 4.

These documents were almost certainly drafted by Henry Venn, though unsigned.

Circulars and Other Papers

To Be Found in Archives G/AZI/1

No. 27, Oct. 5, 1841
> To secretaries of local associations on preserving the independence of the Church Missionary Society. See *M.R.*, Oct. 1841, pp. 441-443. This circular was reissued in Nov. 1849 with a note to say that the Committee, after eight years' experience, endorsed the original circular.

No. 30, Dec. 13, 1841
> Statement on the Society's financial position. Important statement on the need to encourage self-support by the local church. See *C.M.R.*, Vol. xiii, pp. 18-21.

No. 34, Sept. 29, 1842
> Fourah Bay Institution Buildings' Fund. A full description of the Society's policy re higher education. See *C.M.R.*, Vol. xiii, pp. 243-245, and *M.R.* (1842), pp. 441-443.

No. 35, Jan. 27, 1843
> Regulations for the Church Missionary Society's institution at Islington.

No. 36, Jan. 10, 1843
>Letter to local association Secretaries re the Society's financial position. See *M.R.* (1843), pp. 45-47.

No. 39, Nov. 14, 1844
>Correspondence with Archdeacon Samuel Wilberforce re statements made by the Archdeacon to the detriment of the Society. This circular contains the Archdeacon's apology and the withdrawal of certain insinuations.

No. 41, Sept. 5, 1845
>Appeal for subscriptions towards endowment of the bishopric of Prince Rupert's Land.

No. 43, Feb. 9, 1846
>Letter to local association Secretaries urging greater support for the Society.

No. 45, undated
>Letter to local association Secretaries re the Society's Jubilee.

No. 46, Nov. 2, 1848
>Letter addressed to native Christians in areas where the Society was at work conveying message from the Jubilee Meeting of the Society.

No. 49, Oct. 30, 1849
>The Missionaries' Children's Home — a declaration of intention.

No. 50, Jan. 1850
>Statement re comparative economy in administering the affairs of the Church Missionary Society and the Wesleyan Methodist Missionary Society. See G/AZI/2, No. 293 for duplicate.

Nos. 55 and 56, 1850
>A petition of the Church Missionary Society to the House of Commons deprecating the diminishing or removal of the squadron from the west coast of Africa. See *C.M.I.* (1850).

No. 58, April 22, 1850
>Comment by Henry Venn on an appeal by the Bishop of Prince Rupert's Land for help.

No. 59, Nov. 11, 1850
>Minute of Committee on report from a local association as to unfriendly remarks about C.M.S. by S.P.G. See G/AZI/2, No. 279 for duplicate.

No. 61, Jan. 18, 1851
Correspondence re the organization of the Society's affairs in Ireland.

No. 67, Aug. 24, 1852
Letter to the Bishop of Hong Kong re the claim of the American Episcopalian Bishop to exercise episcopal authority over C.M.S. missionaries.

No. 68, Sept. 1852
Official statement re Home for Missionaries' Children.

No. 69, Jan. 1853
An appeal by the Committee to patrons of livings made on behalf of returned missionaries.

No. 70, undated (1853 or 1854)
Suggestions for the improvement of the social and intellectual condition of the native Africans at Sierra Leone.

No. 71, undated (1853 or 1854)
Minute upon the position of native ministers in a mission, and upon the distinction between a mission and the pastoral charge of native converts.

No. 79, June 1854
Circular to missionaries re the finances of the Society, urging more local self-support.

No. 80, June 27, 1854
To missionaries in India urging co-operation with government in likely developments in education. See G/AZI/2, No. 312 for duplicate.

No. 88, Nov. 20, 1855
To missionaries generally re the finances of the Society, urging more local self-support.

No. 89, Dec. 4, 1855
Minute adopted by the Committee seeking to allay anxieties of some missionaries in Bengal as to receiving government grants-in-aid for education. See G/AZI/2, No. 319 for duplicate.

No. 91, April 14, 1856
Minute of Committee on the Society's financial situation.

No. 92, April 14, 1856
Memorial of the Church Missionary Society upon the extension of the Episcopate in India.

No. 95, Dec. 1, 1857
Special appeal for India following the Mutiny. See P.I., Vol. I, No. 2.

No. 97, April 14, 1856
Minute on the uniting of missionary societies. Earlier arguments re-stated and earlier decisions confirmed.

No. 98, April 12, 1858
Letter to a friend re C.M.S. memorial on extension of Episcopate in India. See G/AZI/2, No. 318 for duplicate.

No. 101, July 1858
Ecclesiastical relations of the Church Missionary Society. This document includes Appendix II to the *39th Annual Report,* and notes that the Archbishop of Canterbury and the Bishop of London on approving the statement therein contained became "members of the Society." See P.I., Col. II, No. 2.

No. 108, Feb. 23, 1859
Special appeal for laborers. This document was widely circulated and contains a definition of the qualities looked for in a missionary candidate. See G/AZI/2, No. 283 for duplicate.

No. 109, May 8, 1854
Special appeal for the enlargement of the Society's resources.

No. 113, Oct. 2, 1860
A letter to Mr. Royston, Secretary of the Madras Corresponding Committee, about new plans for the organization of the mission in relation to the local church.

No. 116, July 9, 1861
Minute on the organization of native churches. This is one of the most important statements of policy drawn up by Henry Venn.

No. 130, Mar. 17, 1863
Memorial to the Secretary of State for the Colonies protesting against the policies of Governor Freeman at Lagos.

No. 131, Oct. 12, 1863
Memorial to the Secretary of State for India about the small share being received by the missions from the government's scheme for grants-in-aid for education. See G/AZI/2, No. 351 for duplicate.

No. 132, June 1865
Letter to Secretary of Corresponding Committee in Calcutta on the "Re-marriage of Converts Bill." This is an interesting discussion of the scriptural grounds for the remarriage of the Christian partner, if a previous marriage according to Hindu or Muslim rites had been dissolved. See P.I., Vol. II, No. 40.

No. 134, Mar. 3, 1864
A reply to an article in the *Saturday Review* which had made damaging comments on the Society's financial integrity.

No. 137, July 11, 1864
An appeal from the Committee for increased income. See *C.M.R.*, Vol. ix (new series), 1864.

No. 138, undated
West African Bishopric Fund. An appeal for a discretionary fund for Bishop Crowther.

No. 143, May 8, 1865
Greetings to the Basle Missionary Society on the occasion of its Jubilee.

No. 145, July 10, 1865
Minute on organization of the native church in South India.

No. 148, Oct. 8, 1866
An address to the Sierra Leone Church Missionary Association on the occasion of the Jubilee.

No. 150, Nov. 20, 1866
Minute on the New Zealand Mission raising the question of the withdrawal of the Society, its task being completed with the full establishment of a local church.

No. 151, Jan. 1867
Letter to the Corresponding Committee in Madras stressing the urgency of devolution of authority from the missionaries to the local church.

No. 152, Jan. 1867
Letter to Bishop of Kingston (Jamaica) on the state of the Negroes in Jamaica. An important illustration of Henry Venn's views on missionary policy.

No. 155, Oct. 1867 (Aug. 12, 1867)
Statement on Society's financial position.

No. 158, Feb. 16, 1869
    Memorial to the Secretary of State for India on the slave trade in
    East Africa.

No. 161, June 9, 1870
    Letter to friends of the Society about the Society's financial
    situation. See *C.M.R.*, Vol. xv (new series), June 1870.

No. 163, Dec. 12, 1870
    Minute of the Society on a projected appointment of a missionary
    bishop to Madagascar.

No. 164, Mar. 21, 1871 (see also Nos. 234, 235, 237)
    A reply to criticism of the Minute on Madagascar. This contains an
    important statement on the comity arrangements made between
    missionary societies. See *C.M.I.* (1871).

No. 165, Oct. 1871
    Letter to Archbishop of York re proposal to establish a Central
    Board of Missions.

No. 168, July 8, 1872
    Letter to friends of the Society proposing Dec. 20, 1872, as a day of
    special prayer for more offers for missionary service. See *C.M.I.*
    (1872); *C.M.R.* , Vol. II (second new series), July 1872.

No. 171, Dec. 4, 1866
    Memorandum to Secretary of State for Foreign Affairs re a bishop
    for China.

To Be Found in Archives G/AZI/2

No. 234, 1871
    The Church Missionary Society and the Madagascar bishopric.

No. 235, 1871
    The Madagascar bishopric.

No. 237, Dec. 21, 1870 - Jan. 9, 1871
    Correspondence re Madagascar bishopric.

No. 242, June 1870
    Financial appeal.

No. 255, Jan. 12, 1870
    Minute on polygamy.

No. 257, Sept. 1845
   Papers relative to the education of the natives of India.

No. 260, June 16, 1865
   Letters of instruction to missionaries.

No. 306, Nov. 10, 1869
   Memorandum on the best means of providing episcopal superintendence for a native Christian church beyond Her Majesty's dominions.

No. 345, Jan. 18, 1866
   Memorandum to Secretary of State for the Colonies on the adoption
   by the Synod of Ceylon of a new form of clerical declaration and
   subscription.

No. 373, 1875
   A compilation of documents up to 1875 re consecration of churches
   in India, including a letter from Henry Venn to the Bishop of
   Calcutta, Jan. 10, 1872.

Material to Be Found in Official Reports of the Society, and Not
Otherwise Noted

Missionary Register

Jan. 1842, pp. 48-52.	Statement on financial position of the Society
Sept. 1842, pp. 404-408.	Appeal for funds
Jan. 1845, pp. 53-58.	The origination of the Church Missionary So-ciety
Mar. 1851, pp. 156-159.	Special address to the supporters of the Society on the subject of papal aggression. *C.M.R.,* Vol. xxii, pp. 65-68.

PRINTED MATERIAL ABOUT HENRY VENN

Annals of a Clerical Family, being some account of the family and descendants of William Venn, Vicar of Otterton, Devon, 1600-1621.

by John Venn, F.R.S., F.S.A., Fellow and President of Gonville and Caius College, Cambridge (Publ., London: Macmillan & Co., 1904)

For Henry Venn see pp. 148-174.

Memoir of the Rev. H. Venn — The Missionary Secretariat of Henry Venn, B.D., Prebendary of St. Paul's and Honorary Secretary of the Church Missionary Society.

by William Knight

With an Introductory Biographical Chapter and a Notice of West African Commerce, by his sons John Venn, Senior Fellow of Gonville and Caius College, Cambridge, and Henry Venn, Rector of Clare Portion, Tiverton (Publ., London: Longmans, Green & Co., 1880)

2nd Edition with Portrait and Appendix (Pub. 1881)

N.B. The Appendix contains twelve important documents by Henry Venn:

> Founders of the Church Missionary Society and the First Five Years, 1799-1804.
> Retrospective Address, March 7, 1862.
> Minutes on the Organization of Native Churches.
> Episcopacy in India and Madagascar.
> Politics and Missions.
> Missions in Their Variety.
> Some Eminent Missionaries.
> Independent Action of the Church Missionary Society.
> The Proper Interpretation of the Baptismal Service.
> Commission on Clerical Subscription.
> Ritual Commission.
> Notice on African Commerce.

In Memoriam notice of Henry Venn published in the *Church Missionary Intelligencer*, April 1873, pp. 129-147.

This is probably the best contemporary appraisal of Henry Venn.

In Memoriam notice of Henry Venn published in the *Church Missionary Record* for February 1873, pp. 57-61.

Memorial to the Rev. Henry Venn, B.D., late Prebendary of St. Paul's and for thirty-one years Honorary Secretary of the Church Missionary Society.

The Memorial took the form of a "Henry Venn Native Church Fund."

"To render the Native Churches as speedily as possible self-supporting, self-governing and self-extending was the aim which, in words of his own choosing, Mr. Venn was wont to set before the Committee and himself." P.M., Vol. II, No. 2, Dec. 1, 1873.

A Review of *The Missionary Life and Labours of Francis Xavier* published in the *Weekly Register* of Nov. 8 and 15, 1862. B.M. 4826 bb.35(7).

This intemperately critical review is to be noted chiefly as an example of the *odium theologicum* of the period, an odium of which Henry Venn himself cannot be wholly exonerated.

NOTE

The Archives of the Church Missionary Society contain many hundreds of letters by Henry Venn to correspondents in Britain and abroad. These are to be found in Letter Books arranged for the most part according to the missions concerned, or in Letter Books dealing with the affairs of the Society in Britain.

Henry Venn was an occasional contributor to the *Christian Observer* and from December 1868 till November 1872 acted as Editor.

There are also large numbers of letters addressed to Henry Venn which are in separate Letter Books.

In 1958 Dr. J. A. Venn, President of Queens' College, Cambridge, presented to the Church Missionary Society a large number of documents relating to the Venn family. These include a substantial number of diaries and journals, account books and notes by Henry Venn, together with a number of letters addressed to him. These have all been catalogued and are to be found in the C.M.S. Archives.

Chapter I

THE COMING INTO BEING OF A CHURCH

INTRODUCTION

Henry Venn of the Church Missionary Society and Rufus Anderson of the American Board of Commissioners for Foreign Missions were contemporaries. Fundamentally they both wrestled with the same problems as both sought to "Advance the Gospel."[1] They corresponded with each other. Yet despite the fact that both men arrived at the same formula as indicative of their ambition not only to advance the gospel but to build the church in every land as a self-governing, self-supporting and self-extending unit of the church universal, it would appear that their conviction as to this goal came to each independently. Both were men of wide vision. Circumstances led both to certain broadly similar conclusions.

The following passages from the writings of Henry Venn begin with an article that he wrote for *The Christian Observer* a few months before his death. Its theme, expressed in its title, is the overruling providence of God. This theme appears continually in his letters and published papers. This certainty that the mission of the church was of divine provenance, and wholly dependent upon the working out of the divine purpose, was for Venn a cardinal principle of all his thinking. He was never hesitant about discovering and trying to apply the divine overruling even in the details of everyday life. Such was the deep conviction that determined the tone of all his activities and inspired all his writings.

Precisely because Venn discovered a divine order in the commonplace he was the most practical of men. To "apply" the gospel involved practical measures. It also involved clearsightedness about the human instruments who

51

were to effect those measures. Venn never saw Africans or Asians or European missionaries through rose-colored spectacles. This explains not a little of that paternalism which so clearly emerges in his writings. But it was never a spiritual imperialism that aimed to perpetuate its trusteeship. To help native churches to become self-supporting, self-governing and self-extending was his supreme aim, believing that in this way the gospel would be best propagated.

This chapter ends with Venn's attempt to give guidance on the subject of church discipline in regard to the baptism of polygamists. This is a subject that has divided Christian opinion since Venn's time and still divides it. Venn argued from first principles and these he derived from the Bible. Many would still endorse the argument he developed. Others would want to insist that there are practical problems involved in the social organization of some cultures of which Venn was wholly ignorant. The debate continues.

THE BEGINNING OF A MISSION[2]

It is both interesting and profitable to record the antecedent and concurring providential circumstances which accompany any great enterprise which aims at the glory of God or the benefit of man. There is no surer proof of the good hand of the Lord being in any work than when it is accomplished by the union of various advantages fitted and prepared apart but in due time brought together, and found to be adapted to the accomplishment of a common object, though that object was not primarily in view.

The history of the Church Missionary Society affords many illustrations of this remark, one of which we propose to notice on the present occasion — the selection of Sierra Leone as its first Mission. At that time the place was known only as a part of the pestilential coast of West Africa, and the focus of the cruel slave trade. Now, indeed, the colony contains its native Christian population of 30,000 souls, with its territorial division into parishes having each its native pastor, with its numerous schools, and its seminaries for higher education, both male and female. When Dr. Livingstone visited the colony in 1858, he bore this testimony to its state and progress, addressed not to the Society, but in a letter to Sir R. Murchison, dated March 30, 1858:

> We were at Sierra Leone on Sunday last, and saw an Ordination Service by Bishop Bowen, an energetic, good man. He was a missionary formerly, and a better man for a bishop could not have been. The Sunday is wonderfully observed; as well, I think, as anywhere in Scotland. Looking at the change effected among the people, and comparing the masses here with what we find in parts along the coast

where the benign influence of Christianity has had no effect, the man even who has no nonsense about him would be obliged to confess that England had done some good by her philanthropy, − aye, and an amount of good which will look grand in the eyes of posterity.

The influence of Sierra Leone is greatly extending throughout the 1500 miles which measure the West Coast of Africa, along the whole of which traders and immigrants from Sierra Leone are found, and especially in the vigorous branch missions at Lagos and Abbeokuta and on the banks of the Niger, up to the confluence of two great rivers of Central Africa; and now also Dr. Livingstone pleads for the formation of a colony upon the coast of East Africa, from among the Native Christians on the West Coast, as affording the best hope of introducing civilisation and Christianity into those still benighted regions.

Yet if we compare the various fields of the Church Missionary Society's labours one with another, with respect to their attractiveness in the eyes of the candidates for missionary employment, Sierra Leone unquestionably stands in the lowest place. India and China have more powerful charms. North West America and New Zealand have also theirs. But the name of West Africa creates a shudder, from its supposed unhealthiness and semi-barbarous population. It has been said with truth, that unless Sierra Leone had been taken up by the Society as its first mission, it would have been altogether passed by through the strength of the interest connected with other fields of labour. By commencing with West Africa, the Society set up the highest standard of self-devotion for its missionaries. Every candidate is required to pledge himself to go to any part of the world to which the Committee may send him, and some are sent to West Africa. In the second Report presented by the Society, it is stated as a reason of the failure of English candidates for missionary employment, that the unhealthiness of West Africa was generally alleged as an insurmountable obstacle. Yet happily the Committee determined to persevere in their call for missionaries. They found their first willing labourers among the German Protestants; and to the honour of that country Germans opened the way; though, after a time, the English missionaries were found in sufficient numbers for the work of that mission. We proceed, therefore, to notice some providential circumstances which led to the selection of Sierra Leone as the Society's first missionary station.

1. Thirty-five years before the institution of the Society, the indignant feelings of an English gentleman were aroused by the sight of a wounded negro slave in the streets of London, who had been ill-treated by his master. Granville Sharp was that gentleman, occupying a subordinate situation in the Ordnance Office, but a man of chivalrous philanthropy and dauntless moral courage. He succeeded in rescuing the slave from his master. Seven years later, he took up the cause of another slave, which was brought before Lord Chief

Justice Mansfield for trial, who established by law the glorious principle, that
"as soon as any slave sets his foot on English ground, he becomes free." The
operation of this decision, after ten or fifteen years, was manifested in the
multitude of black men, reckoned at 400, who were beggars in London.
Mr. Sharp, and some other benevolent persons, devised the scheme of
carrying these negroes back to Western Africa, and founding a free settlement
upon that coast. Sierra Leone was the site fixed upon, and in the year 1787
the settlement was commenced. Three years afterwards a company was
formed under the auspices of Mr. Wilberforce, Mr. Henry Thornton, Mr.
Granville Sharp, and other distinguished characters, for promoting the
commercial prosperity of the settlement, and extending its influence as far as
possible on the West Coast. The first fifteen years were marked by long and
arduous struggles with hostile natives, and with internal strife and mutiny.
Once the settlement was plundered and the buildings destroyed by a French
naval expedition, but a more settled and prosperous condition was attained
about the year 1800, and it became a suitable basis for the operations of a
Society for missions to Africa and the East.

The new Society was not, however, suggested by the philanthropic
enterprise just described. By a concurring providence a few London Clergymen, meeting in the Vestry of a London Parsonage, St. Ann's, Blackfriars,
determined to form a Society to fulfil the last commission of the Saviour,
that His Gospel should be preached in all lands. Various fields of labour for
the commencement of missions were scrutinized, but the decision at last fell
upon Sierra Leone.

"In common with the rest of the heathen world, it was included in the
Divine command that the Gospel should be preached to all nations. But here
was a superadded obligation of a debt due to the sons of Africa, for cruelty
and oppression inflicted upon them, during many past generations, by the
accursed slave trade; and therefore they placed a resolution upon record, ere
the Society had struggled through the embarrassments of its first year, that
the first mission should be commenced in the neighbourhood of Sierra Leone,
the centre at that time of the slave trade." (Jubilee Volume).

2. We may notice another providential circumstance which contributed
to the support of the Sierra Leone Mission in its infancy. The Directors of the
Missionary Society had among their number two men personally acquainted
with Africa, namely, John Newton, who had once resided as a slave dealer in
the neighbourhood of Sierra Leone, now an aged minister of a church in
London, and the Rev. Melville Horne, who for a short time had been chaplain
in Sierra Leone; but the providence of God provided a third man eminently
fitted to counsel and guide the Directors of the Society in the person of
Zachary Macaulay. He was descended from an ancient and highly respectable
Scotch family, but being compelled to seek his own fortune, became the
overseer of an estate in Jamaica from 1782 until 1792. Though only in his

nineteenth year when he first arrived in Jamaica, he maintained throughout his course an unblemished integrity of character, and contemplated the condition of the negroes with pious solicitude, and an ever-increasing desire for their temporal and spiritual welfare. In a letter written in 1789, in the prospect of some change in his position, he writes:

> I flatter myself I shall be able, from my freedom from control, to alleviate the hardships of a considerable number of my fellow creatures, and to render the bitter cup of servitude as palatable as possible.

and again:

> There are on the estate between 200 and 300 negroes, whose lives in a manner depend on my care and attention, whose labours I am obliged to direct, whose irregularities I must punish, and whom I must faithfully attend in sickness.

In 1792 Mr. Macaulay returned to England on account of his health, and became known to the friends who were then associated in contending for the abolition of the slave trade, and the support of the settlement in Sierra Leone. The value of Mr. Macaulay's extensive and accurate information, and his powerful writing and firm principles, at once recommended him to these friends, and he was admitted into their confidence and co-operation. They proposed to him to go out to Sierra Leone to occupy the second post in the government of the settlement. Such of his letters as have been preserved which were written at this period, exhibit a noble spirit of resignation to the will of God, to be employed where he might most promote the Divine glory and the welfare of his fellow men. He ultimately went to Sierra Leone, and soon after his arrival he became Governor of the settlement. Through all the troubles and trials of the early days of the settlement, to which allusion has already been made, Mr. Macaulay's wisdom, decision of character, and high Christian principle, gradually gained the ascendancy, and raised the settlement to the position of a well ordered community, though as a commercial enterprise it was a signal failure through the operation of the trade in slaves that then desolated that unhappy coast. The Christian spirit of Mr. Macaulay will be evident from the following extract from one of his letters, in which he describes a rebellion by which his own life was placed in jeopardy, and the colony brought to the eve of destruction, but which evils were averted by the judicious measures and great firmness of mind of Mr. Macaulay.
The extract is as follows:

> After I had finished this letter it has occurred to me, that what I have said would bear too much the appearance of self-confidence and boasting, but God is my witness that I have on no occasion felt more the need of His help, and what a poor, miserable, insignificant, blind,

naked and helpless object man is without Him. What I bless Him for above all is the collectedness of mind He has given me throughout the whole business. He made my way so clear that I scarce felt an embarrassment. He had also blessed me with unusual health, although I expect, from some symptoms I now begin to feel, that I may have an attack of fever ere long. Be it so. He is able to deliver me from that also.

Mr. Macaulay held the government of Sierra Leone for seven years, during which period he once visited England to consult with the Directors of the Company, and with extraordinary self-devotion took his passage from Sierra Leone in a slave ship to the West Indies in order that he might fully acquaint himself with the horrors of the middle passage. Upon his final return to England in 1799, the Directors and his friends generally thought he would be more useful as the Secretary to the Sierra Leone Company at home than as Governor on the coast. He therefore remained in England, and took up his residence on Clapham Common, and was thus brought into immediate connexion with the Directors of the Church Missionary Society, to encourage, guide and strengthen their plans for the Christian Mission in the neighbourhood of Sierra Leone. He was also shortly afterwards appointed Editor of the "Christian Observer" which was then first established, and our early volumes testify to the zeal with which he espoused its interests.

3. The circumstances already described were sufficient to stamp the obligation of a Divine call upon the proposal to go forward with the Sierra Leone Mission; but yet there was one token wanting, which had been granted to the Apostle Paul when he was called to pass from Asia into Europe, and a man of Macedonia appeared with the supplication of "Come over and help us". A sign of this kind was granted in the present instance, for Mr. Macaulay had persuaded several of the leading chiefs in the neighbourhood of Sierra Leone to entrust their sons to his care, for education in England, in the hope that they might return to Africa and become regenerators of their countrymen. In a letter from Henry Thornton, Esq., to Miss Hannah More, he playfully remarks:

> I expect that when Macaulay arrives he will make his triumphal entry into this island with twenty or thirty little black boys and girls at his heels, the trophies that he brings with him from Africa. They have been living chiefly at his house, and have been somewhat instructed already. A zealous man at Edinburgh, Mr. Campbell, has instructed Mr. Macaulay to bring them, having been authorized by some Scotch gentlemen (names unknown) to undertake the whole expense of them.

An establishment was formed for their reception at Clapham, and an instructor was found in a man singularly fitted for the work. Mr. William Greaves was a native of Yorkshire, and brought up under the influence of that revival of true religion of which Mr. Grimshaw of Haworth, and Mr. Venn of Huddersfield, were the eminent leaders. As it was a main object to train up the young Africans to industrial habits, and to introduce through them the arts of civilization into Africa, a proportion of their time in the seminary was spent in such pursuits; and Mr. Greaves possessed an amount of mechanical knowledge, which enabled him to teach them the art of printing and the use of a printing-press, carpentry, and the elements of mechanics. Several of these African lads became promising students, and were brought under the influence of the Christian faith, so that when the two first German missionaries came to England, destined for Sierra Leone, they found, in the seminary at Clapham, the first fruits, it might be hoped, of an African Mission. And herein the invitation was conveyed, "Come over and help us".

The writer of this paper well recollects, in early boyhood, being invited by Mr. Macaulay, one Sunday afternoon, to go with him to the African Seminary, to hear the boys examined in the Bible. They stood in a semicircle round Mr. Macaulay while he questioned them in Scripture history; and Mr. Henry Thornton stood by Mr. Macaulay's side, evidently much interested in the group before him; while Mr. Wilberforce, on the outside of the group, went from boy to boy, patting them on the shoulder as they gave good answers to questions, and giving them each a few words of encouragement, and an admonition to teach the same truths to their countrymen. Messrs. Renner and Hartwig were also present on that occasion.

After four or five years, a few of the number expressed a wish to receive Christian baptism, and eight of them were selected as sufficiently qualified to receive that holy rite. They were baptized at Clapham Church, May 12th, 1805, at the Afternoon Service; and there were present, besides the residents of Clapham, Messrs. Macaulay, Wilberforce, Thornton and others, Lord Gambier, first President of the Church Missionary Society, Lord Muncaster, Charles Grant, Esq., and the Rev. T. Thomason, afterwards of Calcutta . . .

On that occasion, Mr. Venn preached on the text, Colos. iii,11, "Where there is neither Greek nor Jew, circumcision nor uncircumcision, barbarian, Scythian, bond nor free, but Christ is all and in all." An extract from the sermon may interest many of our readers:

> Ye, my Christian brethren of Africa, are witnesses this day that in Christ Jesus there is neither Jew nor Greek, circumcision nor uncircumcision, bond nor free. You can bear testimony to the mild and benevolent spirit of Christianity. If you have been wronged, Christianity has been guiltless of the wrong. She stretches out her arms to invite you, she receives you as brethren, she consoles you with all the comforts of the Gospel of Christ. The Prophet hailed with rapture the day when the Morian's land should stretch out her hands to God. Christ died for you as well as for the Jew, or the Greek, or the Briton. Heaven is open to you as it is to them. The promises of the Gospel are your's as

much as they are their's. We have the same hope of our calling, the same Word of Life, the same promises to cheer us, the same strength to support us.

How encouraging is it to look forward to the glorious scene which will be opened when all the redeemed of Christ shall be assembled together — people of every nation, kindred, and tribe upon earth — a company which no man can number — ten thousand times ten thousand, and thousands of thousands, every petty distinction of jealousy or envy laid aside for ever — all united, as brethren — all perfected in love. Glorious day! Whose heart does not burn with the sacred prospect? who does not, amid the desolation of war, the tumult and destruction, the feuds and jealousies, which agitate the Earth — who does not cry, How long, O Lord, how long? When wilt Thou take to Thee the power and glory, O King of saints, and put an end to the miseries of the world, and let Thy truth and glory prevail?

And now, my African Brethren, it is your part to give thanks to Jesus Christ for the hope to which you are called in Him. If there is any rivalry between nations, let it be only that of striving who can most faithfully serve Christ and show forth His praise. Behold your great benefactor, who laid down His life for you! Direct your whole attention to Him. To Him you owe everything — your life, your comforts, whatever they may be here, your hopes of eternal felicity hereafter. Show, then, by your conduct, your gratitude to Christ. Consider Him as from this day forward your Master and Lord. Devote yourselves to His service. Be assured that His service is perfect freedom. Live no longer to yourselves. You see how much it is your duty to repress all jealousies, envies, pride, anger; how you ought to stifle the rising emotions of discontent and murmuring. Let Christ be all in your esteem. Take pains to understand more fully the excellency of His Word, and the blessing of His salvation. Be careful to live in faithful obedience to His will in all things.

And while you feel, as I trust you do this day, thankful for the mercies vouchsafed to you in Christ — while you rejoice in a hope full of immortality — think upon your poor countrymen who are yet lying in darkness and the shadow of death. Millions amongst them have never heard of the glad tidings of salvation. They know nothing of Christians but as their oppressors: they know nothing of Christ under His true character as a Saviour and Benefactor. No bells call them on the Holy Sabbath to worship in the assembly of Saints. No hope of a better state above cheers them amidst the calamities of life: they rely not on the promise and word of God to support them and to bless them. When they lie upon a dying bed, all before them is the gloom of darkness and uncertainty. Whether there be an hereafter, or of what nature that hereafter is — whether they will be punished or annihilated — they know not. Oh that they could enjoy the consolation and hope which the meanest amongst Christians in our nation may enjoy! Would that some of their own countrymen, who have tasted of the goodness of God, might devote themselves, like the Apostles of old, to the blessed work of making known the name and gospel of Jesus! Pray for them, my friends. If the love of Christ expands your hearts, let the first proof of it appear in this, that you ardently wish and pray that the same benefits which you enjoy may be communicated to your countrymen. This nation was once a heathen nation; and the time may come, yea, will come, when Africa shall embrace the Truth of Christ.

The African Seminary was, however, given up a few years afterwards, partly in consequence of the intention of opening a Seminary in Sierra Leone, but more especially on account of the great mortality which took place among the African students in this country. Only a few returned to Africa, to benefit their countrymen by their Christian example and influence. The presence of such a Seminary however, even for a time, served the purpose of encouraging the Sierra Leone Mission.

This review of the concurring circumstances which attended the establishment of the Sierra Leone Native Church, in three chief particulars, affords to us, at the present day, convincing proof that the hand of the Lord was with the founders of the Church Missionary Society.

And the founders themselves soon felt the need of such an assurance to bear up their spirits against the depressing influence of the news which continually arrived during many successive years, of the death of the missionaries. Often the vessel which brought the account of the arrival of a party of missionaries in Sierra Leone, brought also an account of the death of several among the number; and there were friends at home who urged upon the Committee the duty of giving up a Mission which could not be maintained without a so-called waste of life. In the course of the first twenty years of the Mission no fewer than fifty-three missionaries, or their wives, died at their posts. Subsequently, the mortality of the missionaries was materially reduced, partly by sanitary improvements, and partly by native agency lightening the labours of European missionaries, so that latterly the rate of mortality has not exceeded that of the West Indies, or many parts of India. It is hoped, however, that the high standard of self-devotion and self-sacrifice which animated the early missionaries to West Africa, has not been lowered. Instances happily are occurring, both at home and abroad, in which the agents of this Society are not only risking their lives to accomplish its objects, but cheerfully sacrificing all that the world would regard as most valuable in life; whilst thousands of missionary collectors go forth weekly or monthly to receive the contributions of the poor, animated by the simple motive of love to Christ, which motive would have sufficient strength to carry them into unhealthy climates or arduous labour, if called to the same by their Divine Master. While this spirit prevails in the Society, there need be no fear of the failure of its resources, or of the want of suitable labourers for carrying on its glorious work.

ON HELPING A NATIVE CHURCH TO BE SELF-SUPPORTING [3]

It has always been a recognised principle of the Committee, in carrying
on the operations of the Society, that Native Converts should be habituated
to the idea that the support of a Native Ministry must eventually fall upon
themselves; as, in their heathen state, they have been accustomed to bear the
expense of Heathen Ministration. The present position of the Society renders
it more than ever important that this principle should be carried out to the
utmost practicable extent. By this course, the Committee would be preparing
the way for the transfer of such Native Christian Congregations to the regular
Ecclesiastical Establishment; and leave themselves at liberty to go forward in
the work of breaking up the fallow-ground of Heathenism, which is the
peculiar province of a Missionary Society. The assertion of this principle is
not intended, however, to interfere with measures for the endowment and
establishment of a Native Church; but it is hoped that it may rather facilitate
and prepare the way for that desirable ultimate object.

A NATIVE MINISTRY [4]

The results of the Niger Expedition have supplied still stronger motives
to the adoption of the most effective measures possible for training Africans
as Religious Teachers: —

1. It has afforded additional and very painful proofs of the baneful
influence of the climate of West Africa on European constitutions: so much
so, that all parties are agreed, that to benefit Africa extensively, by imparting
to her our religious and social blessings, Africans themselves must be the
principal agents.

2. The important and cheering fact has been established, that both
Chiefs and people are willing to receive instruction from Black Men, even of
such as they know to have been in a state of slavery; and that such Black
Men, trained in the Schools and Institutions of the Society in Sierra Leone,
are capable of acceptably imparting it. This fact is so peculiarly hopeful for
Africa that, in corroboration of it, the Committee quote the following
passage from the ... Letter of Mr. Schön: —

> I have frequently had occasion to allude, in my Journal, to the utility
> of Native Agency. The remarks there made are supported by facts,
> which cannot be contradicted: and if there should be anything wanting
> to compensate me for feelings of disappointment in the results of the
> Niger Expedition in other respects, I acknowledge with gratitude to
> God, that the information obtained on this subject is more than a
> counterbalance. It not only demonstrates to us, that the designs for
> which the Expedition has been chiefly undertaken will, in the course of

events, be carried out by Natives; but, that the Nations in the interior acknowledge the superiority over themselves of their own country-people who have received instruction, and are willing, nay anxious, to see them return, and to be instructed by them in the habits of civilized life, and especially in the truths of the Gospel.

The following occurrence is related by Mr. Schön in his Journal. Describing his intercourse with Obi, King of Ibo, he says:

I opened the English Bible, and made Simon Jonas read a few verses to him, and translate them into Ibo. The verses he read were some of the Beatitudes of our Saviour, in the Fifth Chapter of St. Matthew. Obi was uncommonly taken with this. That a White Man could read and write, was a matter of course; but that a Black Man — an Ibo man — a slave in times past — should know these wonderful things too, was more than he could ever have anticipated. He seized his hand and pressed it most heartily. "You must stop with me! You must teach me and my people! "

LETTER TO AN AFRICAN[5]

We have read your journals with great interest — they are very well written and convey to us a great deal of information which we wish to receive: keep up writing all you see which relates to the great object of your Mission, and also your feelings in respect of your work: — that we may know the better what to ask of God on your behalf and for your country's sake.

Ever keep in mind the *one* subject of your mission — to make known the Redeemer's love and the treasures of grace, happiness and glory which are opened to us through the knowledge and faith of Him. Remember that it is to affect the heart that you must chiefly aim. It will be easy to inform the understanding when the heart is inclined to listen. I have always had great hope in the African heart — I know that the Lord has given to your countrymen warm affections and I am sure that when the love of Christ is apprehended by them, through the Holy Spirit's influence, they will become devoted followers and zealous preachers of Christ.

THE ESTABLISHMENT OF A NATIVE CHURCH[6]

The fact that the numerous Native-Christian Congregations in many of the Missions of the Church Missionary Society now occupy the chief time and attention of our Missionaries, has forced upon the Committee the considera-tion of the best means of so relieving missionaries from the pastoral charge of those already converted to the faith, that they may be enabled to carry forward *the extension* of the work among the Heathen.

The Committee have taken advantage of the presence in England of some of their most experienced Missionaries to confer with them upon this subject; and have adopted the present Minute in reference to the same.

1.   A tendency exists in every Mission to occupy the time and labours of the Missionary in the home duties of Schools and pastoral ministrations, and even when two or more Missionaries are united in the same field of labour, these home duties are still the chief object of attention, each sharing in them to the hindrance or neglect of direct missionary work.

2.   It is very true that Native Converts, both invite, and in a measure require, the constant care of a native Christian ministry − and that in the supply of their spiritual wants there will always be room for the application of additional time and attention. But if a limit be not placed to this occupation of the time of a missionary, the whole resources of the Society will be exhausted in maintaining the ground already gained, instead of making fresh inroads upon Heathenism.

3.   The best remedy for the tendency here described, is to be found in the preparation of a NATIVE MINISTRY capable of undertaking the pastoral charge of Native Christian flocks, under the general superintendence of the Missionaries, whose time and strength will be proportionately released for the direct work of a Mission − the evangelization of the Heathen. In proportion also as such a Native Ministry can be introduced, the Mission will become firmly rooted in the soil, and the resources of the Society will be set free for the "regions beyond"!

4.   This view of a Native ministry should be kept in sight from the first commencement of a Native Church, otherwise the Missionary will insensibly become the Pastor, and the Native Teachers who may be trained up will be employed rather as Missionaries than as Native Pastors, and will, as agents of an European Society, imbibe European tastes and habits; instead of regarding themselves as ministers, or servants in the Lord of the Native population with which they are to be in every way identified.

5.   The Committee are indeed happy to reckon among their Missionaries several Native ministers, who now act as Evangelists among their countrymen, and who superintend other Native labourers. But these should be regarded as exceptions to the rule of *a Native Ministry,* properly so-called. They are not Native Pastors but the agents of a Society foreign to their country; they possess qualifications and literary attainments of a higher order than those necessarily required in Native Pastors. They are brought into nearer con- nexion with European Society, sit in the Committees and take part in the administration of the affairs of the Society; whereas a Native Pastor should never be trained up in habits and expectations too far removed above his countrymen. He is ultimately to receive his support from them, − or if

supported by endowment, the amount of such support will necessarily be regulated according to Native habits and modes of life.

6. Missionaries should remember that it is upon the training up and location of such *Native Pastors* as we have described that their own labours and the resources of the Society will be best economised; and that a preparation will be made for the transfer of Missionary labours to the surrounding Heathen.

It is important ever to keep in view what has been happily termed "the Euthanasia of a Mission", where the Missionary is surrounded by well-trained Native congregations under Native Pastors, when he gradually and wisely abridges his own labours, and relaxes his superintendence over the Pastors till they are able to sustain their own Christian ordinances, and the District ceases to be a Missionary field, and passes into Christian parishes under the constituted ecclesiastical authorities.

ON MISSIONARY POLICY IN REGARD TO THE GROWTH OF A NATIVE CHURCH[7]

. . . I notice all that you have said respecting the uncertainty and often the treachery of your native Teachers, and deeply sympathise in your disappointments: But the full survey of the whole Mission Field which my position enables me to take convinces me that our present work is to *spread* the knowledge of the Truth as widely as it can be done with any tolerable degree of efficiency, and we must wait before we can expect to see much spiritual progress in native Christians till a larger body of converts have been given to us, and till they form a Community amongst themselves of Christian mechanics, and men of property, and above all Christian mothers — and of such a Community God will raise up as he has always done in his true Church bright examples of his power and grace. But while a few scattered converts are living amongst the heathen, in an artificial state of dependence upon Christian Europeans I think we must not be surprised at the weakness and often the hypocrisy which manifests itself . . .

ON EXCITING A MISSIONARY SPIRIT IN A NATIVE CHURCH[8]

. . . The fourth special point on which the Committee will speak, is that of cherishing a missionary spirit in each Native Church. The Committee have lately been made more than ever aware of the fact that Native Converts do not generally lay themselves out to bring over their countrymen to the truth. In some Missions indeed this spirit has happily manifested itself from the first, such as in New Zealand and in Yoruba. But in mission fields, in which the Native population is accustomed to look up to their European Rulers as the doers of everything, the Converts are too apt to expect that they shall be supported and kept in leading strings by their Missionaries, and that it is only the Missionary's or the paid Teacher's duty to bring others of their countrymen into the same comfortable fold. The case needs but to be stated to exhibit the warning and the duty that every convert should be instructed from his conversion in the duty of labouring for his self-support, and for the support of Missions to his Countrymen, and to lay himself out as a Missionary among his relations and friends to bring them to the truth. Since the pecuniary pressure upon the Society has crippled its grants to the Missions, it has suddenly appeared that the Native Converts were in many cases ready and willing to do far more themselves than was expected. In Tinnevelly, also, where the Native Converts had already contributed largely of their means, a new and blessed advance had been made by their sending out Catechists from among themselves to labour in Ceylon among the Tamil Coolies and into North Tinnevelly to labour with the itinerating Missionaries. In this latter case, the proposal was made by Mr. Ragland that each of the larger Districts should bear the expense of one Native Catechist to labour for a month. This it was thought would be a pecuniary burden which they could bear. It was tried — the Catechist returned to his District at the end of the month, and reported his labours. At once new light and life entered the minds of the Native Converts, they had tasted the sweets of doing something for Missions — they resolved to support two Catechists for the whole year, and one man at once agreed to go for two months for each year at his own charges.

Let this illustration stir you up to excite and cherish the Missionary spirit from the first. It will often give a reality, a vigor, an independence to native Christianity which it now wants. We should hear less of the feebleness of Native Converts and of their inability to help themselves — and above all the work would spread as we may say of itself, and such an extension would soon appear, as we have hitherto almost ceased to expect — waiting as we too idly say, for the outpouring of the Holy Spirit. True, we depend wholly upon that outpouring. The present Season is a glorious Missionary season. But we are sure that the gift is not granted to an extent which we are not prepared to recognize — that our want of faith does not stint the manifestation of the Giver. Let us use every means in the confidence of hope, in the dependence of humility, in the thought of faith, and God will put a new song into our mouths . . .

A NATIVE MINISTRY[9]

. . . In the year 1848 the Committee took advantage of the presence of several of their most experienced Missionaries to confer with them upon the subject of Native Ministers: and they adopted a series of resolutions upon the subject, which have been acted upon in several Missions, have been frequently reviewed by the Parent Committee, and have received some additional remarks from time to time, in explanation or enlargement of their meaning.

The main principles of the Resolutions have been generally approved by the Missionaries of the Society: and the Parent Committee is more and more confirmed in their propriety and importance.

The Resolutions of 1848 having been printed and circulated it will only be necessary to refer to them in the present memorandum. The *first* Resolution provides that a Native should only be ordained when there is some body of Native Christians to whom he may act as a Native Pastor — so that he may have a Church or District assigned to him, in which he may minister, under the general superintendence and direction of a Missionary, until he is proved to be qualified for a more independent position.

It is assumed by this Regulation that the work of evangelizing the heathen is best carried out by European Missionaries and Native Catechists — and that it is not advisable to employ Native Ministers in this department but that ordination should only be connected with the Pastorate. This was the rule generally observed in the early progress of Christianity — the instruction of Enquirers is the special office of a Catechist. Many considerations point out the propriety of this Course — one of which is that if Native Ministers were associated in the work of Evangelization they must necessarily assume too much of the European status. As Clergymen of the Church of England, they would appear before their countrymen as belonging to a different class, and as the well-paid agents of a foreign Society. This was the ground alleged by one of our most superior Brahmin Catechists, against receiving ordination — he was apprehensive that it would deprive him of influence with his unconverted countrymen and the Parent Committee fully appreciated the motive.

By pursuing the proposed course, the Catechists will be taught to view ordination as specially uniting them with the Native Church — as the seal of the pastoral relation. They will perceive that they are ordained to an office in the Native Church and not to an office in the Church Missionary Society. It is equally important for the sake of the Native Church to cherish these feelings and for the sake of the Society to discourage the notion that Native Ministers are to be dependent upon its funds.

The Second regulation, however, holds out the expectation to Native Pastors of a true Missionary spirit, that after sufficient trial and experience they may attain to the position of Missionaries, and occupy such a position as many Native Ministers already fill, namely John Dewasaygan, S. Crowther, H. Budd and others.

The third Resolution lays down the principle which is to decide the salary of a native minister. The Committee has since adopted a course which leaves the question of a native minister's salary to the discussion of local Committees abroad, namely that the Parent Committee should only give the salary of a Catechist to those who are ordained, the highest in the scale, but nothing beyond a Catechist's salary: and that whatever addition may be thought necessary upon ordination should be supplied by local funds, without pledging the Parent Committee to keep up such addition.

The fourth regulation advises the establishment of a Native Pastors Fund in every mission where there are organised congregations of Native Christians. This fund should be formed both by Endowments and by periodical contributions. If the Native Minister receives the addition to his salary wholly or in part out of this fund, it will tend to cherish still more effectually the feeling of identity with the Native Church to which reference has been made in a former paragraph.

The fifth regulation refers to the status of those Native Missionaries — They can be so advanced only be a direct vote of the Parent Committee. Upon such appointment they will become the recognized Agents of the Society and receive their whole salary from its funds, and be eligible to all local Committees of the Society.

The Parent Committee require that in the case of every candidate for holy orders in the presentation of the Society, three Missionaries of the Society should concur in the recommendation, giving their separate testimony, in the form of a letter to the Corresponding Committee, to his fitness. These testimonials, if approved of, to be referred home with the account of the sphere of labour in which he is to act as Pastor, for the final sanction of the Parent Committee.

It is scarcely necessary to explain that by the distinction between Native Pastor and Native Missionary in their Memorandum, it is not supposed that the Native Pastor will confine his labours to the Christian Congregation — He will of course labour for the conversion of the heathen in so far as he has time and opportunity, but the pastorate will be the distinguishing feature of his office . . .

THE ORGANIZATION OF NATIVE CHURCHES[10]

1. The work of Modern Missionaries is of a two-fold character. The heathen are to be brought to the knowledge of Christ and the converts who embrace the truth are to be trained up in Christian habits, and to be formed into a native Christian Church. These two branches are essentially distinct; yet it is only of late years that the distinction has been recognized by appointing Missionaries to the purely Evangelistic branch under the designation of Itinerating Missionaries, in contradistinction from "Station" Missionaries.

2. The Missionary whose labours are blest to the gathering in of converts, naturally desires to keep his converts under his own charge, to

minister to them as a Pastor, and to rule them as a native congregation. So the two branches have become blended together; hence also the principles necessary for the Evangelistic work, one of which is "taking nothing of the Gentiles" have insensibly influenced the formation of the native Christian Church — as if the word had been "taking nothing of the Christians." Whereas the Scriptural basis of the pastoral relation, within the Church of Christ, is "they that preach the Gospel should live of the Gospel" — "the ox that treadeth out the corn should eat of the same"; so that while the Missionary properly receives his support from a foreign source, the native Pastor should receive his from the Native Church.

3. Under this system, the Missionary takes charge of classes of Candidates for Baptism, Classes of Candidates for the Lord's Supper, and Communicants-classes. The Missionary advances the converts from one class to another at his discretion. When the converts become too numerous or too scattered for the individual ministry of the Missionary, he appoints a Catechist or other Teacher, and the Society pays him. The Society establishes Schools and pays for the Teachers. As the Mission advances, the number of Readers, Catechists, and Ordained Pastors, of Schools and Schoolmasters, is increased. But all is dependent upon the Missionary: and all the agency is provided for at the cost of the Society.

4. The evil incident to this system is threefold:

(1) In respect of the Missionary: his hands soon become so full that his time and energy are wholly occupied by the converts, and he extends his personal labours to the heathen in a continually decreasing ratio. His work also involves more or less of secularity and account keeping. The character of a simple Missionary is complicated with that of the director and paymaster of the Mission.

(2) In respect of the converts: they naturally imbibe the notion that all is to be done for them — they are dependents upon a foreign Mission, rather than members of a Native Church. There may be the individual spiritual life, but there is no corporate life: though the converts may amount to thousands in number they are powerless as a body. The principles of self-support, self-government, and self-extension are wanting; — on which depends the breath of life in a Native Church.

(3) In respect of the Missionary Society: the system entails a vast and increasing expense in its oldest Missions; so that instead of advancing to "the regions beyond", it is detained upon old ground: it is involved in disputes about native salaries, pensions, repairs of buildings, etc.: and as the generation baptized in infancy rise up under this system, the Society has found itself in the false position of ministering to a population of nominal Christians, who in many instances give no assistance to the progress of the Gospel.

5. This system of Church Missions often contrasts unfavourably with the

Missions of other denominations, supporting their own Teachers and of their self-exertion for the extension of the Gospel: − as in the case of the American Baptist Mission among the Karens of Burmah, of the Independents among the Armenians of Asia Minor, and of the wonderful preservation and increase of Christianity in Madagascar after the expulsion of European Missionaries. The unfavourable contrast may be explained by the fact that other denominations are accustomed to take part in the elementary organization of their Churches at home, and therefore more readily carry out that organization in the Missions. Whereas in our Church the Clergy find everything relating to elementary organisation settled by the Law of the Land: − as in the provision of tithes, of church-rates, of other customary payments, in the constitution of parishes, and in parish officers, our Clergy are not prepared for the question of Church organization; and therefore in the Missions they exercise the ministry of the Word without reference to the non-existence of the organization by which it is supported at home.

6. This imperfection in Church Missions must be remedied by keeping in mind the distinction between evangelizing the heathen, and the ministering to the Native Church; and by introducing into the Native Church that elementary organisation which may give it "corporate life", and prepare it for its full development under a native ministry and an indigenous Episcopate.

7. For the introduction of such elementary organisation into the Native Church the following principles may be laid down:−

Principles

I.   It is expedient that native converts should be trained, at as early a stage as possible, upon a system of self-government, and of contributing to the support of their own native Teachers.

II.   It is expedient that contributions should be made by the converts themselves for their own Christian instruction, and for schools for their children; and that for this purpose a Native Church Fund for an assigned Missionary District should be established, into which the contributions should be paid. The Fund must, at first, be mainly sustained by grants from the Missionary Society, these grants to be diminished as the native contributions spring up. Whilst the fund receives grants from the Society, the Parent Committee must direct the mode of its management.

III. It is expedient that the native Teachers should be divided into two classes, namely −

(1) Those who are employed as assistants to the Missionary in his evangelistic work, and who are paid by the Society.

(2) Those who are employed in pastoral work amongst the native Christians, who are to be paid out of the Native Church Fund, whether Schoolmasters, Readers, Catechists, or Ordained Pastors, as the case may be; so that they be regarded as the ministerial agents of

the Native Church, and not as the salaried agents of a Missionary Society.

IV. It is expedient that the arrangements which may be made in the missions should from the first have reference to the ultimate settlement of the Native Church, upon the ecclesiastical basis of an *indigenous* Episcopate, independent of foreign aid or superintendence.

Practical Suggestions

To carry out the foregoing principles it is suggested:

8. That, in conformity with Principle I, the converts should be encouraged to form themselves for mutual support and encouragement into *"Christian Companies"* (Acts IV.23. The literal translation would have been "their own friends or relations". The translators of the Bible adopted the term "Company" to denote the new and close brotherhood into which Christians are brought. In Africa the term has already been adopted for their native associations.) The members of such companies should not be too numerous, or too scattered, to prevent their meeting together in familiar religious conference. Local circumstances will decide the convenient number of a company: upon its enlargement beyond that number it should be divided into two or more companies.

One of each company should be selected or approved of, by the Missionary, *as* an elder or *"Christian Headman"*, to call together and preside over the companies, and to report to the Missionary upon the moral and religious condition of his company, and upon the efforts made by the members for extending the knowledge of Christ's truth. Each Christian company should be encouraged to hold *weekly meetings* under its headman, with the occasional presence of the Missionary, for united counsel and action, for reading the Scriptures and prayer, and for making contributions to the Church Fund – if it be only a handful of rice, or more, as God shall prosper them. – (Principle II).

Monthly Meetings of the Christian Headmen should be held under the Missionary, or someone whom he may appoint, at which meetings the headmen should report upon their respective companies, hand over the contributions, receive from the Missionary spiritual counsel and encouragement, and commend their common work, in united prayer, to the great Shepherd and Bishop of Souls.

9. That as long as converts are thus dependent for their Christian instruction upon their headmen, and the occasional ministration of the Missionary or other agents paid by the Society, the work must be regarded as the Evangelistic work of the Society. THE FIRST STEP in the Organization of the Native Church will be taken when any Company, or one or more neighbouring Companies unitedly, shall be formed into a *congregation, having a Schoolmaster, or Native Teacher located amongst them, whose salary is paid*

out of the Native Church Fund. – (Principle III.) This step may be taken as soon as the company or companies so formed into a congregation contribute a fair amount, in the judgement of the Missionary, to the Church Fund.

10. That A SECOND STEP in the organization of the Native Church will be taken when one or more congregations are formed into *a Native Pastorate, under an ordained native, paid by the Native Church Fund.* – (Principle III.) This step may be taken as soon as the congregations are sufficiently advanced, and the payments to the Native Church Fund shall be sufficient to authorize the same, in the judgement of the Missionary and of the Corresponding Committee.

> The Christian Headmen of the Companies comprised within a Native Pastorate should cease to attend the monthly meetings of headmen under the Missionary, and should meet under their native Pastor. As long as the Native Church Fund is under the management of the Missionary Society, the native Pastors, paid out of that Fund, must remain under the general superintendence of some missionary of the Society, who shall be at liberty to minister occasionally in their Churches, and to preside jointly with the native Pastors at the meetings of Headmen and other congregational meetings: the relation between the native Pastor and the Missionary being somewhat analogous to that of Curates with a non-resident Incumbent. (See Society's *Minute on Native Pastors.)*

11. That A THIRD STEP in the organization of the Native Church will be taken when a sufficient number of native Pastorates having been formed, *a District Conference* shall be established, consisting of Pastors and Lay Delegates from each of their congregations, and the European Missionaries of such District: District Conferences should meet periodically for consulting upon the Native Church affairs, as distinguished from the Action of the Society. – (Principle IV).

12. When any considerable District has been thus provided for by an organized Native Church, foreign agency will have no further place in the work, and that District will have been fully prepared for a native Episcopate.

Concluding Remarks

13. There must be a variety of details in carrying into effect these suggestions. A mere outline is given above. But it will be seen that the proposed scheme or organization will prepare the Native Church for ultimately exhibiting in its Congregational and District Conferences, the Counterpart of the Parish, and the Archdeaconry, under the Diocesan Episcopacy of our own Church system.

14. The proposed organization of the Mission Church is adapted to the case as it is, where the Native Church is in a course of formation out of a heathen population by the agency of a Missionary Society with limited

resources. Under such circumstances, a Society must commence its work by accustoming the converts to support their own institutions in the simplest forms; so that the resources of the Mission may be gradually released, and be moved forward to new ground. In other words, the organization must work upwards. When a sufficient *substratum* of self-support is laid in the Native Church, its fuller development will unfold itself, as in the healthy growth of things natural. Had the problem been to organize a mission where ample funds exist in the hands of a Bishop and his Clergy, for the evangelization of a whole district, as well as for the future endowment of its Native Church, the organization might work downwards, beginning with a diocesan Council, forming the converts into districts and parishes, building churches and colleges, etc. These have been too much the leading ideas in modern Missions: and European ideas easily take root in native minds. But past experience seems to shew that such a system, even if the means were provided, would be too apt to create a feeble and dependent native Christian community.

15. The foregoing suggestions must be modified according to the previous system which may have prevailed in a Mission. In older missions the change of system must be very gradual. For when a Mission has grown up in dependence upon European Missionaries and upon native agency salaried by European funds, the attempt to curtail summarily its pecuniary aid, before the introduction of a proper organization, will be like casting a person overboard before he has been taught to swim; it will be a great injustice to the native converts, and may seriously damage the work already accomplished.

16. On the other hand, in new Missions the Missionary may from the first encourage the enquirers to form themselves into companies, for mutual instruction and reading the Scripture and prayer, and for making their weekly collections. It should be enjoined upon each company to enlarge its numbers by prevailing upon others to join in their meetings. The enlargement of a Christian company, so as to require sub-division, should be regarded as a triumph of Christianity, as a festive occasion of congratulation and joy, as men rejoice "when they divide the spoil".

17. If the elementary principles of self-support and self-government and self-extension be thus sown with the seed of the Gospel, we may hope to see the healthy growth and expansion of the Native Church, when the Spirit is poured down from on high, as the flowers of a fertile field multiply under the showers and warmth of summer.

ON EXCITING A MISSIONARY SPIRIT IN A NATIVE CHURCH[11]

As a Parent Committee, we desire, on this occasion, affectionately to encourage and exhort you to strengthen and extend the work of grace which has for so many years been progressing among you.

Let the Missionary brethren and the native clergy labour together in Christian love and hearty co-operation. "Unto every one of us is given grace, according to the measure of the gift of Christ". And, "as every man hath received the gift, even so minister the same one to another, as good stewards of the manifold grace of God." "Sirs! Ye are brethren! " — the people of God dwelling in a land of darkness and of bondage. "Let your light so shine before men, that they may see your good works, and glorify your Father which is in heaven."

But while we thus entreat you as children of the light, to walk as before God, worthy of your Christian profession, the thought at this Season uppermost in our minds is the responsibility resting upon you, as a Native-Christian Church, in the midst of a heathen land, to cultivate and exercise a Missionary spirit. To you (as centuries ago to the Jewish Church, in the prospect of Messiah's advent) is the exhortation this day applicable "Arise shine, for thy light is come and the glory of the Lord is risen upon thee." Yes thy light, Sierra Leone, is come! However dark your West-African coast — however dark the vast continent that stretches far away behind you — upon Sierra Leone the Sun of Righteousness hath risen; and, "blameless and harmless, the Sons of God, without rebuke, in the midst of a wicked and perverse nation, SHINE YE as lights in the world, holding forth the word of life." Ye are the salt of Africa! Let not the salt lose its savour. Ye are the light of Africa! Put not your lighted candle under a bushel, but set it on a candlestick, that it may give light both far and near.

You know, Christian brethren, how European Christians, since the beginning of the present century, have never grown weary in sending you their sons and daughters, bearing on their lips the message of grace. You know full well how, as one and another, after a brief interval of labour, has laid down his life for the Gospel's sake in Africa, the supply of Missionary brethren and sisters has never failed. Whatever other heathen fields waited, Sierra Leone never waited *long* for the faithful labourer. Christian charity, and an honorable sense of justice, have never allowed Great Britain to forget the wrongs of Africa. In some measure, at least, Christian England has now for many a year remembered you for good. We wish, dear brethren, this day to lead you faithfully to enquire how far YOU are remembering your duty to *yourselves!* Shall ENGLAND remember Africa, but AFRICA forget *herself?* Rather, shall not Africa? — we speak to the Christian natives of your favoured peninsula (men gathered from almost every nation and tribe of your vast continent) — shall not Africa? you who hear or read this Jubilee Address! — will you not call to mind this day, as in the solemn presence of the Lord, your duty, as His disciples, to your heathen countrymen?

Oh, let this Jubilee year in Sierra Leone prove indeed a Jubilee to Africa. Let the silver trumpet ring its joyous notes throughout the land, that slaves to sin and Satan may become the freedmen of Jesus Christ!

We wish, dear brethren, to encourage you, as a Native Christian Church of many years' growth and standing, to deeds of manly enterprise and independent effort.

The Parent Committee will therefore direct your thoughts to a field of labour, to which their own thoughts have lately been directed with much anxiety, namely, the tribes which border upon the Colony, or which visit you from the interior. It is a cause of humiliation and reproach to the West-African Mission that, till the present year, not one book of Holy Scripture has been given in the native tongue to any of these tribes. The Gospel of St. Matthew has happily been printed in Timneh, and the rest of the holy volume is in course of translation; but there is the Mendi, the Vei, and the Sherbro, almost untouched.

There are settlements of natives speaking these languages on each side of the border, but no adequate efforts have yet been put forth to encourage these people to read and write their own language, or to spread in the vernacular language of their countrymen the wonderful works of God, with which they may themselves have become acquainted through their knowledge of the English tongue . . .

. . . Let the Native Church of Sierra Leone prove itself an effective basis of operations beyond the Colony. Let pious men, who can speak any of the languages surrounding the Colony, be sought out, and encouraged and trained to act as Catechists, and sent out at the charge of the Native Church. Let men who have the love of Christ in their hearts learn one of these native languages and offer themselves to this work. Let the many native traders and book-keepers who visit the rivers carry with them Primers and portions of the Scriptures, and encourage the people to teach the children to read and write their own tongue.

Such a movement would have a blessed reaction upon the Native Church itself and bring into its own bosom richer blessings than it dispenses to others.

And then, beyond the neighbourhood of the Colony the Parent Committee would point to the Niger and Bonny rivers, where additional labourers are urgently needed, which correspond with the Ceylon and Mauritius of the Indian Sea.

The Church Missionary Society still retains its motto "for Africa and the East". It will rejoice to enlarge its expenditure upon the regions beyond Sierra Leone. It will be ready to supply European pioneers, but their labours must be multiplied a hundred-fold by native agency. For the training of such agency the Society has provided a Grammar School, which, under God's blessing, has proved a great success; and now the Fourah-Bay Institution has been re-opened.

The Fourah-Bay Institution, while open to all who seek a Christian and liberal education, is more especially a Missionary Institution. Like its elder sister in Islington (where many Africans — as Bishop Crowther and others —

have been received and educated), it is open to all who are animated by a Missionary spirit, and possess the requisite judgement and talent. A new Principal has just been appointed, in whose piety, learning and ability we repose the fullest confidence. Under his superintendence it is hoped that many valuable native Missionaries to the interior, as well as native parochial clergymen will be raised. Let the Native Church in Sierra Leone avail herself of such a precious opportunity. Let the Clergy, while they press home upon their flocks, the duty of Native Missions to Africa, remind them of the advantages of the Fourah-Bay Institution. Let them seek out their best young men as candidates for admission, and do their part to raise the Institution to such a position of honour and usefulness in the Colony as shall make it a real blessing, not to Sierra Leone alone, but to Africa herself.

There is work for all. Every Christian must be a Missionary, if his Christianity is vital and effective. Your calling in life may be a humble one, and it may be your duty to "abide therein"; nevertheless, in that calling, who may not speak of Christ, and extol His love and grace? Yet, beyond this, there is special work, full of honour and responsibility, to which God gives, as He sees right, a special call. Distant lands must be visited: The Gospel must be preached there: The Scriptures must be translated: Churches must be founded! The work is divinely appointed, and He who has appointed the work will not fail to confer the gifts and graces needful for its accomplishment. On some, such gifts seem conferred from infancy: by others, such qualifications must be acquired by diligent study and perseverance. Now, let each enquire, What am I doing for Christ? Something you *ought* to do! In the spirit of the great Apostle to the Gentiles, ask – "Lord, what wilt thou have *me* to do? " And who can tell but of you, too, it may be said – "He is a chosen vessel unto me to bear my name before the Gentiles."

Your earnest prayers are needed. Your contributions, too, are needed. Your own personal service is also needed. Your Saviour who gave Himself for you, commands you to give yourself to Him. And, dear brethren, in forwarding you our congratulations on the occasion of your Jubilee, and commending these thoughts to your prayerful consideration, with what more delightful words, as a motive to gratitude and incentive to effort, can we bid you an affectionate FAREWELL, than those of the Apostle – "Ye know the Grace of our Lord Jesus Christ, that, though He was rich, yet for your sakes He became poor, that ye through His poverty might be rich."

ON STEPS TOWARDS HELPING A NATIVE CHURCH TO BECOME SELF-SUPPORTING, SELF-GOVERNING AND SELF-EXTENDING[12]

... 7. Under the new system, a Church Council will be formed, the three native Ministers being members of it. The Corresponding Committee will appoint a Chairman, either a Missionary, or the Secretary of the Corresponding Committee, or one of the Native Ministers when their number increases. The Chairman will appoint two other members of the Church Council, of any race or position. The lay members of the Congregation will appoint three more. The Council is to be appointed periodically, annually, probably, at first, so that members may be changed as they are found suitable or unsuitable, and the balance of European and native influence may be adjusted from time to time.

8. The Council will meet periodically, say once a month, or every fortnight, "to consult upon the interests of the Native Church, and for the general superintendence of its affairs". The reports of the subordinate agents, as well as of the Native Pastors, will be presented to the Council. A Native Church Fund having been constituted, the Society's grant will be remitted monthly to the Council as a grant in aid of the Native Church Fund. If the Native Church Fund increases, the Council will decide what new agency shall be instituted.

9. In all these arrangements no change is made in the direct Mission work. All preaching and school superintendence will go on as before. The European Missionaries will have their districts, exterior to the Native Pastoral Districts and in such Missionary districts no change whatever will take place. The only changes will be in the superintendence and payment of the Native Pastors and their work. The responsibility of this superintendence will no longer rest upon the Missionaries and Corresponding Committee, but upon the Bishop and ecclesiastical authorities, as in the case of all new churches erected in the diocese. The Society will still maintain its influence by its aid to the Native Church Fund and by its representatives in the Council.

10.(ii). Another misapprehension has arisen, the Parent Committee fears, in the notion that the *new system draws an absolute line between ministering to the Native Christians, and ministering to the heathen,* cutting off the latter department wholly from the Native Church Agency, and assigning it to the Missionary Society. Far otherwise. The whole organisation is founded upon the three principles — self-support, self-government, and self-extension. Self-extension implies missionary action and missionary success.

11. The Missionary aspect of the Native Church is prominently put forward in the Minutes on Native Church organisation. One of the principal objects of the Christian companies, into which it is suggested that the converts should form themselves, is to concert and adopt plans for bringing their countrymen into the Christian Church. The Native Fund, also, will be available, after providing for the Pastor and church expenses, for the support of Scripture-readers and for Catechists among the heathen. Hence the limits of each Native Pastorate should include a portion of the heathen population, more or less, according to the zeal of the Native congregation. Fostered by the European Mission, which works side by side, and which keeps up the true

standard of aggressive Christianity, the Native Church may ultimately become the more efficient Missionary Agency, as of old, when from the Church of Thessalonica, "sounded forth the word of the Lord, not only in Macedonia and Achaia, but also in every place, their faith to Godward was spread abroad."

12. (iii) A third misapprehension the Parent Committee would desire to notice. It is alleged that the *system is so complicated and artificial, that it will not be perpetuated in the Native Church,* after the agency of a foreign Mission is withdrawn and the Native Church is left to itself.

13. The Parent Committee fully admit that the system they are endeavouring to establish supposes far more zeal, spiritual life, and activity in the Native Church than are usually seen in the quiet working of a Church in a Christian land; and they fear that there is great danger of a Native Christian Church, even in the midst of heathenism, settling down in complacency with the Christian ministrations which it enjoys, without attempting to exercise any aggressive influence upon surrounding heathenism. It would not be difficult, alas! to point out such instances, even in the present early period of missionary labours. This experience and sense of danger urge the Parent Committee to prepare the Churches which their Missionaries gather out from among the heathen, to become centres of aggressive action, spreading light and life to all around. This they believe to be in accordance with the primitive and Apostolic standard.

14. The idea of assimilating a mission Church to a parish or congregation in an established Christian Community is likely to mislead, if applied to countries only partially evangelized; and yet it may be observed that the elements of the proposed new system have always been resorted to, even in the settled Christian Communities, in seasons of awakened Christian zeal and life. The meeting together of earnest Christians in small companies, conferences of clergy and laity on questions touching the advancement of true religion, a craving for synodical action in the Church, — these are universally the features of spiritual life; and the scheme proposed by the Committee is only an attempt to bring these principles into operation in the Mission Churches of the Society.

15. (iv) There is only one other misapprehension which the Committee will notice. It has been objected, that *in the new system the European element is too prominent,* and, in fact, depresses the Native: and that an European Chairman, with a veto, and the appointment of two members of the Church Council, will give the Council more the character of an European than a Native institution. But it will be seen that the printed regulations do not require an European Chairman, or even a single European member of the Council. Though, in the first instance, and while the tentative and transition stage lasts, it may be advisable to give a preponderating influence to European Missionaries, yet as the Native Councillors become efficient, and as the native

contributions enlarge, and the Society's grant in aid is diminished, the European element will be gradually withdrawn, until the Native Church becomes wholly free and independent.

16. Having thus endeavoured to remove some of the objections which have been alleged against the proposed new system for the organization of Native Churches in the Missions, the Parent Committee would point to the probable effect of a *Native Institution* for spreading Christianity, such as the action of the Native Church Council will exhibit, upon the heathen at large. Even now, many heathen subscribe to Christian schools and to the erection of Christian churches; it may be anticipated, therefore, that to the Native Church Fund, administered by Native Councillors, contributions will flow from that large and increasing class of the heathen who respect without embracing Christianity. The Eurasian Community, as well as the European, will feel a special interest in helping forward an indigenous movement.

17. But above all, the system is calculated to give confidence and self-reliance to the Native Christians, and to quicken their zeal and liberality. In Calcutta, one self-supporting Native congregation, originating with the Free-Church Missions, has existed three or four years, independent of missionary Societies. It prints and publishes an annual Report; and Missionaries in various parts of North India have spoken of the encouragement which this single instance of a self-supporting and self-governing Native Christian Institution has given to the Native converts of other denominations. At Agra, a Native Church Council was lately established, and a Native Christian of some wealth was elected a Councillor. He had hitherto been a retiring member of the Christian Church, but now, feeling an official responsibility, he urged the Council to undertake the erection of a new church, subscribed liberally and collected subscriptions for it; having, as he said, long hoped that Missionaries would one day build a church in that part of the city. These are specimens of the advantages which will be gained to the cause of Christianity, when the Native Church shall assume before the people the aspect of a national and not a foreign institution.

18. The Parent Committee have sufficiently pointed out in their printed Minutes on Church organization, that some change of the present system is required, in order to relieve overworked Missionaries from the position of Pastors, secular agents and paymasters, and to set them free for the general direction of evangelistic work. For as long as a Mission mainly depends upon its Missionaries, their hands are soon filled; and the work is also checked by the limited resources of the Missionary Society. But the proposed system, if it succeeds, has the power of expansion to any extent. Self-extension has no external limits.

19. The Parent Committee, in thus urging upon their Corresponding Committee, and upon their Missionaries, the system which appears to them most adapted to sustain and enlarge the Native Churches in the midst of

heathenism, are not going beyond their province. While they earnestly
anticipate the time when these Native Churches will become independent of
all Missionary influences, it is their duty to prepare them for this independence before they relinquish their connexion with them. They have had a
lamentable warning in the Mission in the West Indies against too hasty a
withdrawal from a Mission field. They have had great encouragement in their
attempts to organize a Church while still in their care by the experience in
West Africa. They regard it, therefore, as a very solemn obligation resting
upon every Missionary Society to train up their infant Churches "in the way
they should go". But at the same time they are ready to submit their plans
for correction to friends on the spot, and to consider of any other plans
which may claim a fairer prospect of success . . .

THE ORGANIZATION OF NATIVE CHURCHES[13]

... It may be said with truth, that hopes of the future progress of negro
conversion were unduly raised by a state of religious excitement consequent
upon emancipation. The people believed that they owed the boon more
immediately to the friends of Christian Missions. They soon afterwards began
to feel the pecuniary pressures and evils of a transition state.

But after making all allowances on these accounts, the inquiry is still
forced upon us, why the fair commencement of a prosperous Mission was so
soon checked, and why the negroes of West Africa have so far progressed in
civilization and Christianity beyond the negroes of Jamaica. There can be no
doubt on the minds of those who have watched the progress of modern
Missions that a chief cause of the failure of the Jamaica Mission has been the
deficiency of negro teachers for the negro race. The congregations were not
organized *upon the principles of a native Church,* but under the false idea
expressed by the Committee, and already quoted, that they would "fall
naturally, as it were, into the general ecclesiastical establishment of the
island." Had they been English settlers, as in Australia, this might have been
the case; but race distinctions, not sufficiently understood at that period of
Missions, introduced an element which defeated the best hopes of the
Society.

It may be said to have been only lately discovered in the science of
Missions, that when the Missionary is of another and superior race than his
converts he must not attempt to be their *Pastor;* though they will be bound
to him by personal attachment and by a sense of the benefits received from
him, yet if he continues to act as their Pastor they will not form a vigorous
Native Church, but as a general rule they will remain in a dependent
condition, and make but little progress in spiritual attainments. The same
congregation, under competent native Pastors, would become more self-
reliant, and their religion would be of a more manly, home character.

PROBLEMS FACING NEW CHURCHES[14]

... The Committee of the Church Missionary Society having learnt that cases have occurred in the Missions, of baptized converts, who reside among the heathen, falling into the practice of polygamy; and having been also requested by some of their Missionaries to explain their views upon the question of the admission of polygamists to Christian baptism; the following Minute upon the sinfulness of polygamy generally, as well as upon the particular question alluded to, is printed and circulated for the information of the Missionaries of the Society." ...

... After this review of the Scriptural arguments against polygamy, there should be no difficulty on the part of the Missionaries in plainly stating to the heathen or Mahommedans that the practice is contrary to the will of God. The natural conscience of every man must bear some witness, however faint, to this truth. The condemnation of the practice by the Roman law and by other heathen nations, is a testimony to this fact. The original creation of one man and one woman, may be appealed to as enforcing the true nature of Marriage. The saving alive in the Ark of men with one wife each, which is a type of admission into the Church of Christ, together with the providential equality of the sexes in every land, and at all times, may be pointed out as corroborative testimony to the continued force of the original institution. Various other moral considerations may be urged, to show that upon the principles of natural religion the practice is unlawful. Much may thus be done to inculcate upon the native mind right notions of marriage, before the question arises of their admission as candidates for Christian baptism, as well as to inspire all who have embraced Christianity with a just abhorrence of the practice of polygamy.

The foregoing review will also help to decide the question of the admission of a polygamist to baptism. The sin may have been commenced in ignorance, but its continuance, after Christian instruction, must bring guilt upon the conscience. The polygamy which is prohibited by the law of God is not only the *taking,* but the *having* and *retaining* more than one wife. Baptism, upon every view of the ordinance, carries with it a public profession of submission to the law of Christ, which the polygamist habitually violates. In the case of those, especially, who are baptised according to the adult service of the Church of England, no man can honestly declare that he will "obediently keep God's commandments, and walk in the same all the days of his Life", when he purposes to live with two or more women, as wives, at the same time.

Or the argument may be thus shortly given:

A state of polygamy is unlawful within the Church of Christ, even though commenced in ignorance: —

1. Because it has been declared by God to be contrary to the Divine

institution of marriage.

2. Because it has been pronounced adultery by Christ.

3. Because it is written: "Let every man have his own wife, and let every woman have her own husband."

Therefore a polygamist cannot be lawfully admitted by baptism into the Church of Christ.

It has been argued in favour of admitting polygamists into the Christian Church, that there is no precept in the New Testament, nor any Canon of the Early Church, forbidding their baptism.

But the Holy Scripture forbids not the baptism of an offender against the Divine laws, but only the offence.

With respect to the early Church, this explanation is given in the oriental Canons which bear the name of St. Basil the Great, in the year 340. The 80th Canon declares: "The Fathers say nothing of polygamy as being brutish and a thing unagreeable to human nature. To us it appears a greater sin than fornication."

It has been objected also, that if polygamists be thus absolutely condemned, and if baptism be refused to those who have more than one wife, it will compel men to put away those who have been regarded as their wives. This however was obviously the dilemma in which our Lord placed many to whom his words respecting divorce were addressed. All the practical difficulties apprehended in the one case belong to the other.

It has been argued, indeed, that Christ himself forbids a man to put away his wife, but it seems to be forgotten, that this prohibition applies only to the true wife to whom he is joined under the Universal Law "They twain shall be one flesh". The so-called second marriage is no marriage upon the principles of natural and revealed religion, but an unlawful connexion. Compare with the Divine Law "Let every man have his own wife, and every wife her own husband," the licentious precept of the Koran, "Take in marriage of such other women as please you, two, or three, or four, and no more." This is a clear case in which the law of men makes the law of God of none effect: and as the law of God overruled the law of Corban amongst the Jews, so it must be in this case: or to take an instance very likely to occur in the present day, if a heathen in his ignorance has entered into an obligation to sacrifice to an idol, he is released from such obligation when the law of God is made known to him.

A case is recorded in the Book of Ezra, which should have great weight with those who argue the question upon considerations derived from the hardships to women and children who may be put away. During the captivity the people of Israel, Priests and Levites, had married heathen wives. Much might have been pleaded in respect of such wives and their children; but under Ezra's remonstrances the people determined, "Now, therefore, let us make a covenant with our God to put away all the wives and such as are born of them, according to the Counsel of my Lord, and of those that tremble at the Commandment of our God: and let it be done according to the Law." (Ezra x.3). The last clauses of this text intimate that a proper reverence for the Word of God will overcome a variety of perplexing questions which may otherwise entangle a scrupulous mind.

At the same time, as far as marriage constitutes a civil contract by the Law or custom of any country, it must be explained to the converts that they are bound to fulfil such obligations by providing for the wife or children, and in every other lawful way repairing the injury which a separation may occasion to the woman, while they repudiate cohabitation. Serious difficulties will doubtless sometimes occur, as in every transition from a wrong to a right course of action. These difficulties will vary according to the laws of marriage and divorce in different countries; cases must therefore be dealt with according to circumstances. Whatever unhappiness or injury may result from an act of religious duty must often be borne as the fruit of an original fault, though that fault may have been committed in ignorance.

It must be added, however, that the *practical* difficulties of the case are far less than might be supposed. It is only a few, of the higher and wealthier classes, who can afford to keep many wives. The lower classes, the poor to whom, especially, the Gospel is preached, seldom take second wives. In many countries where, in common parlance, polygamy is said to prevail, one woman only is regarded as the wife, and the rest as concubines. And it has not yet been pleaded that a man should keep his concubines when he enters the Christian Church.

It has been alleged that by refusing baptism to polygamists, converts may be kept out of the Church of Christ, and deprived of further instruction, and that the heathen may be the more prejudiced against the truth.

To this allegation it might be answered generally, that many other things in the Christian system will appear hard sayings to some who will go back. But it is not necessary to repel a polygamist from Christian instruction; baptism may be deferred until increasing light in the minds of the parties, or the Providence of God, remove difficulties out of the way. It is the testimony of many Missionaries that comparatively few polygamists seek baptism for the natural conscience feels the difficulty, and shrinks from a Christian profession, however favourably disposed in other respects: it is scarcely possible to conceive that one who truly believes in God would be willing to continue in a course of polygamy after he knows the truth. There is little fear of *sincere* converts therefore being repelled; while the fact of each Christian convert being the husband of one wife, in a land of sensuality, is both a test of sincerity, and a striking evidence of the power of religion. This produces a general impression amongst the reflecting members of the community favourable to Christianity.

It has been the main object of these remarks to place the question simply upon Scriptural grounds. But it must be remembered that many obvious evils must arise from the admission of polygamists to baptism. It would be very hard to convince baptized converts, tempted to sin, that there is any real difference between admitting a polygamist into the Christian Church, and allowing polygamy to those already within it; or that it is just to put a polygamist out of the Church, who has become such after baptism, when another polygamist who had become such before baptism, might be admitted, and remain one of its members.

It must also be added, that much greater danger arises from any apparent toleration of polygamy than many Christians would suppose. Doubts or suggestions respecting the strictness of the original law of marriage, and inferences from the example of the Patriarchs, have ever found too ready entrance into the corrupt heart of baptized men. In many periods of Church History this root of bitterness has sprung up, and many have been defiled. Even at the close of the last century, a question respecting the lawfulness of polygamy was introduced, and spread amongst religious people, to a most pernicious extent. The commentator Scott, upon the passage in St. Matthew, already quoted, speaks of the serious evils which he had witnessed from unwarrantable inferences from our Lord's words. The present day has witnessed the fearful abominations of the Mormonites. These things are enough to warn Christians against anything which tends to unsettle the original and universal law of marriage — "They twain shall be one flesh."

Notes

1   R. Pierce Beaver, *To Advance the Gospel* (Grand Rapids: Eerdmans, 1967), pp. 36-37.
2   "Providential Antecedents of the Sierra Leone Mission." P., Vol. II, No. 19. (*The Christian Observer*, No. 419, November 1872.) This was the last article produced by Henry Venn before his death.
3   G/AZI/1, No. 30, Dec. 13, 1841. Extract from an address of the Committee of C.M.S. on the present financial situation. Signed by Henry Venn and other Secretaries.
4   G/AZI/1, No. 34, Sept. 29, 1842. Fourah Bay Institution Buildings' Fund. Signed
·   by H. V. and other Secretaries.
5   CA2/L1, pp. 50-51, April 17, 1847. Extract from a letter to an African, Mr. W. Marsh at Bedagary (Nigeria).
6   G/AZI/1, No. 71, Pars. 1-6. Undated, probably 1853 or 1854. Minute upon the position of native ministers in a mission, and upon the distinction between a mission and the pastoral charge of native converts. Internal evidence would seem to make it virtually certain that this Minute, albeit unsigned, would have been drafted by Henry Venn.
7   CI.1/L4, p. 251, December 13, 1854. Extract from letter to a missionary, the Rev. R. M. Lamb, in N. India.

8 CI.1/L4, pp. 293-295, June 1, 1855. Extract from letter of instructions to missionaries.

9 CI.1/L4, pp. 386-388, Aug. 4, 1856. Extract from a memorandum on the views of the Committee upon presenting for ordination native catechists in their employment.

10 G/AZI/1, No. 116, July 9, 1861. This Minute was submitted to the Society's missionaries and managing committees – not by way of positive instructions, but to direct attention to a matter of great and increasing importance.

11 G/AZI/1, No. 148, Oct. 8, 1866. The address of the Committee and Secretaries to the Sierra Leone Church Missionary Association, Oct. 8, 1866.

12 G/AZI/1, No. 151, Jan. 1867. Extracts from a letter to the Corresponding Committee in Madras on Native Church Organisation, dealing with some misapprehensions about proposed changes.

13 G/AZI/1, No. 152, Jan. 1867. Extract from letter of Henry Venn to the Bishop of Kingston (Jamaica) on the state of the Negroes of Jamaica.

14 G/AZI/2, No. 255, Jan. 12, 1857. Extract from a Minute of the Committee. The Minute began by a study of a large number of scriptural passages.

Chapter II

THE CALLING AND WORK OF A MISSIONARY

INTRODUCTION

Venn's vision of native churches, rooted in the soil of their own culture and history, depended upon a supply of men who would, as missionaries, take the good news of salvation to those who had never heard it. And Venn, as the first four extracts make clear, was seized of the vital importance that missionaries should be living exemplars of the gospel they preached. This was the continuing burden of his correspondence with missionaries.

The other passages provide a fair sample of the vast correspondence that Venn carried on with missionaries all through his secretariat. The last to be quoted is a Letter of Instructions to all missionaries on the subject of the annual letter every missionary was expected to write reporting on his work. The spiritual, no less than practical, importance of such letters is here masterfully portrayed. Elsewhere, an extract from his life of Francis Xavier holds up that great missionary to emulation on this point (p. 180).

Venn is sometimes accused of having failed to see the missionary as having a place within the structure of the native church. His preoccupation with "the regions beyond" and his view about "the euthanasia of the mission" (p. 63) are cited to illustrate this failure. So to read Venn is to misunderstand him. His primary concern, after the preaching of the gospel, was the building up of a native church. He saw clearly the danger that missionary paternalism would be likely to result in missionaries trying to retain control of the native church and so to stifle its true development. How very right he was! His great concern, which can be seen in such passages as will be found on pages 66-71, was to get the foreign missionary out of any

85

position of control. But that is not to say that he saw no place for the missionary *within* the structure of the church. Venn's own strong sense of church order and his efforts to extend the Episcopate overseas implied the organization of the church into dioceses. The missionary would certainly be part of the structure of the life of the diocese. But in the vast majority of situations with which Venn had to deal that was a development that could only come with time. The immediate task was to build up a native church. Where Venn was far ahead of almost all his contemporaries and of all too many of the men who came after him, was in seeing the danger for the native church of domination by the foreign missionary.

LETTER TO A MISSIONARY[1]

... Now let me urge upon you, my dear Brother, to commence or carry on your intercourse with your fellow labourer in the spirit of Christian unity and joint supplication for direction and blessing upon your labours. We have too low notions of the value of Christian love, we regard it too much in respect of the *comfort* of it — we forget the *power* it exerts. Fellow labourers, without vigorous love in exercise amongst them, lose half their efficiency. This arises in some measure from natural causes, but much more from supernatural ones. The Holy Spirit will not dwell where love is wanting. Therefore the success which can alone come from him fails.

But how is love to be kept in exercise? The grand means is by joint prayer — Two friends of a former age whose love to each other was most conspicuous and who were both of them most eminent in the revival of God's work in the Church of England, I allude to my own grandfather whose name I bear and Mr. Simeon of Cambridge — never spent part of a day together without praying together — and often more than once.

May the Lord increase you more and more in this and every other grace — may he warm your own heart with a Saviour's love — may he stamp upon your soul his own divine image that you may be an Epistle of Christ known and read of all men. May He give you the rich fruit of souls truly converted to him for your reward . . .

LETTER TO A MISSIONARY[2]

... Imperfect as my knowledge of the case thus is, I cannot let this mail go without expressing to you the great anxiety I feel that you should not be betrayed into language or take any step under the influence of irritated feelings which you may afterwards regret: and which may hinder your usefulness.

My dear Brother, we must all meet in this angular world with many things calculated to irritate our feelings — and I have heard enough of the effect of the Indian climate to make large allowances. But these are just the occasions for the trial of our faith and of our love to our blessed Saviour and of our conformity with his temper and disposition. Your appointment to Benares was made under full consideration of the leadings of Providence — and under prayer for divine direction. At every step of your progress towards the post you now occupy divine direction has been sought. Surely you should not contemplate a change to another sphere of labor without such evident direction as may satisfy any candid Christian mind. Surely it is no reason for the Steward of the Lord to relinquish his post because he is subjected to inconveniences which might be removed upon proper remonstrance. We must have higher motives and reasons for determining our conduct in each serious step of our course. . .

LETTER TO A MISSIONARY[3]

. . . I am happy to say that our Society continues to enjoy a peculiar calm and prosperity in all its home operations — and I trust that this blessed respite from anxious questions and controversies will be improved by us to the more abundant exercise of intercessory prayer on behalf of our dear Brethren who are engaged in the work abroad. That the Lord may both enlarge and unite all your hearts by the effusion of the spirit of love. This is the grace chiefly needed at the present day, both in respect of the laborers themselves and the efficiency of their labours . . .

LETTER OF INSTRUCTIONS TO MISSIONARIES[4]

. . . The first subject is the duty of mutual confidence and cordial co-operation amongst all Missionary labourers, especially those of the same Society or station.

In the early stage of a Mission each labourer has much work to do which may be accomplished singly and independently of others; such as preaching to the heathen; teaching the catechumens; instituting schools, translational labours, etc., in all this he may do much work alone. However desirable for his own spirit that he should have frequent conference with his brethren yet the work proceeds in his particular department.

But when the second stage is attained and Christian congregations have been formed, and native Teachers have been appointed, more or less approaching to the character of Native Pastors, then new duties and responsibilities arise and there is an urgent necessity for cordial union and co-operation between the fellow labourers in the Mission: for mutual confidence, for frequent counsel, and joint deliberation.

It now becomes necessary that each labourer should look beyond his particular sphere, should consider the end to be kept in view, and how the various plans in operation may combine together towards the attainment of that end.

That end is not the multiplication of Missionary Stations over the whole land, but the establishment of a few well selected and strong stations, where the foundations of a native Church may be wisely laid; where a native agency may be trained to carry forward the work, independently of Missionary assistance; so that the Missionary stations may become radiant points amidst the surrounding gloom; centres of faith, hope and charity; affording at once the source and the standard of Christian truth and morals to the rising Native Church.

All Missionary proceedings should be arranged in reference to this enlarged view of the subject, and to the ultimate results of our measures. But how shall we secure this unity of purpose without the mutual dependence, and combined influence, of each part of the Mission? And how shall this be accomplished unless there be mutual confidence and frequent consultation and united prayer on the part of those who conduct Missionary operations? And how can these exist unless there be Christian love and mutual forbearance and ready conversion and self-sacrifice, and a holy determination to keep the Unity of the Spirit in the bond of peace? . . .

ON THE IMPORTANCE OF LEARNING THE LANGUAGE OF THE PEOPLE[5]

. . . The Committee have a deep sense of the importance of the work to which you are appointed. The experience of the last 50 years of Missionary labour has proved that the three great desiderata are first, the early settlement of the orthography of a new language, secondly the preparation of valuable elementary and reading books in the vernacular, thirdly, the early circulation of God's pure Word amongst the converts. These are the roots of a sound growth in a Mission. They can be effectually accomplished only by the labour of those to whom God has given the special gifts, which in our day supply the miracle of Pentecost . . .

ON THE PROGRESS OF A MISSION[6]

. . . It is important ever to bear in mind what may be called the normal progress of Missionary operations, which may be thus represented:

The first stage is that in which a single Missionary goes forth upon a vast undertaking, attempts such part of the work as circumstances may suggest — but has not strength or agency enough effectually to follow out his plans — he earnestly appeals for help, he is distracted between conflicting claims upon his time. Such is the commencement of a Mission.

The second stage of progress is when there is a sufficient Missionary force to allow of a systematic arrangement between station duties and itinerant preaching: whether by setting apart labourers for each department or by an alternation of duties. This is the establishment of a Mission.

As the work prospers a third stage is characterized by the institution of central, normal and training schools to supply several stations with School-masters, Catechists and eventually Native Pastors. This is the era of the Extension of the Mission. These branches of the work may all be carried on within the compass of one city, as in Benares: or as in Tinnevelly many stations may be dotted over three or 4,000 square miles — while the central educational establishments are at Palamcotta, and itinerant Missionary work is kept up within the circuits of the stations in the regions beyond.

Real progress in a Mission depends upon keeping up both station duties and itinerary. The efficiency and success of the one is inseparably connected with the efficiency and success of the other. In the one case a station may wear a very promising Christian appearance, but if there be not a putting forth of Missionary effort and continual accessions from the surrounding heathen, the work within the Christian enclosure will languish and turn into disappointment. In the other case a spirit of inquiry may be excited throughout a district, but if there be not Christian villages and congregations at hand to point to as living witnesses of a Native Christianity, and as asylums for the persecuted or timid, if there be not trained native teachers to sustain the movement, a spirit of slumber deeper than before will creep over the District. Let not therefore the itinerant Missionary and the Station Missionary underrate each other's labours. If the one department may be compared to the foliage of the tree, the other is the root. The roots must be striking deep into the soil, while the summer shoots are multiplying . . .

THE WORK OF A MISSIONARY[7]

. . . You are going forth, dear brethren, at a season of peculiar interest in many respects. The state of our beloved Church at home — the state of India, to which your destination has been fixed by the Committee — the state of the world at large — each of these topics might suggest many important reflections bearing upon your enterprise.

One peculiar characteristic of the present times is the changeableness and uncertainty of the human mind. The opinions which had been apparently rooted and fixed in men's minds are relinquished, and the very opposite are embraced: Feelings which lately identified with the national character, are now cast aside by a large proportion of the Community: Society has no longer the security which once existed as to the principles of men who occupy its various stations. Amidst such a state of things it is of the utmost importance that those who are to co-operate in any great work should thoroughly understand each other.

The Committee confidently trust that such an understanding exists between you and themselves. The principles on which the Church Missionary Society has long since taken and maintained her stand are concisely explained by the terms "protestant and evangelical": Terms which, through *evil report and good report* this Society has ever chosen as her motto. It is upon the faith that these principles shall regulate all the proceedings and all the agencies of the Society, that the funds are contributed and the very existence of the Society is maintained. If therefore there be any departure from these principles, faith is broken with the Society, and the party who thus violates good faith is bound by every principle of justice and honour to withdraw from the Society. The principles which the Committee would thus uphold are only an expansion of the very title of the Society − "The *Church* Missionary Society! " For they are the principles of our beloved Church as it came forth from the hands of its Protestant founders, and have been by them embodied in its articles and formularies.

It is not the object of the Committee in making these remarks to cherish in you, or to indulge in themselves, any spirit of controversy − any narrow or party feelings − far otherwise! They desire only that you and they should clearly understand each other, just as the Patron of a Living at home when nominating an Incumbent − or an Incumbent when appointing a Curate; desire to have a clear understanding of the faith and expectations on which this engagement is formed.

And when through the good providence of our God you shall have entered upon your work abroad all that the Committee desire to hear from you is that you stand fast in the Lord, and give up yourselves wholly to the work to which you are called; namely to preach the Gospel of the grace of God to the heathen in all the simplicity and fulness with which it reveals itself in the open volume of inspiration. The Committee would earnestly commend to your frequent perusal the late Metropolitan charge of the Bishop of Calcutta, a copy of which will be given to each of you, and specially would they direct your attention to that part of it in which the Bishop advises his reverend brethren to abstain from controversy unless where an evident necessity may call for it. Such advice is doubly valuable for Missionaries: and the words of the Charge which close this sentiment are words which deserve to be written in letters of gold. "It is not so much argument which we want, as grace, the secret gentle effusions of grace upon all our hearts. This will give us a riper knowledge of the Bible, a firmer grasp of the capital doctrines of the gospel, a more full apprehension of the person and glory of Christ, a deeper sense of the evil of sin; a warmer love to God and man: a more holy spirit of abstraction from the world, and a more fervent temper of prayer and communion with God".

The State of India is one, also, which presents peculiar interests to those who are now entering upon Missionary work. Every frank account bears evidence of the movement which is going on, of the critical character of the present moment with reference to the direction of that movement, whether to good or evil. Alas! how utterly inadequate, and in the eyes of men of this world, contemptible does the instrumentality of a few scattered Missionaries appear! one to 100,000 heathens and how insufficient for these things does the Missionary appear in his own eyes when he compares his weakness, poverty and insufficiency with the magnitude of the work to which he is called!

"It may seem (says the pious Archbishop Leighton) a poor despicable business, that a frail man speak a few words to his perishing fellow sinners; yet look upon it as the way wherein God communicates happiness to them that believe, and works that believing unto happiness, alters the whole frame of the soul, and makes a new creation. Consider it thus which is the true notion and then what so precious! Let the world disesteem it as they will: know ye that it is the power of God unto salvation. The preaching of the cross is to them that perish foolishness, but unto them that are saved it is the power of God says the Apostle."

Another agency, second only to that of the preaching of the Gospel which Missionary work comprises is that of scriptural education, because education apart from religious instruction is only instructing the movement without directing it; or, perhaps, imparting to it an evil bias. Yet at present there exists in India a vast apparatus of education from which religion is excluded — is *"barred out"* to use the forcible expression which, thirty years ago, was adopted by a late noble Governor General of India; Lord Teignmouth — and has again been employed by the Bishop of Calcutta in his Metropolitan Charge, in order to express their solemn conviction of the impolicy as well as impiety of such a course of proceedings.

But while Christianity is thus "barred out" from Government schools how doubly important is it that Missionary schools conducted upon a more enlightened principle — should be maintained in the highest state of efficiency — and should be adapted to the most advanced stages of intellectual improvement.

The Committee specially allude to this subject because two of you dear brethren will have to labour in immediate connection with such educational establishments. They would desire that you should ever remember that your educational duties must be made *Missionary* work; by being carried on in a Missionary spirit, and directed to the great end of Missions — the conversion of the soul to Christ. When so conducted it is a work not beneath the hearty aspirations of the most devoted piety and the highest order of talent. More especially is this true when such establishments are directed, as all those of this Society ever have been to the training up, under God's blessing, of a native ministry. Here a wide and glorious field of usefulness opens before the Society in which the minds of the wisest Christian philanthropists have delighted to expatiate. It is impossible to calculate the benefit which in the present transition state of India is conferred by raising up well educated and pious young men for native teachers . . .

LETTER OF INSTRUCTIONS TO A MISSIONARY[8]

. . . Here (Garruckpore) also an experiment has been made of training up Native Christians in habits of industry and profitable employment, upon a farm, reclaimed from the wilderness, where converts and adults brought up in Orphan Schools, are located in a little Christian village, with its school and its consecrated Church.

This interesting Christian Community is situated about four miles from the populous native town of Garruckpore, where a Missionary of the Society, the Revd. J. P. Mengé resides.

It is the Committee's wish that while Mr. Mengé devotes himself to the general Missionary duties, such as preaching to the heathen, and superintending schools, and preparing native books, — you should regard as your special charge the native Church in the wilderness, and by exercising a constant and vigilant pastoral superintendence over them endeavour to build them up in our most holy faith.

The experience of all who have laboured in India testifies to the need of European superintendence to secure, under God, strength and consistency of Christian character in our converts. Even those who are most sincere in their profession of the Christian faith cannot be trusted alone. The depressing effect of heathen descent and of the long servitude of the Natives of India to other nations, manifests itself most affectingly in the feebleness of many of the rising Christian Churches. This is especially the case where a large proportion has been received as orphans from their heathen parents, and baptized in their infancy. They will need to be trained up in Christian habits and taught to apply Christian principles to the daily duties and occurrences of life, as a careful mother in this country teaches her children during the early years of childhood . . .

LETTER TO A MISSIONARY[9]

. . . In the multiplicity of engagements which fall upon the Secretaries at home it is impossible to keep up that individual correspondence which we should desire, with our several Missionaries — but believe me, my dear Brother, there is not one in whose welfare we do not feel a deep interest, and whose communications we do not look for and welcome with Christian sympathy and brotherly affection. We greatly value quarterly journals: and the regular communication between England and India has now removed every obstacle to their regular transmission. Even though nothing may have occurred of a marked kind, these journals are valuable on many accounts — both to the Missionary himself, and to the Parent Committee. Situated as you are in the metropolis of India your thoughts must be conversant with a multitude of subjects connected with the advance of our blessed Redeemer's kingdom, which might afford matter of deep interest and much usefulness. Brother Long has in the course of last year sent us several more acceptable letters of this kind. Ever bear in mind that Missionaries have a power and privilege, beyond any others, of exciting the zeal and animating the prayers of the Church at home by their own communications, which may be circulated, in the Society's publications to a vàst extent, and which are read and talked over by thousands of the Lord's children. How great then is their responsibility! Oh that they might all act up to it! That after looking up to Him "from whom cometh the preparation of the heart in man and the answer of the tongue" — they may pour forth the fulness of their hearts into the ear of the Christian public: and awaken Christian Churches to some just sense of their duty towards heathen lands. The time is short in every sense — great events are rapidly approaching. How long the present facilities for preaching the Gospel may continue — How long you and I may be permitted to engage in this honored work — Oh let us work and strive to stir each other up and work while it is day . . .

LETTER TO A MISSIONARY[10]

. . . I praise Him for your safe arrival at your post of labour — for the vigour with which you can enter upon it — for the favourable account you give of it notwithstanding our fears — for the heart cheering account of your conference at Krishnaghar — and the most satisfactory testimony you bear to the advancement of the work of grace amongst the native Christians in this district. I had just been preparing the Report of the North Indian Mission — from the documents before me I was somewhat cast down — and feared that no visible blessing from the Lord had been manifested during the last year. But your testimony has been a real cordial and will contribute some bright rays to gladden many hearts in Exeter Hall in the forthcoming Report . . .

LETTER TO A MISSIONARY[11]

. . . You will see that the Committee authorise the Calcutta Corresponding Committee to appoint either Mr. Reuther or Mr. Droese to visit and sojourn for a time at Bhagalpore, for the purpose of ascertaining what are the peculiar encouragements for Missionary exertions in that locality; but the Committee are not prepared at present to take up this or any other fresh station without a strong providential call.

The first principle of the Society is to provide adequate thought for the fair trial of its existing stations. A single Missionary at a Station who may be overwhelmed with work and liable to be frequently interrupted by ill health, cannot be said to afford such a fair trial; but Hawes at Jampore, Mr. Lamb at Meerut and Mr. Mengé at Gorruckpore are instances in point. It is better to relinquish a Station than to sustain it in an inefficient state without the prospect of improvement.

Upon this principle there must be a providential call before we enter upon new ground. This providential call must be looked for in the favourable feelings of the people towards the reception of Christianity, and in the peculiar facilities for Missionary operations, on a large scale, in the locality, rather than in the lure of special funds or the earnest desire of the residents, who normally take a deeper interest in their own immediate locality than in any other.

In the early days of Missionary History the latter inducements were the only grounds upon which we could act, but in the present advanced state of Missions and with all India open before us, and with other countries inviting our labours, we must be guided by other considerations . . .

CIRCULAR TO THE SOCIETY'S MISSIONARIES[12]

Dear Brethren,

The completion of the first half of their financial year has led the Committee once more to review their financial position. The result shows an increase, under the head "Association", of above £1800 over the receipts of the first six months of last year — more than half of this sum however is due to a large remittance from Ireland, usually kept back till towards the close of the year. There has been a diminution of legacies to the extent of £1500 below last year, and nearly to the same extent below the average of the last five years; while there has been an increase of about £2000 in Benefactions over what had been received up to September 30, 1854, and nearly £2500 over the average. There appears on the whole an aggregate increase of somewhat more than £3000 over the receipts at the corresponding period of 1854; but of less than £2000 over the average of five years. But the year commenced with a debt of £5621 and several Missionaries have since been added to the list.

The Committee, therefore, are unable to reduce the estimate made at the beginning of the year, that an increase of at least £11,000 over the receipts of last year is requisite to place the Society free from embarrassment at the commencement of the ensuing financial year.

We have recently been reminded by one of our Missionaries of a remark in Cecil's *Remains:* "When a man becomes a Christian he is written upon as it were *to be provided for,* and he ought therefore to notice as he goes on how Providence does provide for him". The Committee very thankfully acknowledge the marked way in which the Lord has hitherto provided for the wants of the Society; and especially for the manner in which it has pleased Him from time to time to assist them in seasons of financial difficulty, and they entertain a firm confidence that He will not fail them at the present crisis.

It must, however, be noticed that the great pressure arising from the war and the consequent increase of taxation and the cost of all the necessaries of life at home, continues unabated; while new demands are perpetually made upon the charity of the public: and that it would therefore be unreasonable to expect that the Society's income should remain unaffected: and though the income of the six months just elapsed affords but imperfect data for estimating that of the entire year, the statement above made is sufficient to suggest the utmost caution. In the good Providence of God the Committee would hope that their resources will not be diminished; but they dare not reckon upon a continuance of that rapid increase which had marked the few years immediately preceding the outbreak of War. They are therefore quite unable to remove the restrictions they have been compelled to put upon their foreign expenditure.

On the contrary, they feel it right afresh to lay upon their Corresponding Committees and Missionaries the state of their finances, and once again to remind them, in all confidence and affection, that it is a burden providentially imposed upon the Society at large.

It may be useful to recapitulate the principal points to which attention has already been directed; and the Committee do this the more cheerfully because they have been so much encouraged by the ready response with which their former communications have been met; and by the efforts made to supply abroad the lack of service at home. This spirit they are persuaded will re-act powerfully upon friends in England, and thus a double blessing may result out of a present trial.

1. The Committee desire to encourage a sustained effort to throw as much as possible of the work upon the self-supporting system.

Here the Committee cannot but notice that while their prayers under their financial difficulties have been heard and answered in a direct manner by the large donations received during the course of the present year, it has pleased God to give an indirect answer to prayer, yet more precious than the direct answer. The crisis had led not only to a distinct and, happily, to a great extent, to a successful effort to husband the resources of the Society, but, what is vastly more important, it has developed the resources of the infant churches planted through its instrumentability in New Zealand, Africa, India, and America; and initiated or given a fresh impulse to exertions which the Committee trust will not only establish an important principle, but sensibly and permanently relieve the Society of a large expenditure incurred in the maintenance of schools, in buildings and other matters, which should more properly be charged to the account of the Native Congregations themselves. In Sierra Leone, a definite scheme has been suggested and heartily taken up which will in a few years transfer the support of the Schools entirely to the Colony; and the Committee very thankfully acknowledge the progress made in the same direction in other of their foreign stations.

In connexion with this subject the Committee must remark, that in laying the foundations of a Native ministry, Missionaries should bear in mind that ordained Natives, so far as they are employed in ministering to the wants of Christian congregations, belong to a settled rather than to a Missionary Church, and hence, while the Committee readily acknowledge an obligation to assist its infant churches during their transition state, they cannot but feel that the maturity which justifies the location of a Native pastor in charge of a fixed congregation, also involves the obligation on the part of this people to contribute something to his support. They are sensible of the exertions which have been made to secure endowments for such pastors, and will continue to encourage them as they have hitherto done, according to the Jubilee regulations, by making grants to meet sums raised in the Missions for this purpose. Meanwhile the rule which is already in operation in Western Africa, viz.: to continue to an ordained Native the salary he has received while employed as a Catechist, leaving any increase of salary which may be deemed requisite to be provided independently − should be applied to all other Missions, as far as circumstances will allow. The case of those Natives who are employed in the capacity of Missionaries, strictly so called, is special, and must be determined by the circumstances of the case.

2. Another remark has been somewhat unexpectedly forced upon the attention of the Committee by the suggestion of the Missionaries themselves in sôme of the Society's stations, namely, the retrenchment of unnecessary expenses, by the closing of inefficient Schools, dismissing supernumerary or inefficient agents, curtailing needless travelling expenses, and checking other similar outlays of money, which there is always a tendency to continue, after the necessity in which they originated has passed away; and which from time to time require a careful revision.

3. It will be necessary to postpone many desirable objects, and more particularly buildings, which can be dispensed with for the present.

4. The Committee would also hope that increased contributions either by special Donations or by new or enlarged Subscriptions, may be obtained abroad, and more particularly in India, where the pressure of the times is less severely felt than in England.

5. It is most important to bear in mind, that concurrently with the straitened state of their resources, openings of more than ordinary promise are presenting themselves on every side. New fields of labour can be entered upon only after mature deliberation; but when those present features indicative of a decisive providential call, and men present themselves for the work, the Committee dare not refuse to entertain invitations to come over and help perishing nations. If, then, means enlarged in proportion to an enlarging work be not afforded by the Christian Public, however painful it may be to curtail existing station expenses, and however great the obligation to sustain the work in which God has already largely blessed their efforts, the Committee are constrained to consider whether their present missions cannot be efficiently carried on at a diminished cost, before they can bring themselves to pause in their onward movement where the door is providentially opening before them. They earnestly pray that they may not be compelled to adopt the last most painful alternative of declining to send out suitable Missionaries who are willing to go, until the means for their future support are afforded.

Commending this subject to your prayerful consideration and to the blessing of Almighty God.

ON THE TRAINING OF MISSIONARIES AT THE SOCIETY'S INSTITUTION AT ISLINGTON[13]

... I must bear my testimony to the evident success of the Institution in training young men, often from the very commencement of their education, to become well-furnished Ministers of Christ. I had the experience of five years as Tutor of Queens' College Cambridge and I have been for 15 years a Visitor of the Islington Institution: and I can state that the men presented for ordination from Islington have been fully on a par with the *best* men from Cambridge in respect of Theological knowledge and a knowledge of the Scriptures in the original.

The present Bishop of London has repeatedly and publicly expressed his entire satisfaction with the results of this instruction at Islington, as manifested in his ordinations.

The importance of the Institution to our Society consists in the furnishing us with a supply of men, with whose character and capabilities we are thoroughly acquainted and of whose services we can either prospectively or promptly avail ourselves according to the exigencies of the Mission . . .

LETTER OF INSTRUCTIONS TO ALL MISSIONARIES ON THE IMPORTANCE OF ANNUAL LETTERS[14]

You are about to proceed to the Mission Fields of North India, Western India, South India and New Zealand, to which you have been appointed, there to be associated with others of your brethren who have preceded you, that you may be fellow-labourers with them in the Gospel of Christ, to the glory of God and the salvation of sinners. They on their departure received their respective instructions, and to those Instructions the Committee would refer you as comprising all that they could desire to say to you, on the general character of your work, the tone and temper in which it ought to be commenced and carried on, and your need of the grace that is in Christ Jesus, that you may be sustained under difficulties and trials.

On the present occasion, the Committee propose to address themselves to a special subject, directing your attention to that exclusively. Its importance, as they conceive, justifies their doing so. It is of universal application to all Missionaries. The diverse fields of labour to which Missionaries are appointed must necessitate considerable dissimilarity in the Instructions delivered to them. Missionary work in its detail presents a great variety of aspect, and the counsel which would be most pertinent in one case, would be quite irrelevant in another. But the subject to which the Committee would confine themselves today, applies with equal force to every Missionary, whatever the peculiarities of his work; and, intimately connected as it is with the well-being of the Missionary cause, and the hopes we entertain of its being deepened and strengthened into increased efficiency, has a powerful claim on the prayerful consideration of all. It has to do with the well-being of the Church at home. It has to do with the well-being of the work abroad. There is therefore an importance connected with it which the Committee have long felt, and they gladly avail themselves of this present opportunity to give it due consideration and prominence.

The subject to which the Committee refer is the duty which devolves on every Missionary to present to the Society, and through the Society to the Church at large, regular and faithful transcripts of the Missionary work as it comes under his own personal observation.

There is Scriptural example to direct us in this matter. On a reference to the Acts, the 13th chapter, we are informed, that when at Antioch there were congregated "certain prophets and teachers", two from amongst the number, Barnabas and Saul, were specially designated by the Holy Ghost to go forth and preach the Gospel in the districts around. "Separate me Barnabas and Saul for the work whereunto I have called them." Such is the hope we entertain respecting you beloved brethren – "that you are inwardly moved by the Holy Ghost to take upon you this office and ministration;" and our desire is that you should go forth with our heartfelt prayers and sympathy, just as Barnabas and Saul went forth with the prayers and sympathy of the Christians at Antioch, who, "when they had fasted and prayed, laid their hands on them, and sent them away". The particulars of the labour in which they engaged, the places which they visited, and the reception which they met, are then detailed in this and the succeeding chapter, until their return to Antioch, "from whence they had been recommended to the grace of God for the work which they had fulfilled;" and immediately on their arrival, as a primary duty which ought not to be neglected, they gathered the Church together, and "rehearsed all that God had done with them." So again, in the next chapter (the 15th) when deputed to visit Jerusalem in connection with a certain question, as they "passed through Phenice and Samaria", they declared "the conversion of the Gentiles" causing "great joy unto all the brethren. And when they were come to Jerusalem, they were received of the Church, and of the Apostles and Elders, and they declared all things that God had done with them." On a subsequent visit to Jerusalem, as detailed in the Acts, the 21st Chapter, we find Paul pursuing the same course, and declaring "particularly what things God had wrought among the Gentiles by his ministry". The original Greek shows that there must have been much of minute detail in his narrative – *exēgeito kath hen hekaston ōn epoiēsen ho theos en tois ethnesin dia tēs diakonias autou.*

It is important that the Missionary should ever bear in mind his responsibilities to the Church at home in the discharge of this duty. The Missionary interest at home is the heart of all that is going forward in distant parts. Those foreign efforts are the expression of this home interest. Sympathy between them must be maintained, and the work abroad must re-act beneficially on the interest at home, if that interest is to be kept up, and if the undertakings it has put forth are to be vigorously prosecuted. A forcible analogy, illustrative of the subject, may be found in the organization of the human frame. The heart is the fountain from whence the vital streams diffuse themselves through every artery and vein, and hence the pulsation of life, and the capability of effort, which pervade the members. Yet, if the heart give, it receives in return. The members are in various ways employed in ministering to the requirements of the central reservoir, so that there may be no enfeebling of its action, and all unite in reciprocating supplies to that from whence they are all supplied. So, wherever a Missionary is located, and there is the expenditure of interest connected with the commencement and prosecution of Missionary work, there ought to be from thence a grateful re-action and the remittance of that information which is the very material that holy love, the love that is of God, love to Christ and to souls, by its peculiar action, transubstantiates into increased sympathy and increased effort.

The Committee are the more anxious to place this duty before their Missionaries in the clear and Scriptural light which they conceive belongs to it, because misapprehensions may arise respecting it, which, wherever they exist, must interfere with its performance. The intelligence transmitted from the diverse points of Missionary occupation varies considerably. From many quarters it is fresh and abundant. From others there is regular communication, but of an official and formal character; while from some only occasional letters arrive, which are not such as to enable the Committee to identify themselves, as intimately as they would desire, with the efforts of their brethren, and to feel themselves in that close sympathy with them which they are anxious to maintain.

The withholding of information, when it does occur, may be accounted for in various ways. There is sometimes a morbid sensitiveness on the part of a Missionary as to the publication of details; and, shrinking from the idea of having his work submitted to the public eye, he confines himself in his reports to generalities. But the work is not the Missionary's. It is the Lord's work. It is what Christ hath wrought by the Missionary that we seek to know; and *that,* no private individual is justified in withholding from the Society and the Church. It is not with him to decide on that point. He has no option in the matter. So Paul felt. In his Epistle to the Romans, xv, 18, he says expressly, "I will not dare to speak of any of those things which Christ hath not wrought by me, to make the Gentiles obedient, by word and deed;" but of those things which Christ had wrought by him he found himself, at the proper time and occasion, constrained to speak, as he immediately proceeds to do in the next verse — "Through mighty signs and wonders, by the power of the Spirit of God; so that from Jerusalem, and round about unto Illyricum, I have fully preached the Gospel of Christ."

Again, some are deterred by the fear of ministering to the selfish and vain-glorious principle, of the stirrings of which every Christian man is in a greater or less degree painfully sensible, and of the necessity of subjugating which he is equally convinced. The pride of the human heart finds materials to feed upon in every change of outward circumstance, and that pride may be gratified in the very reserve which had been resorted to in the hope of starving it. The expulsive power of a new and divine affection, increasing love to the Lord Jesus Christ, and elevation of soul to Him, under a sense of benefits continually received, constitutes the only true corrective. But the attempt to escape one temptation, by the avoidance of duty is the sure way to fall into some other.

The hindrance, to which the Committee refer, will be much lessened by the simple consideration, that whatever work the Missionary is permitted to do is not so much his, as the Lord's. All are but instruments. He selects such as it may be His pleasure to employ, apportioning them their proper spheres and callings, whether ministerial work at home, or Missionary work abroad, and carrying forward, through their instrumentality, that which He has purposed should be done. His whole mystical body is rendered available to this end. He works in and by His willing people and directs them to the performance of such good works as He has before ordained that they should walk in. But the results produced are His, not ours. The works done, the fruits yielded, are the Lord's; and it is His pleasure that such should be made known, for the encouragement and comfort of His people – "O give thanks unto the Lord; call upon His name; make known His deeds among the people. Sing unto Him, sing psalms unto Him: talk ye of all His wondrous works." (Ps.cv.1,2.) "One generation shall praise Thy works to another, and shall declare Thy mighty acts ... All Thy works shall praise Thee, O Lord; and Thy saints shall bless Thee. They shall speak of the glory of Thy kingdom, and talk of Thy power; to make known to the sons of men His mighty acts, and the glorious majesty of His kingdom." (Ps.cxliv). So the Saviour once enjoined, "Go home to thy friends, and tell them how great things the Lord hath done for thee, and hath had compassion on thee." (Mark v.19).

The Committee would further observe, that it is not any partial view of the work which they desire, but a faithful transcript of it, as it is – its difficulties as well as its encouragements, its reverses as well as its successes. They wish to know as much of it, when it is under a cloud, as when the sunshine of the Divine favour is unequivocally resting upon it. It is only as the narration is thus faithful, that it can be profitable to the Church.

The beneficial effects of a conscientious discharge of this duty are manifold. It is advantageous to the Church, beneficial to the Missionary cause, healthful to the Missionary, and promotive of the best interests of his own particular station.

It is advantageous to the Church, for it developes interest, quickens sympathy, and brings into exercise the varied graces of the Christian character. Faithful transcripts of the Missionary work will necessarily be of varying aspect. There will be the dark ground of heathen ignorance, and the welcome relief of the Gospel in its renewing action. There will be the Missionary's hopes, and the Missionary's fears; the faithful few who are his crown of rejoicing, and the unstable many who go back and walk no more with him. But all will be profitable. The clouds and the sunshine, the storm and the tranquil season, temper each other. There will be enough of encouragement to "thank God, and take courage"; and enough of difficulty and disappointment to remind us of our complete dependence on the Lord. The hearts of Christians at home will be moved in sympathy with their Missionary friends abroad, and they will be enabled to "rejoice with them that do rejoice, and weep with them that weep". The work, as presented in its varied aspect, will elicit, now the thanksgivings, now the earnest supplications, of the Lord's people, just as the hand brings forth from an instrument, sounds, now joyous, now moving; and in each God is glorified.

The Missionary cause in general, the discharge of this duty will prove in many respects beneficial. There will be an increased acquaintance with the nature of the work in which we are engaged. The necessities of the heathen will be better understood, and the desire to help them be increased proportionately. The conviction will be strengthened that far more ought to be done, and there will be a clearer perception as to the way in which we ought to do it. As, in analytical science, various experiments bring out principles, so, in the variety of details submitted from various quarters, we are enabled to distinguish between the permanent characteristics of Missionary work, and such as are only local and incidental; between the changes wherewith it is sure to be affected, wherever it be prosecuted, and such as are occasional and exceptive. We are taught, so to speak, the philosophy of Missions. We are forewarned alike against over-sanguine hopes and depressing fears. We are prepared for vicissitudes. But we are confirmed in the conviction that the work is the Lord's and the issue sure. Thus the work becomes more and more a work of faith; there is less of excitement, but more of principle; and in this, provision is made for stedfast persistence in its prosecution, amidst whatsoever difficulties.

To be thus in close connection with home will be of first importance to each Missionary, and to the work in which he is personally engaged. Friends become familiarized with the details of each particular station, and are thus increasingly interested in its welfare. They know its wants, and they are moved to prayer on its behalf. The information they receive respecting it makes them acquainted with its peculiar features, and when they would pray they know what petitions to offer up. And as with his work, so with the Missionary. He is had in remembrance by his brethren. He is enriched by their prayers; while he who isolates himself by silence, and withdraws himself from this communion, must not be surprised if he find himself proportionably impoverished. More frankness of intercourse with his brethren would ensure to him more perceptible support and comfort. St. Paul was sensible of this. He would not have his Christian friends at Corinth (2 Cor. i.8) ignorant of the trouble which came upon him at Ephesus. And why? Because he desired to be helped by their prayers. He believed that such prayers were efficacious to help – "Ye also helping together by prayer for us." He looked forward to many a similar time of difficulty; but he took courage in believing that like deliverances, to that which he had so recently experienced, would be vouchsafed him – "who delivered us from so great a death, and doth deliver: in whom we trust that He will yet deliver us;" and he desired their prayers, not only that he might be helped, but when, in answer to their prayers, the deliverance which had been sought had been conceded, "that for the gift bestowed upon us by the means of many persons thanks may be given by many on our behalf." The Missionary who is duly sensible of his position will earnestly desire the prayers of his brethren: and they *are* so desired. There is no one entreaty urged more continuously from every portion of the Missionary field. But if the brethren abroad would be helped by the prayers of those who are at home, they must, in the discharge of the duty on which the Committee have expressed themselves, help the Church to pray.

In conclusion, the Committee would observe, that if the duty in question be thus important, it is well worth the time which may be expended on it. They are quite aware of the many responsibilities which engage the attention of their Missionaries. Still, they have the less hesitation in urging the claims of this particular service, persuaded as they are that it is an expenditure of time and thought which will not be lost, but will be sure to bring back a rich return. Neither in these observations do they mean to imply that the duty under consideration has not been strongly felt, and extensively acted upon, throughout the wide circle of the stations in connection with the Church Missionary Society. They desire to record, with much thankfulness, the full and punctual communications which it is their privilege to receive. Their object, with reference to the general body of their Missionaries, is not so much to correct a deficiency, as to strengthen a conviction already existing, and to encourage you, beloved Brethren, who are now going forth to the Mission-field, to the punctual discharge of a duty, of which so happy an example is being set you by so many of your brethren.

There is now one special act in the discharge of this duty which the Committee have to recommend, and which it is the main object of these instructions to enjoin upon each of their Missionaries, in various parts of the world. It is, that every Missionary, besides the transmission of the ordinary Reports and Journals – which, passing through the hands of the various Corresponding Committees, are not unfrequently delayed before they reach us – should, at the close of each year, transmit to the Parent Committee a digest of his labours and proceedings, in the form of an *Annual Letter:* a copy of which should be sent to the Corresponding Committee. This Annual Letter, if sent early in each year, will reach the Committee while they are engaged in the preparation of the Annual Report, and will materially assist in that work . . . Such an annual review will be profitable to yourselves. It will afford to you the opportunity of considering whether you have in ought deteriorated from that simplicity and earnestness of purpose, by which you were actuated when you first put your hand to this work of faith and labour of love, and of seeking in earnest prayer those refreshings from the presence of the Lord, whereby He is able to revive His work in the hearts of His people.

Notes

1   CI.1/L3, pp. 291-292, December 5, 1846. Extract from letter to the Rev. J. P. Mengé.
2   CI.1/L3, pp. 137-138, Jan. 7, 1845. Extract from letter to Rev. E. Johnson.
3   CI.1/L3, p. 117, Sept. 7, 1844. Extract from letter to the Rev. J. Innes.
4   CI.1/L3, pp. 324-325, May 24, 1847. Extract from letter of instructions to Rev. J. Hasel and Rev. M. Wilkinson.
5   CI.1/L5, p. 67, Oct. 1, 1858. Extract from letter of instructions to a missionary proceeding to India.
6   CI.1/L4, pp. 176-177, Aug. 26, 1853. Extract from letter of instructions to missionaries proceeding to India.
7   CI.1/L3 (1842-1851), 7 July 1843, pp. 46-50. Extract from letter of instructions to Rev. G. Johnson and Mrs. Johnson on going to Calcutta.
8   CI.1/L3, pp. 276-279, December 1, 1846. Extract from letter of instructions to Mr. Alexander Acheson.
9   CI.1/L3, p. 147, March, 24, 1845. Extract from letter to the Rev. J. T. Osborne.
10 CI.1/L3, pp. 151-152, April 24, 1845. Extract from letter to the Rev. J. J. Weitbrecht.
11 CI.1/L3, pp. 459-460, October 19, 1849. Extract from letter to the Rev. G. G. Cuthbert.
12 G/AZI/1, No. 88, November 20, 1855.
13 G/ACI/5, May 9, 1846, pp. 117-118. To Archdeacon Musgrave.
14 M.P., Vol. II, No. 14, June 16, 1854.

Chapter III

THE PRINCIPLES AND WORKING OF A MISSIONARY SOCIETY

INTRODUCTION

Venn was clear that if missionaries were to fulfil their vocation they needed the support of a society whose members, sharing that vocation, were pledged to their support. This sense of a deep personal commitment, which united the missionary abroad with his supporters at home, lay at the very heart of the principle of voluntary association. Venn believed that a missionary society, based on this principle, was the best possible agency for spreading the gospel. There are substantial grounds for holding the conviction that this principle is as valid today as it was in Venn's time. This is not to claim that such voluntary associations of persons, animated by the same convictions, are the only agents of mission. There are many agencies. Nor was Venn ever jealous of the activities of others. This volume contains illustrations of his wide sympathies (see the chapter on "Ecumenicity"). But he was deeply convinced that the "Voluntary Principle," by which men and women agreed not only on the goal but on the means to reach it and were united to pursue it, had a validity of its own in the work of the gospel.

How Venn thought about this in broad principle can be seen in the two long documents that come first in this chapter. One is a sermon in which the very points he makes about the character of one of his predecessors illuminate his own, and illustrate his convictions as to the spiritual basis of the Society he served. The second is a wide-ranging review of thirty years in the history of the Church Missionary Society.

These two long documents provide a background for the understanding of the shorter extracts that follow. In the first of these the word "secularity" is used in a fashion unfamiliar to most readers today. By "secularity" Venn meant complete absorption in matters secondary to the primary object of preaching the gospel. That Venn did not despise the "secondary" is amply demonstrated throughout this volume. But he was always anxious about any tendency for the "secondary" to become "primary." Some of the ambivalence of his thinking about education, for instance, illustrates this anxiety. In a word, in Venn's thinking, "secularity" means preoccupation with what is secondary. It bears no relation to what today is meant by secularism or secularization.

A SERMON ON I PETER 4:10-11[1]

As every man hath received the gift, even so minister the same one to another, as good stewards of the manifold grace of God.

If any man speak, let him speak as the oracles of God: if any man minister, let him do it as of the ability which God giveth: that God in all things may be glorified through Jesus Christ, to whom be praise and dominion for ever and ever. Amen.

A great Christian principle is laid down in this passage, which, though it frequently occurs in the Sacred Volume, is scarcely in any other place so fully developed. It is, that all the endowments of a man, mental and spiritual, all the wealth and influence which he possesses, are the gift of God – the spontaneous and unmerited emanation of Divine Love – of the *manifold grace of God.*

To a certain extent this principle is readily admitted by Christians; for all are willing to trace up whatever good thing they possess to the bounty of their Heavenly Benefactor. But too many withdraw their assent when the principle is urged to the extent to which the text carries it; namely, that these gifts are not made over to us absolutely; that we are not the proprietors of them; that we are only stewards of the *manifold grace of God:* so that no man is at liberty to say before God, of any thing he has acquired or inherited, "May I not do what I will with my own? " The things we possess are only committed to us to be dispensed through our hands to the objects or persons for which God has designed them.

The principle is, however, carried to a still further extent by the Apostle: for he reminds us that this dispensation of grace, and our stewardship therein, are ordained for the glory of God. Though *good-will toward man* is indeed stamped upon every part of the Gospel, yet is the great end, to which all the designs of Providence and of Grace tend, and to which, therefore, the thoughts and desires of the servant of God should ever tend, *That God in all things may be glorified through Jesus Christ.*

Through Jesus Christ. The *manifold grace of God* flows to us through our crucified and exalted Redeemer. The dispensation of the Gospel is *the manifestation of the.glory of God in the face of Jesus Christ.* (2 Cor.iv.6.) As we can receive nothing but through Christ the Mediator; so neither can we render any glory to God, either by our lips or in our lives, but in and through Him, *whom God hath given to be the head over all things to the Church.*

Now, to embrace this great principle in all its fulness, and thus to glorify God in all things through Jesus Christ, is no common attainment. It requires a clear apprehension of the great truths of the Gospel; a power of redeeming love upon the heart; and an entire renunciation of our own righteousness and strength, such as few, even among the best Christians, alas! attain unto. So that when our attention is called by the dispensation of Providence to a rare example of this high Christian character, it is our sacred duty to adore the grace of God manifested therein, and to hold up that example for the encouragement and instruction of the Church of Christ.

Such an occasion has brought me here this day. It has pleased God to gather into His garner, *at a full age, like a shock of corn in his season,* a venerated Clergyman, well-known in this parish – the late Josiah Pratt, whose great distinction it was to have been the Secretary of the Church Missionary Society during twenty-two of the earliest years of its history. It was mainly at his instance that the Missionary College was established in this parish; which has formed a link of so close and interesting a kind between the parish and the Society, that the Committee gladly availed themselves of the kind proposal of your Vicar that one of their number should preach on the occasion of his death.

Under these circumstances I now appear before you; and I have chosen a text which will not only afford me scope for the illustration of the character of our late friend, as *a good steward of the manifold grace of God,* but at the same time guard us against all undue attempts to exalt the man, and prompt us, in unison with the ever-predominant desire of his own heart, to give all the glory to God through Jesus Christ. Lift up your hearts with mine, my Christian friends, in that devout Doxology which the Apostle (abruptly but most appropriately) introduces into the text – *To Him be praise and dominion for ever and ever. Amen.*

I purpose, by God's assistance –

I. To point out some of the important effects which follow the cordial adoption of the great principle of the text.

II. To illustrate them by a reference to the character and labours of our deceased friend, especially in connexion with those great Missionary efforts of the Church of England which will cause his name to be held in *everlasting remembrance* (Psalm cxii.6.)

I. I proceed, in the first place, to point out some of the important effects which follow the cordial adoption of the great principle of the text.

1. The first effect which I will notice of the great principle of the text is, to abase the pride of man and to exalt the glory of the Lord.

Though the whole dispensation of the Gospel is fitted to humble man – to show us our nothingness – to convince us of our forfeiture of every claim upon the Divine favour, and that we must be wholly dependent upon the *manifold grace of God;* yet still is pride ready to rise within our breasts upon any little acquisition which we obtain above others: so that we continually need the admonition of the Apostle – *I say, through the grace given unto me, to every man that is among you, not to think of himself more highly than he ought to think; but to think soberly, according as God hath dealt to every man the measure of faith. (Rom.xii.3.)* And what argument can be used more effectual to check the rising of pride than the pointed question – *Who maketh thee to differ from another? and what hast thou that thou didst not receive? Now, if thou didst receive it, why dost thou glory, as if thou hadst not received it? (1 Cor.iv.7.)*

When we look upon the Church, and see how God employs various instruments to accomplish His purposes – often those which we should have judged to be least fitted for success, every man working according to the ability that God giveth; – when we trace the hand of God in the insignificant beginnings of the most grand designs, and mark, on the other hand, how often human wisdom and power come to nothing; – we are prepared to respond to the sublime words of St. Paul – *God hath chosen the foolish things of the world to confound the wise; and God hath chosen the weak things of the world to confound the things which are mighty; and base things of the world, and things which are despised, hath God chosen, yea, and things which are not, to bring to nought things that are: that no flesh should glory in his presence . . . that, according as it is written, He that glorieth, let him glory in the Lord.*

2. A second blessed effect which will flow from the cordial adoption of this principle is, that it will cause a man to abound in *works of faith and labours of love.*

The great antagonist principle to such zeal is selfishness. So strong is this corrupt nature, that St. Paul says, even of Christians of his own day – *All seek their own, not the things which are Jesus Christ's.*

What more effectual antidote to selfishness can there be, than the conviction that nothing is our own – that all our gifts are to tend, not to our own aggrandizement, but to the glory of God? When the chain is thus loosened by which a man is bound to his wealth, he becomes ready to distribute and glad to communicate. The desire to live to the glory of God is an active principle, infusing energy into the whole man, and providing full employment for the affections and faculties which it has already disengaged from the grasp of the world.

We learn from the text, and from the connexion in which it stands, how wide is the circle of duties to which it will prompt us — *Use hospitality one to another* (says the Apostle) *without grudging.*

The "hospitality" spoken of in the New Testament was not merely the interchange of friendly entertainments, but, from the peculiar circumstances of Christianity at that period, the term had reference chiefly to the hospitable entertainment or pecuniary support of those who suffered temporal loss or exile through their attachment to the Gospel, or who went forth as preachers and missionaries in its cause. According to the words of St. John in his Third Epistle, *Beloved, thou doest faithfully whatsoever thou doest to the brethren, and to strangers; which have borne witness of thy charity before the church: whom if thou bring forward on their journey after a godly sort, thou shalt do well: because that for his name's sake they went forth, taking nothing of the Gentiles. We therefore ought to receive such, that we might be fellow helpers to the truth.* But whether we give a more or less restricted meaning to the term "hospitality", the next words comprehend the whole range of philan-thropic beneficence: *As every man hath received the gift, even so let him minister the same.*

The term "gift" is equivalent to the term "talent" in our Saviour's parable, and comprehends whatever faculty or possession can be made useful to man, or can advance the glory of God. And in the exercise of these gifts and talents, let the *largeness* of the divine bounty to us give us a largeness of heart in devising liberal things. Let the *freeness* of that bounty teach us to *do good and lend, hoping for nothing again;* that we may *be the children of the Highest;* for he is kind to the unthankful, and to the evil (Luke vi.35). Let the unweariedness of the divine bounty to us, which *giveth liberally and upbraideth not,* teach us to be patient, and long-suffering, and persevering in our labours of love without being discouraged, though we see no fruit of our toil. But a whole discourse would be insufficient to unfold the full meaning of the precept — *As ye have received* any gift, *even so minister the same one to another, as good stewards of the manifold grace of God.*

If any man speak, whether in public or private, upon spiritual subjects, *let him speak as the oracles of God;* i.e. in strict conformity with the Holy Scriptures as the sole standard of faith and practice. Let him be careful to represent things in the same proportions and relations in which the Scriptures do. Let the Word of Christ dwell in him so richly, in all wisdom, that his speech may, like the sacred oracles themselves, minister grace unto the hearers.

If any man minister, let him do it as of the ability that God giveth. This may have a primary reference to the office of deacons, yet it comprehends every other kind of service. The expression, *as of the ability that God giveth,* is also very emphatic: it implies that we should put forth our utmost strength, inasmuch as that strength is provided by the Lord, who is the Leader of the work, and who has supplied the means for its performance – *hōs exi ischuos hēs, chorēgi ho theos.*

3. I will mention only one other important effect as following from the cordial adoption of the great evangelical principle of the text; namely, that it lays the surest foundation for union and sympathy amongst all who labour in the cause of Christ.

For what can be more effectual in promoting Christian union, than the consideration that we are all stewards of the *manifold grace of God,* receiving our several gifts and abilities from Him, and all working toward the same great end – the glory of our God and Saviour.

To show this more clearly, I will refer to two passages of Scripture, in which St. Paul lays down the same principle, and expressly connects it with Christian union and co-operation.

In Romans xii.6. the Apostle speaks almost in the very words of the text: *Having then gifts differing according to the grace that is given to us, whether prophecy, let us prophesy according to the proportion of faith; or ministry, let us wait on our ministering.* And these words form the main strength of his argument for union amongst Christians; declaring, in the verse immediately preceding – *So we, being many, are one body in Christ, and every one members one of another;* and closing the passage with the comprehensive injunction, *Let love be without dissimulation.*

In the fourth chapter of the Ephesians, the Apostle exhorts Christians to keep *the unity of the Spirit in the bond of peace,* seeing that *there is one body, and one Spirit . . . one hope of* our *calling, one Lord, one faith, one baptism, one God and Father of all.* And to enforce this exhortation, he adds the principle of the text – *But unto every one of us is given grace according to the measure of the gift of Christ.* And then, having described the various gifts in the different orders and administrations of the Church, as ordained for the edifying of the body of Christ, he closes the subject with a reference to the final issue of Christian unity – *Till we all come in the unity of the faith, and of the knowledge of the Son of God, unto a perfect man, unto the measure of the stature of the fulness of Christ.*

Such are some of the blessed fruits of the principle unfolded to us in the words of the text. So effectually does it tend to abase man, and to exalt the Lord; to put strength into the soul for activity and perseverance in doing good; and to cherish mutual sympathy, and a cordial union amongst Christians.

II. I now proceed, in the second place, to illustrate the principles we have been considering, by the life and labours of our late venerated friend.

The several points which have come under our view will serve, with remarkable exactness, to depict his character. Indeed, it was the contemplation of his life and labours which suggested the text for the present occasion: it seemed to me to afford the very key to his whole character. In him the *manifold grace of God* was most evident; and most faithfully did he acquit himself as *a steward* of the gifts of God, and diligently did he minister *as of the ability which God had given him.*

The foundation of his Christian character was laid in deep experimental piety. While yet a youth, his heart was given up to the Lord, and he no longer considered himself as his own, but the Lord's, who had bought him with a price. There was, in a remarkable degree, the stamp of REALITY upon his religion. He evidently felt and spoke and acted on every occasion as one who referred every thing to the hand of God – as one who had tasted the powers of the world to come.

Taking the text for our guide, I would notice some of the most remarkable points in his character.

He was a man who had eminently overcome the natural selfishness of the human heart. He lived not for himself, but for others. Many can bear testimony of him, as St. Paul did of Timothy, they *know the proof of him,* that he sought not his own, but the things that are Jesus Christ's.

The unweariedness of his labours was truly extraordinary: few men are capable of such continuous exertion as he endured; and still fewer would give themselves up to toil herein, not for a temporal reward, but to send a blessing to distant lands.

As a preacher, his ministrations pre-eminently exhibited the characteristic of the text: he spake *as the oracles of God.* Scripture was the staple of his instructions. It was plain and unadorned, but fervent and weighty Scriptural instruction.

But I do not propose to sketch at any length his personal or his ministerial excellencies. It is chiefly in connexion with Missions that I shall endeavour to review his character.

In this connexion I would notice, as a peculiar qualification for his work, that *largeness of heart,* which could embrace the necessities of all his fellow-creatures, and earnestly seek the extension of Christ's Kingdom throughout the world: for while he was an active supporter of home charities, his sympathies were especially drawn forth in the exercise of that "primitive hospitality" to which I have alluded. I have heard from the lips of many a Missionary affecting testimonies to his tender sympathy and paternal regard toward them from the first hour that they devoted themselves to the work of the Society. He bore them continually upon his heart: though absent from them in the body, still present with them in spirit, joying and beholding their success and prosperity.

This largeness of heart was not the fruit of his connexion with the Church Missionary Society: rather, the establishment and extension of that Society was the result of this noble quality of his mind. Nor was it restricted in its exercise to the operations of this one Society: for being animated and regulated by the principle laid down in the text, it manifested itself in a genuine catholicity of spirit.

He heartily rejoiced in the success of all who were labouring in the cause of Christ, and willingly co-operated with them as far as he had opportunity. Though his whole soul seemed devoted to the interests of one great Society, yet he was far above all petty jealousy or party spirit in respect of other kindred Institutions. When, in the year 1819, a Royal Letter was issued on behalf of the venerable Society for the Propagation of the Gospel – an advantage which he could not hope to obtain for his own Society – he drew up and published, though without his name, an Abstract of the designs and proceedings of that Society, with a view of enabling the Clergy to plead its cause with better advantage, in obedience to the Royal mandate. This Publication was dedicated to the Prelates and Clergy of the Church in these words: "With an earnest hope and prayer that it may be rendered the means of cherishing throughout the Established Church of these Realms a spirit of holy zeal and enlarged charity for the conversion of the Heathen."

The same spirit was manifested in the hearty sympathy which he bore toward all whom he believed to be engaged in the Lord's work, though in a separate line in which he could not conscientiously join.

Mr. Pratt was firmly attached to the Church of England as settled at the Reformation. He spoke of it as "the pillar and ground of the truth:" he believed it to be destined to become the grand instrument in the conversion of the world. He had a very high sense of the importance of Ecclesiastical order and discipline. He laboured unremittingly to excite and mature a Missionary spirit amongst the Clergy and members of the Church; yet he gave abundant proof that it was his heart's desire to keep *the unity of the Spirit in the bond of peace* toward all other Christian Bodies. The principle embodied in one of the fundamental Regulations of the Church Missionary Society, namely, "That a friendly intercourse shall be maintained with other Protestant Societies engaged in the same benevolent design of propagating the Gospel of Jesus Christ," was fully carried out by Mr. Pratt during the years of his Secretaryship. In this spirit he projected, and for many years conducted as Editor, the "Missionary Register;" which, while it gives chief prominence to the labours of the Church Missionary Society, embraces, at the same time, a review of the proceedings of all other kindred Societies, and exhibits them with the candour and sympathy due to those who are fellowhelpers in the Lord.

There is, however, one expression of the text to which I would more especially direct your attention, as setting before us the character of this excellent man in a point of view most honourable to him, and most instructive to ourselves: *If any man minister, let him do it as of the ability which God giveth.*

Mr. Pratt seems to have discerned most accurately that precise line of labour which constituted the ability which God had given to him; and convinced that herein he was following the call of God, he pursued it with constancy and perseverance, and never deviated from it to grasp any other distinction. That precise line was, to take a practical view of all questions connected with the Evangelization of the World. It was his part to mature measures, devised by himself or others, for the accomplishment of this end; to carry them out in detail; to combine the varied efforts of zealous friends at home; and to preserve a consistency in all the operations of the Society abroad. For this work a man was needed possessing a mind comprehensive in its views, sound in its judgment, candid towards objectors, practical in its character, prompt and patient in execution. Such was Josiah Pratt. He had the rare faculty of taking a wide and comprehensive, but at the same time, a thoroughly practical view of questions. There was nothing minute about the character of his mind; yet it was most admirable in following out his plans in detail.

The vast extent to which the operations of the Missionary Society were, under his direction, extended, yet with sound practical wisdom in all its departments, affords a standing proof of this statement. And many other proofs might be cited in connexion with other great undertakings.

For instance; the first conception of a most useful periodical publication, the "Christian Observer", originated with him, and received from him that catholic and spiritual tone which has rendered it essentially serviceable to the cause of vital Christianity. He was the Editor of that Journal at its commencement.[2]

When the British and Foreign Bible Society was first established, Mr. Pratt was selected as one of the Secretaries; and though he held that office for only a few weeks, and then, with characteristic humility, proposed one whom he thought better suited for some of the peculiarities of the post; yet in that short interval he conceived and brought to a successful issue some measures, of which, according to the testimony of the Historian of that Society, subsequent experience has shown the uncommon sagacity and forethought with which they were devised.[3]

Having now considered some of the chief features of the character of our venerated friend, in connexion with the work of Missions, it will be instructive to notice the good providence of God in raising up such a man for his particular day, and in so qualifying him with the ability necessary for the work to which he was called.

At an earlier age, when the revival of true Religion began in our Church, there was needed a class of men, not only bold and uncompromising in the preaching of the truth, but also of striking and attractive powers of elocution, prepared to stand forward as *signs and wonders.* (Isaiah viii.18). Such men were raised up in Whitefield, Romaine, Walker, Newton, and many others. When they had, by God's signal blessing on their warning voice, kindled in many souls some zeal for the Saviour's name, there needed another class of character – men fitted for more retired labours – to carry out, in their practical application, the great principles of the Gospel to which the Church was awakening; and such men were found in Scott, Simeon, Venn, Owen, Pratt. This generation, with the advantage of intimate personal association with their predecessors, and animated by the same principles of action, yet in the altered circumstances of Christian society, exerted themselves in another line, *as of the ability God had given them.*

The connexion of our deceased friend with the generation of zealous men who preceded him was of a close and interesting kind.

When the late venerable and indefatigable John Riland removed from the Curacy of Huddersfield to the Church of St. Mary's, Birmingham, which was connected with a large and crowded population, he happily obtained the aid of several pious Laymen to assist him in his pastoral labours, by exercising a Christian influence and oversight, each over a few assigned families, and communicating with their Minister at stated intervals. The father of Mr. Pratt was one of the most valued of those *fellowhelpers in the Lord.* With such a pastoral and parental example before him Mr. Pratt was trained in his early years; and being, in the first instance, designed for a mercantile life, he acquired habits of business which were of essential service to him in his labours as Secretary of the Church Missionary Society, and which he always regarded as a providential assistance in the work.

And here I cannot but stop, to address a word to the many fathers of families now before me, whose circumstances are very similar to those of Mr. Pratt's father, and remind them of the important gift which they may be preparing for the advantage of the Ministry of the Word, by training up their children to habits of activity, and to a love of doing good on sound Christian principles.

After a few years spent in the Curacy of a country town – Bewdley, in Worcestershire – he became the assistant of the Rev. R. Cecil, in London, and afterward of the venerable Mr. Newton. Thus signally was he prepared, and providentially designated, for the great work of his maturer years: thus faithfully did he *minister as of the ability which God gave him.*

To complete our review of the life and labours of our venerated friend, we must now take a rapid survey of the wonderful manner in which it pleased God to prosper the work of his hands.

At the time he undertook the Secretaryship of the Church Missionary Society it was in its early infancy. It had been formally established, about four years previously, at a meeting of sixteen London Clergymen, the venerable John Newton being amongst the number, on the 12th of April, 1799, at which Mr. Pratt was present. The Rev. Thomas Scott was the first Secretary. After about four years, upon Mr. Scott's removal from London, Mr. Pratt succeeded to the office. But hitherto no Missionary had been engaged, no Mission had been attempted, and the income of the Society amounted only to £1200.

In 1804, a Mission was commenced on the West Coast of Africa, at Sierra Leone, by sending out two Lutheran Clergymen. For several years this was the only Mission of the Society; and it demanded no common share of wisdom, perseverance and decision, and, above all, of faith, to bear up against a variety of adverse and changing circumstances, and the fearful mortality of Europeans on that coast.

In 1809 were sent out the first Christian Teachers in New Zealand; and many and anxious were the deliberations of the conductors of this Society with the zealous Chaplain of New South-Wales, the late Rev. S. Marsden, ere they attempted to send a Mission to the land of those dreaded savages.

But the most important period of Mr. Pratt's labours was in the year 1812, upon the renewal of the East-India Company's Charter, when a wide door was opened for Missionary exertion in India, and a new impulse was given to all the friends of that sacred cause. Then it was that all the faculties of Mr. Pratt's mind were summoned to take full advantage of the important crisis; and eminently were his efforts prospered. Through his personal labours, plans were devised and put into a train of execution — men were engaged as Missionaries — influential friends were brought to co-operate together; and thirty years subsequent experience has proved that the good hand of his God was with him at that eventful day.

In the year 1815 a Mission was commenced in South India; in 1816, in North India; in 1818 and 1819 the operations of the Society were extended to Ceylon and Bombay. To this Society was given the high honour of sending out the first Clergyman of the Church of England who went to India as a Missionary.

During these same years a Mission was commenced in the West Indies, and one at Malta, for the benefit of the vast countries bordering upon the Mediterranean.

In the year 1822 a ninth Mission was undertaken to North-West America; so that when Mr. Pratt resigned the Secretaryship of the Society in the spring of 1824, the Society had nine separate Missions widely spread over the globe, in which 36 Missionaries and 26 European Catechists were labouring, with 265 Schools and above 13,000 Scholars, and an income of above £37,000.

And after Mr. Pratt resigned the onerous duties of the Secretaryship, he had the privilege of witnessing, during a period of the same length as that during which he had held office, the operations of the Society — conducted by those whom he had trained to the work and animated by his example — still increasing, still owned and blessed of God: so that he lived to see 93 Stations occupied by the Society; 113 Clergymen, 9 of them Native or Country-born, labouring in its Missions; 50 other European Teachers, and above 1,000 Native Teachers; its Congregations, gathered from the heathen, so numerous, that even the Communicants exceed 8,000; the Scholars in its Schools, 35,000; and its income £100,000.

The *first* official act of Mr. Pratt was, to meet, as one of sixteen Clergymen, all without wealth or rank, to form the Society: the *last* was, to stand forth at a Special Meeting of the Society, when it had attained to this eminence, and to advocate the adoption of a proposal made by the Bishop of London and the Archbishop of Canterbury, for the purpose of receiving the Society into more direct connexion with the Heads of the Church.

Seldom has it been given to one man to witness such fruits from labours which he was so justly entitled, humanly speaking, to call his own; but of which he ever disclaimed all the merit and glory.

It remains that I should, in conclusion, return to the final words of the text – *that God in all things may be glorified through Jesus Christ.* This was the motto of the life of our dear friend – this was his dying testimony. Had it been our privilege to visit the chamber of sickness, or the death-bed of that most indefatigable, most useful, and most successful man of God, think you that you would have heard him exulting in the fruit of his labours, and receiving the congratulations of friends at the retrospect of a well-spent life? I am no advocate for gratifying an unsanctified curiosity, which would eagerly seize upon the last sayings of a man; I am aware that we should not unveil to public gaze scenes of so solemn, and often so private a character; but I shall not be violating this propriety, if, on the present occasion, I say, that from the lips of this holy man, when the fatal tendency of the disease became manifest, you would have heard only the accents of deep self-abasement for past unprofitableness, for sins of omission, and for lost opportunities; of earnest supplications for pardon and mercy through the blood and righteousness of the Lord Jesus Christ; and earnest exhortations to all around him to work while it is called to-day.

The very last words in which he audibly joined, only a few minutes before his admission into the eternal joy of his Lord, were –

Open now the living fountain,
Whence the healing streams do flow:
Let the fiery cloudy pillar
Lead me all my journey through.
Strong Deliverer!
Be thou still my strength and shield!

To the world, such a scene as this appears a mystery. But ye, dear Brethren, have not so learned Christ. You will see in this a holy consistency with his past life and labours and character, and the very secret of all his past success. In these self-abasing views of himself, in this exaltation of the Saviour, lay the strength of this man of God, as truly as did the strength of Samson in his Nazarite vow.

To God, then, be all the glory of the eminent services of this His faithful servant! Let us adore His mercy for having spared him so long to bless, and animate, and instruct us with his presence. Let us learn, each in our several callings and stations, to follow more diligently and faithfully them who through faith and patience now inherit the promises. Let us banish selfishness from our bosoms by the mighty influence of the love of Christ. Remember that God divideth to every man severally as He will. All cannot be what Mr. Pratt was; very few can imitate him in the peculiarities of his position and abilities; but all may *minister as of the ability which God giveth.* This is the great lesson we learn from the example before us — that to *minister as of the ability* (be it great, or be it small) *which God giveth* is the highest glory, and the surest way of success for those who labour in the work of the Lord. All may, and, if they hope for his success, MUST, have their whole heart brought under the powerful influence of the great doctrines of the Gospel. These must be the soul of all our moral machinery and labours, as well as the ground of our own personal salvation. With respect especially to that great Society which will ever be identified with the name of Josiah Pratt, I will only say, may God give grace to those who have succeeded to his labours, that it may continue to be identified with the very same principles as he infused into all its regulations and proceedings while he presided over it in the days of its most rapid progress and success!

I close this discourse with the words which he himself delivered on the last great public occasion to which I have already alluded:

"THE PRINCIPLES OF THIS SOCIETY, WHICH ARE THOSE OF AN APOSTOLICAL CHURCH PROPERLY CARRIED OUT, HAVE BEEN THE GREAT CAUSE OF ITS SUCCESS. If, then, the least sacrifice of those principles were to be made, I would protest against it. I would rather leave the Society than continue in it if it were to lose its characteristic and vital principle of upholding the great doctrine of justification by faith in the Lord Jesus Christ as the ground of a sinner's hope for salvation with God."

THE WORK OF A MISSIONARY SOCIETY[4]

I had the privilege of addressing the Islington Clerical Meeting in 1846, and again in 1856, upon a kindred subject to that which has been assigned to me this day. On the first occasion I reviewed the progress of the Church Missionary Society for the ten years preceding, namely, from 1836 to 1845. On the second occasion I reviewed the next decade, from 1846 to 1855. If I had waited another year another period of ten years would have been completed. On the present occasion, however, I will treat of the third decade, for though it lacks the returns of last year, I can easily supply them by estimate.

The review of three decades of years in such a great work is a solemn undertaking. It is an attempt to mark the progress of Christ's kingdom during a whole generation, as far as exhibited in the fruits of the operations of the Church Missionary Society. And when I reflect, that during the whole of these three decades I have been permitted to take a prominent part in the direction of the Society, I might well hide my face in confusion upon the retrospect of innumerable personal failures and deficiencies and unprofitableness. But called as I have been, in the providence of God, to the post I occupy, I am bound to sacrifice all personal considerations, and to offer the poor tribute of my long and intimate acquaintance with the subject towards the setting forth of the Lord's work, if haply He may bless the offering, to the furtherance of the Saviour's glory, and to the quickening of the Church at home to increased zeal in the blessed work. May the blood of the Covenant remove the stain of past delinquency, and may the Holy Spirit guide and enlighten our minds; for it is His prerogative to "separate" and to send forth Missionaries for the work whereunto He hath called them, and to preside over the whole enterprise.

The terms of the question before me would embrace the labours of the sister *Society for the Propagation of the Gospel,* and of the *Society for promoting Christianity among the Jews.* But the time will not allow me to travel, on this occasion, beyond the limits of the operations of the Society with which I am officially connected, and to which my address was, on two former occasions, confined.

Before I attempt to answer the question, whether the Missionary efforts of the United Church of England and Ireland are adequate to her responsibilities, you must allow me to clear the ground for the inquiry by two cautions.

First, let me say, I do not regard the Christian Church as bound to send out Missionaries enough to attempt at once to occupy all non-Christian lands. There is a danger of regarding all heathendom as a field to be evangelized by European and American Missionaries. It is a common calculation, "One clergyman to two or three thousand at home; one to two or three millions abroad: Manchester has so many; Benares not a twentieth part." Now, all such calculations – though to a certain extent they may be useful as showing how very little we are doing – are apt to mislead the mind. One single fact will show the impossibility of evangelizing the heathen world by the agency of European and American Missionaries. Transplant the whole clergy of England into China, place them as they are placed here, so many clergymen to so many people, and what would be the consequence? You would have supplied just one-twentieth part of the population of China. Nineteen out of twenty parts would have been unsupplied, even if every clergyman in England had migrated to China. What, then, is the duty of the Christian church under the present dispensation? It is, not to spread their Missionaries over the whole heathen population, but to establish in each district, and especially where there are separate languages, a self-supporting, self-governing, self-extending native Church. And what is the duty of the mother Church towards such native daughter Churches? Not to supply an European pastorate, but to prepare native pastors for native converts, and to endeavour, by divine help, to fix the spiritual standard in such Churches by securing for them a supply of the Vernacular Scriptures, and a sound theological literature, which, in this country, and in the English language, so happily abounds.

My second caution is, that you must not regard the Christian Church as bound to send out Missionaries beyond the supply she can afford of men of the right spirit, which is a very limited supply compared with the whole number of the clergy at home. It is a common saying, that in the Mission field there is work for all. Some say, "Send out your spiritual men, but send out also your earnest men, although they may not be so spiritual, or so well instructed in the truth as you could desire; establish schools, build churches, subdivide dioceses, and Christianity must prevail." Must prevail! What security have we that when you send out unstable Missionaries they will not themselves adopt the speculations of heathenism, and be carried away from the faith when they enter into controversy with the Brahmin or Kaffir? Send out these feeble Christians! What can they establish but a feeble, nominal, native Christianity? And if I have learnt any one lesson in my long experience of Christian Missions, it is this, that a feeble Christianity is a hindrance, and not a support or encouragement to a Mission. A feeble, nominal Christianity is the great obstacle to the conversion of the world. In the emphatic language of the Metropolitan of India, in a lately-published document: "An inefficient or inconsistent clergyman is an evil scarcely to be endured even in a long-settled Church, and in one just struggling to maturity would be absolutely fatal to its growth in grace and the extension of its borders." The supply of true Missionaries – men of firm faith, men of intelligence, men of zeal, men of power – is very limited; and if we will not send out "reeds shaken by the wind," we must wait till the Spirit of God has revived the work at home before there can be any general sending forth of ministers abroad.

The question, therefore, which I propose to discuss is narrowed to this issue: Is the United Church of England and Ireland putting forth, through the agency of the Church Missionary Society, Missionary efforts adequate to her resources and to her responsibilities? And perhaps I should limit it still further: Are the evangelical members of the Church fulfilling their duty in carrying on the Missions of which their fathers and predecessors wisely and zealously laid the foundations? It must, I think, be acknowledged by all, that the Missions to the heathen, now so popular and so much honoured in the Church of Christ, were first enkindled as a feeble spark amongst the evangelical revivalists of the last century. The cause was brought forward by a few unnoticed men, acting on the principle of individual responsibility. Thomas Scott, the first Secretary, said, "I can do but little, but that little I will do for the conversion of the world". And with the increase of evangelical religion the cause of Missions to the heathen advanced. It grew with its growth and strengthened with its strength. During the first half of the existence of the Church Missionary Society there was scarcely any aid rendered except by those who loved and valued, and personally embraced the doctrines of divine grace. Now, indeed, the case is greatly altered. Where there was apathy, indifference, scorn, and even contempt for the Missionary cause, there is now commendation and encouragement. Under these altered and more favourable circumstances have the evangelical clergy fully availed themselves of the opportunity afforded to them for enlarging the operations of this Society?

In answering this question I will first take a very brief retrospect of our work during the last twenty years. I will then examine the prospect of the fulfilment of our Missionary duties in future years.

I. The Retrospect

My review of the decade from 1836 to 1845 was printed as a pamphlet, and widely circulated. I presented a sketch of the success of Missions as exhibited in a tabular view of the number of communicants in the several Missions of the Society for the ten years. It was distinctly pointed out that such statistics can only give a very partial view of the success of Missions. God may be carrying forward a mighty revolution in the thoughts and habits of millions, which meets the eye of the Missionary only in a few isolated outbreaks. Nevertheless, the number of communicants exhibits to a certain extent the progress of a *Mission,* though not the progress of the *work.*

> Under the strict discipline of all the Missions of the Society, every communicant is registered, and any open inconsistency with his Christian profession incurs his suspension from the sacred ordinance of the Lord's Supper. The communicants, therefore, are the nucleus of the native Church. It is from these we select our native helpers, and from these, in a great measure, sounds out the word of life to their countrymen. A large induction of facts will show, that for every communicant there will be on an average five or six native converts (including baptized children), and five times the number of heathen brought under the sound of the Gospel, and made acquainted with its leading facts. I am justified, therefore, in speaking of the number of communicants as representing the visible results of Missionary labours.

I showed that, in the first decade, there has been in every Mission a gradual increase of communicants, so that they had increased in ten years sevenfold. I quoted the pointed testimony of the then Bishop of Madras, after a visitation of the province of Tinnevelly, that "every faithful missionary who might be placed in the unoccupied parts of the province of Tinnevelly would have at once 1500 or 2000 fresh inquirers gathered around him, who would lay aside their idolatry, and submit themselves to Christian instruction." Upon such facts as these I grounded an appeal, that if the Church at home would put forth a proportionate energy for the next ten years, we might look for another sevenfold increase.

I have this day to confess that the anticipated results have not been reached. The Church at home did not put forth any proportionate energy. Our income is only half as much more as it was twenty years ago. The European labourers have only been increased about sixty per cent in the twenty years. Hence, had the Lord given us a sevenfold increase, we should not have had the Missionaries on the field to house the harvest. Surely this fact affords one answer to the question, "Is the Church of England fulfilling her office as a Missionary Church? " The extent and influence of evangelical truth in the Church have very largely increased. Has her Missionary zeal increased proportionably? Nay, is there not reason to fear that in many places it has somewhat retrograded; that the warm sympathy and self-denying exertions in our cause which animated many of the early friends of the Society have become more rare of late; that Missionary meetings have become less interesting?

But let us look abroad and inquire into the increase of Missions; we shall find that, instead of sevenfold at the end of ten years, the increase has not reached threefold at the end of twenty years. The number of communicants was, in 1845, over 9000; in 1865 they may be reckoned 26,000 including those who have been transferred to the care of settled pastors, both European and native, in Sierra Leone, the West Indies, and New Zealand; yet this increase, so far below what was anticipated, exhibits a far larger proportion, it is feared, than that of the increase of zeal in the Church at home.

The retrospect of the last twenty years is of a chequered character: there have been judgements as well as mercies. Let me briefly touch upon each topic.

Besides the discouragements arising from the scantiness of our resources, the Society has of late been subjected, in the providence of God, to many severe trials and hindrances. In New Zealand, the unhappy wars which have raged have led to the breaking up of many flourishing stations, and to the dispersion of the people, and so from 2000 to 3000 of our communicants have been lost to our lists. We must add the lamentable war in the Yoruba Mission; in China, the irruption of the insurgents into the Ningpo Mission; and in India the great Mutiny of 1857, which arrested for a time the progress of our Mission in North India. Such checks to the Lord's work from war and rebellion are among the mysteries of Providence to the world. But to him who is instructed in the history of God's dealings with His Church they are only evidences of the dispensation under which at present His sovereign will has placed His people, to magnify His grace in overruling evil to good and temporal death to spiritual life. So we regard that recent great calamity in

South India, when a mighty wave of the sea in the bay of Bengal swept harmlessly by the accursed Temple of Juggernauth, and poured its fury upon Masulipatam, to the destruction of one of the most interesting of our Missions, sweeping down a whole city, carrying off 30,000 inhabitants by a sudden death, sparing the lives of the Missionaries, but leaving them destitute of the necessaries of life, even of clothing, bread and water.

The great lesson we should draw from these discouragements is, that the work of Missions is no smooth and easy work which the people of God may contemplate with composure, and help forward with an annual donation, but otherwise not draw their hand from their bosom. Oh no; the success of Missions cannot be achieved without "great conflict" on the part of those who share the honour of helping them forward, without the exercise of a firm faith, and the wrestling in prayer for a blessing. And can it be said that in this respect the Church at home has fulfilled its obligation? As the Missions have expanded through God's blessing upon them, the responsibilities of the work have increased, and the perils have been enlarged. Has prayer abounded in behalf of the Society in the same proportion? Is the subject of Missions spread with corresponding fervour before the throne of grace, in the social circle, in clerical meetings, in special prayer-meetings connected with the Anniversaries of Associations? We fear that, if tried by such tests, the Missionary zeal of the Church will be found wanting.

But I will pass on to a more cheerful theme, and point out some of the chief mercies and encouragements in our work abroad which strike me as most characteristic of the period under review. I will select four:

1. The extension of the area of our Missions.
2. The introduction of the principle of self-support into Missions.
3. The Native ministry.
4. The movement in the public mind of heathendom towards Christianity.

1. First, there has been a great extension of the area of our Missions since 1845. It has been already stated that the increase of our income and of our European Missionaries has slowly progressed till they have become half as much more than they were twenty years ago. Now, with such limited means at their disposal, the Committee of the Church Missionary Society might have declined to extend their Missions, and have been content with carrying on the Missions which they had already formed, upon the plea that the means furnished to them would not be more than sufficient for the annual increase of expenditure required in prosperous Missions. Many a time has the Committee been solicited to pour all its resources into the fields thus occupied, and not to go to regions beyond till those fields were completely evangelized. But the Committee had respect to the pattern of the first promulgation of the Gospel in apostolic times, when Missions were spread

over the known world by occupying great centres of national intercourse, though it was often done in feeble force. Thus they determined to act upon a large faith, and to lay foundations for evangelizing the chief heathen and Mohammedan countries of the world, in preparation for the time when the Church at home should awake to its great responsibilities, and to the force of its Saviour's last command, and send forth a sufficient supply of labourers to build upon these foundations.

Let me give a hasty sketch of the extension which has been accomplished in the last twenty years. In West Africa the Yoruba Mission has been more than doubled in the extent of the field occupied; and during the last decade a Mission has been established on the river Niger which, if God prosper the enterprise, will open an intercourse with the vast interior of Central Africa from the limits of the influence of Sierra Leone in the west for 2000 miles towards the east. In the Mediterranean Mission the year 1846 witnessed only the support of three small Missions at Syra, Smyrna, and Cairo. Cairo has been dropped, but there has been added the country of Palestine, with the two centres of Judaea and Galilee, Jerusalem and Nazareth, and a direct Turkish Mission has been opened at Constantinople, the religious citadel and metropolis of all Islam. In Western India the Mission has been extended by itinerating labour from Malligaum throughout the large district of Kandeish, and from Junir in the Deccan, and, more recently, in the northern portion of the Nizam's territory at Aurungabad, thus taking Missionary occupation of those parts of the Bombay Presidency not already occupied by other Missionary Societies. In North India, besides several new stations in Bengal and the North-west Provinces, including a Mission to the Santals and two stations in the kingdom of Oude, at Lucknow and Fyzabad, our operations have been extended into the Punjab, which has been grasped by four important border stations – Kangra, Peshawur, Derajat, Mooltan – connected with the central station of Umritsur. And, having so reached the limits of the British empire of India, our Missionaries at Peshawur are attempting to penetrate even Central Asia, through the Afghans and other hill tribes, as well as to establish a Mission in the far-famed valley of Cashmere. In South India, the Tinnevelly province has been covered, in all the parts not previously occupied, by the itinerating Mission of the North. In Travancore the interesting hill tribes of the Arrians and the slaves in the plain have been largely evangelized. In the Telegu country two interior stations have been occupied – Ellore and Bezwada – and a new Mission opened to the Kois on the Godavery. In Ceylon two interesting branches of Missionary operations have been introduced; among the 100,000 Indian coolies in the coffee plantations and among the ancient inhabitants of the central Kandian districts. During the last decade the Mauritius Mission was commenced amongst the 200,000 immigrant Indian coolies in that island, and the Gospel is preached in the three chief Indian languages. From thence a Mission has been opened in Madagascar, and the intercourse between Mauritius and East Africa will infuse new life into that Mission. In the China Mission, twenty years ago, only one solitary station was maintained; but, since then, Ningpo, Fuh-chau, and Hong-Kong have been occupied to the south, and Pekin, the capital of the enormous empire of China, to the north. In North-west America the Missions have been spread over the greater part of the country east of the Rocky Mountains, by trebling the number of stations; while they have been extended 2000 miles, from the Red River to the Arctic Circle on the Mackenzie River; and on the other side of the Rocky Mountains a most flourishing Mission has been opened among the Indians on the shores of the North Pacific.

I have detained you by this geographical review, because it is most important, in these days, to show what this Society has done and is doing for the extension of Christ's kingdom. Let Societies be judged of by the work which the God of Missions enables them to effect, not by the narrow marks of the colour of their complexion or their age. I hesitate not to affirm that the amount of Missionary extension which I have sketched, during the last twenty years, would have been a great success for any new Society to have achieved; but when it is regarded as the extension to regions beyond, whilst all its older Missions were being sustained, consolidated, and built up in faith and knowledge — it exhibits results which call for unfeigned gratitude and praise to the great Head of the Church, in putting this honour upon the Society's instrumentality.

2. A second marked characteristic of Missions during the last twenty years is the introduction of the principle of self-support in the older Missions of the Society. In Sierra Leone, during the second decade, the experiment was made of casting upon the people the support of their elementary schools, for which the Society was paying £800 a-year. This sum the Society proposed to reduce gradually by one-fifth each successive year. The people assembled in their several congregations, and determined to raise at once the whole sum necessary for the support of their schools, and to fund the Society's grants. This was accomplished. During the third decade, the support of their native pastors was thrown upon them. They willingly undertook the responsibility of nine native pastors, at a total cost of £600 a-year, and immediately raised their stipends. And after thus nobly providing for the education and ministrations of the native Church they have contributed more liberally than ever to the Bible Society and to the Church Missionary Society, raising for these Societies more than £300 a-year, over and above their native church funds. Such pecuniary exertions, it will be said, bespeak a people of some energy and wealth. Undoubtedly; the negro has a head for business and a heart for religion; and let the facts which the West-African Mission discloses answer the speculations of the present day as to his position in the intelligent creation. In New Zealand the contributions of the natives in land, produce,

and money, for the endowment of the native Church, have been very liberal in proportion to their means. The fact is, that up to this time all the unordained native teachers, amounting to several hundred, are gratuitous, working for their support in their cultivations while they minister to their countrymen. *Their* contributions are, therefore, in the form of endowments for an educated ministry and for a native bishopric. In South India the contributions of the native converts have been hitherto devoted to various benevolent and Missionary purposes; for it was thought better to introduce among them the habit of giving in that form. But within the last few years the support of native pastors has been proposed to them, and they have willingly responded to the appeal; so that, in one district, the veteran Missionary Thomas reports seventeen congregations ready to support as many native pastors, and other neighbouring districts would more than double that number. The native Churches in Tinnevelly already raise 13,574 rupees annually for religious and benevolent purposes, which, according to the value of money, estimated by the wages of labour, would be equivalent to £7000 a-year in this country, or about 17s 6d for every Christian family among a rural and labouring population. In one village, containing 400 families, the contributions last year amounted to a sum equivalent to £2 for each family. I need not dwell on the prodigious advance beyond the first stage of Missions which such results exhibit, nor upon the healthy tone, independent action, and self-extension which will always characterize self-supporting churches. The great majority, indeed, of our native congregations in other Missions have not reached the measure of contributions in Sierra Leone or Tinnevelly. But the principle being established in the Missions of the Society, the practice will gradually prevail as Churches are able to adopt it.

3. I now come to a third great Missionary encouragement, which marks the retrospect of the last twenty years, namely, the success of the native ministry. At the commencement of the period now under review, a native ministry was regarded as an experiment, to be cautiously entered upon, with a long diaconate and an European superintendent. The Society has now had the experience of about eighty ordained native teachers, in nearly all the Missions of the Society, and every year has given accumulated proof that they are enabled to fulfil the ministry they have received of the Lord. Some have proved powerful preachers, able to rivet the attention of, and to edify the largest congregations; others have been skilful and wise pastors of a flock and helpers of their faith. Judged by Anglo-Saxon ideas they are sometimes pronounced unable to stand alone; but judged by a larger and wiser rule they are found to be fully qualified for standard-bearers in a native Church, and their efficiency will increase in proportion as they are instructed in biblical knowledge, and accustomed to co-operate in council and in the ecclesiastical administration. In New Zealand three Annual Synods have been held in the Diocese of Waiapu, at which native ministers and native lay members of the

Church sat in deliberation and passed canons, and the Bishop pronounces these Synods a great success. But the crowning success of the native ministry is the appointment of a negro minister to be a Bishop of the United Church of England and Ireland, consecrated under the royal licence. The first year of Bishop Crowther's Episcopate has not yet closed; but it is not too soon to speak of the admirable humility, wise forethought and large-minded spirit in which he has laid out his plans, and won golden opinions from all who have had the opportunity of judging of his administrative powers. The effect of this appointment upon the whole of the native ministry throughout our Missions has been remarkable. It has given them a lively demonstration of the truth that a native Church is not to be kept too long in a state of dependence, but that the mother Church will commit the superintendence to a native Bishop as soon as the native church is ripe for such a measure. By this a great impulse has been given to native ministers to cultivate a manly independence of mind, and to recognise the responsibilities of their position. In Tinnevelly, the senior Missionary, Mr. Thomas, has brought before large assemblies of the head-men and catechists the proposal of a native bishop to superintend the native Churches, and has met with a cordial and intelligent response.

4. A fourth remarkable encouragement of Missionary labour which has characterized the period under review is the indications of the rising of a public sentiment in favour of Christianity. The Missionary is now generally recognised as the trustworthy friend of the native race, and exercises an indirect influence over the multitude who witness his behaviour, though they cannot accept his teaching. The Indian mutiny brought out this fact beyond contradiction. The internal wars in Africa and New Zealand have proved it. The native newspapers of India confirm it. This influence in India, combined with the intellectual enlightenment which Government education has introduced, has rendered the educated classes a promising field of Missionary labour. Light has thus broken in upon the thick darkness. In the eloquent language of Sir Herbert Edwardes — "Where have they got the light? From the feeble tapers which Missionary Societies have kept flickering alive in scattered Mission homes for sixty years, amidst darkness, discouragements, and scorn. Missions in India have begun to tell. God grant that we may see their triumph in our day."

And now I must once more revert to the question which I have to answer. With such rich encouragements in the work abroad, and with such crowning blessings granted to the native Churches founded by this Society, has the Church at home expanded its charity and enlarged its exertions according to the measure of the gratitude due to the great Head of the Church for so honouring its instrumentality? The meagre results of the last twenty years in the supply of men and means give a sad response to this enquiry.

II. The Prospect

I must now turn, as I proposed, to THE PROSPECT abroad and at home for the future.

Abroad all is bright and encouraging. The difficulties in the way of extension we once experienced from the unsuitable climate of Africa to the European constitution have been alleviated by the extensive employment of native agency. In India the positive obstacles to Missionary success from Governmental connexion with idolatry have been abolished. A cold neutrality, and often the official discountenance of Missionary operations, which once proved a great hindrance, have been mercifully replaced by the general respect, and often the zealous co-operation and cordial sympathy of the authorities. Grants-in-aid to Mission schools were conceded by the Government on the very ground of the utility of Missions to the general interests of the country. In the Punjab, a great Missionary Conference was held two years ago, in which the highest civil and military officers sat in council with the Missionaries, and united with them in prayer; such a public and happy encouragement may well be set against years of past indifference and hostility. In China the country has been opened to our Missionaries, just in proportion as they have been prepared to branch out. The consular restrictions of the five ports are at an end, and now Missionaries may penetrate in every direction throughout the interior.

The difficulties of languages have been overcome, in a great degree, in every Mission-field. Bibles in the vernacular are provided in rich abundance, through the liberality of the British and Foreign Bible Society. Philological skill has been so brought to bear upon the reduction of unwritten languages, that portions of the Scripture are prepared as soon as Missionaries have entered a new country.

Even the lamentable wars in Africa and New Zealand may yet be overruled to the progress of Christianity, as the great Indian mutiny has been overruled.

But what is the prospect *at home* of the supply of sufficient means for the extension of the work abroad? Here I hesitate to pronounce the prospect either bright or encouraging. The insufficiency of our income cripples all our operations, and makes us sometimes tremble lest we should have carried Missionary extension beyond our supports in the zeal and faith of Christians at home. Yet I can affirm before God that we have not taken one step in advance without much prayer and the fullest consideration, or without the conviction that we were following the call of God, and the glorious footsteps of his providence. We are not ungrateful to those numerous and zealous friends who have raised our income to its present amount; but now, for seven years, it has hovered over the same limit. Our Associations — the Missionary barometer — have vibrated above and below £100,000. But during these seven years the openings in new and promising fields, and the call for increased labourers from all our old Missions, have been most inviting and most earnest. And during these seven years the wealth of the nation, and we trust also the power of the gospel, have increased. Why then does not our income continue to rise as it did in former years? We have endeavoured carefully to investigate this subject, and my clerical brethren must bear with me while I faithfully state the result. We are assured that there is a large amount of pecuniary aid available for our cause, but it is not applied for. The parochial clergy have the key in their hand which would unlock this treasury, but they will not, speaking of them as a body, apply the key to the lock. The proportion of clergy throughout the country, who allow of appeals to their congregations for the Church Missionary Society, is little more than one out of four or five. And in this small proportion of pulpits, in which we have an opportunity of pleading our cause before the people, too often the interest is confined to the day of the Anniversary; nothing is done to inform the people, or to keep the cause before their minds. Here, you will allow, is cause of discouragement; but this is not our chief discouragement. Our fear is, lest the cause of the Church Missionary Society should be allowed to droop in the house of its friends. The multiplicity of calls upon the evangelical clergy of the present day is one reason; an erroneous impression that the Church Missionary Society can take care of itself is another reason. But I will not probe the matter further: the fact is, that we have not, at this day, the same number of whole-hearted, self-denying advocates that we had twenty or thirty years ago. When Charles Shorting was taken to glory, he scarcely left his equal in aiding our cause throughout a large district; when George Hodgson fell at his post at York, we lost one who, with the aid of a brother, had raised the proportion of churches in Yorkshire, contributing to our Society, to a greater ratio than that of any other county in the kingdom. Many men of like mind still survive, and show what one zealous friend can, by personal exertion, achieve. A single congregation in a chapel in a watering place sends us up £750 a year.[5] We have honorary district Secretaries who preach their twenty or thirty sermons for us in the year. But we want more such to fill up our thinned ranks, and to extend our lines; and for such I appeal on this occasion. The evangelical clergy are increased in London tenfold since I first entered Orders as a Curate of a City church, but our funds scarcely fourfold. I pray God that these hints may touch the hearts of some of my younger brethren in the ministry who will rally round the Society, and help it to assume a more firm, and even aggressive position for the time to come.

Upon one other point only will I touch in conclusion – What is the prospect of the Church at home fulfilling its duty in supplying men for the extension of our work? We know that we have been sometimes blamed for being too strict in our selection of Missionaries. It is curious to see how the charges against the Society, as against the children of wisdom of old, run into opposite extremes. Twenty years ago the charge against the Church Missionary Society was, that it was no Church Society. I was myself at some pains to draw up a paper to show that it was a true Church Society. Now the attack is from an opposite quarter; and because we are a Church Society we are reproached with the charge of a sectional spirit in the selection of our men, and that we do not send out a fair proportion of various kinds of ministers found in the Church at home. They are said to be all of one hue. We are charged with exacting tests of doctrine narrower than the doctrine of our Church. To such charges – if they deserve the name of charges – we reply that we take the best men who offer themselves to us according to the standard fixed by the fathers and founders of our Society – a standard confirmed by the practical experience of every year in the Mission-field as comprising the only qualifications which can win souls to Christ. Our standard we proclaim in all our publications. We seek men who have so felt the constraining love of Christ as to be weaned by it from the love of this world, and to be willing to spend and be spent for Him; men who know what true conversion of the soul is by personal experience, and can testify to others that they have found the pearl of great price. It is by no formula of doctrine that we judge, but by the spirit of the men. It is forty-six years since I first entered the Committee-room in Salisbury-square, and there has been no change of standard, no uncertainty of selection. We kept on our steady course when the wind blew from the biting north-east, and now that it has veered round to the soft south-west we shall not alter our course. Speaking in this Memorial Hall, I cannot resist a reference to the memorable words of Bishop Daniel Wilson in his sixth Charge (1851) – "The Society has much gratified me by a most decided protest against Romanism; no silence, no hesitation, no ambiguities as to the line they take. I beg also to mark with warm approbation their great care in the choice of their Missionaries. This is a primary point." It is to the evangelical clergy that the Committee look for help in this most essential particular – the supply of men of the right sort. Let them look out for such: let them test their qualifications as spiritual teachers: let them train for a time, and then recommend them to the Committee. In this way many of the most valuable Missionaries have been brought forward. And will not the younger clergy and the students of our Universities, who feel the obligation of the Church to fulfil her duty as a Missionary Church, ask themselves the question – Why should not I go? The call of Christ to his ministers to go into all the world and to preach the Gospel to every creature is a general call; but if no providential impediment can be alleged, it becomes a personal and a special call. May the Lord make it an *effectual* call; and thus thrust forth labourers into his vineyard!

I have thus endeavoured to set before this Meeting, once more, at the close of a third decade, the position and future prospects of the Church Missionary Society. I have stated the principles which guide the Committee in the administration of its affairs. By these principles, and by the results which God has graciously given to their labours, they desire to be judged. These principles have carried them through sixty years, have guided them in early difficulties, have matured their experience, and have enabled them safely to ride out many a storm. These principles have embedded themselves deep in our hearts, as the shades of the evening of life close in upon us; and our most earnest desire is to commit them to younger and stronger hands unsullied and uncompromised.

ON THE WORK OF A MISSIONARY SOCIETY[6]

The Church Missionary Society has always made the preaching of the Gospel its first work, and has proposed this work as the grand motive to its candidates. I am fully aware also of the facts you state respecting the impediments to this work arising from the large amount of secularity in our Missions. But I greatly doubt whether this arises from the system. I conceive it arises from the men themselves. I see the same thing at home. I see hundreds entering the Ministry with the determination of making the preaching of the Gospel their first work, but nine-tenths are engulfed in the vortex of secularity, in schools, or societies, or literature, or a thousand other ways. I conceive that the secularity of our Missions as you describe it is far less than the secularity of the home Ministry and I have long come to the conclusion that the irresistible tendency to secularity is the great snare and bane of the Church of Christ, and a snare not so much arising from the integral system as from the fallen nature of man.

In the importance of imparting to our rising Christian population the best education which they are capable of receiving, I fully agree with you. We are exerting all the means in our power to secure this.

ON THE WORKING OF A MISSIONARY SOCIETY[7]

My Dear Friend,

The Committee are now looking about for a new Secretary to supply the place of our late beloved coadjutor Mr. Fox.

The importance of the office has always appeared very great in the estimation of those who were best acquainted with the working of the Society: but never more so than at the present moment, when the Jubilee commemoration has shewn us how strong a position the Society occupies in the Church: and how much its influence and means may be enlarged by bringing its claims forward in suitable publications, and by proper methods: and how much its foreign operations need additional guidance and encouragement in the way of correspondence with the Missionaries.

I enter into these particulars to shew the special qualifications which we desire to secure in our new Secretary; in addition to the fundamental requisite of a heart under the full influence of the grace of Christ — we need habits of business — literary competency — and enlargement of mind.

We earnestly entreat your prayers in our behalf that we may be directed to the right man. And we request you also to look round upon the zealous young friends of the Society in your acquaintance — and to favour us with the names of any one whom you may think likely to suit and to accept the invitation.

Mr. Fox was Assistant Secretary. And the Committee enquire for a Secretary *or* Assistant Secretary: reserving to themselves the offer of the one or other office according to the maturity of the qualifications which they have named.

The difference of Salary would be £200 and £300.

Commending our whole work to your Christian Sympathy and prayers.

THE SECRETARIAT OF THE SOCIETY[8]

It is more than half a century since I first took my seat in the Committee. Perhaps I may, then, be allowed a few words at the close of so long a period, which comprises nearly two generations of men. In such a work as this it is absolutely necessary that a large and generous confidence should be reposed in the Secretaries. There can be no practical danger of their confidence being disappointed as long as the Committee shall uphold the principle of equality of responsibility among the Secretaries, and the practice of forming their decisions by general agreement rather than by casting votes . . . The Secretaries of our Society are the originators of the measures to be passed, the chief authorities on its principles and practice, and must often act upon their own discretion in cases of emergency, and in confidential interviews with Church or State authorities. At the same time I must bear my testimony that this large confidence reposed in the Secretaries is not inconsistent with the independence of judgment and ultimate supremacy on the part of the Committee.

ON THE INDEPENDENCE OF A VOLUNTARY SOCIETY[9]

. . . The Society is clearly at liberty to hold meetings and to send Deputations to any parish in the kingdom.

In exercising this liberty, Christian prudence and forbearance are undoubtedly necessary. The Society has never causelessly forced itself into parishes with an offensive opposition to the parochial clergy.

But on the other hand where the Society has been accustomed to hold its meetings it can never consent to discontinue them merely at the bidding of the Incumbent, because he has changed his mind or has entered upon the pastoral of the parish in which such meetings are to be held. This would be allowing a spiritual dominion over the charitable feelings and actions of the people which the Church of England has never recognised.

The Church Missionary Society is not singular in having to resist this assumption. The case occurred not long ago when the Incumbent of Leamington objected at a public meeting to his own Diocesan taking the chair for a pastoral aid meeting . . .

THE VOLUNTARY PRINCIPLE[10]

. . . The Committee of the Church Missionary Society have been informed that Resolutions were adopted at a Diocesan Conference in the Diocese of Salisbury, August 9, 1871, and the opinion of this Committee has been asked respecting them. The Resolutions are:

I. "That this Conference are of opinion that it is desirable to institute a permanent Synod in the Diocese of Salisbury."

II. "That the Synod consist of the following official members: The Lords-Lieutenant and the High Sheriffs of the two counties (being communicants), the Dean of the Cathedral, the three Archdeacons, and the Chancellor of the Diocese; and of Clergymen elected by the Clergy, and Laymen (being communicants) elected by the Lay-churchmen of the parishes, to serve for each division of the Rural Deaneries of the Diocese, in the proportion of four Clergymen and six Laymen for each Sub-Deanery, undertaking to serve for three years."

III. "That the duty of the Synod be two-fold: first, with the consent of the Societies now engaged in those duties, to take charge of the chief operations conducted by voluntary Associations within the Diocese, such as those of Church Education, the supply of Clergy and of Churches, and Church Missions; and, secondly, to be of conference and counsel with the Bishop in regard of ecclesiastical affairs of importance to the Diocese."

The Committee fully recognise the friendly feeling manifested towards the Society by the proposal to assist in collecting funds and in promoting its interests in the Diocese; but as the proposal would in a great measure supersede the present system of its Association arrangements, it is necessary to compare together the two systems, with the view of estimating their relative advantages.

The Associations of the Church Missionary Society are voluntary combinations of its friends, which elect their committees, officers, and collectors.

hold anniversary meetings and solicit the Clergy to grant them sermons with collections. The Parent Committee maintain a large staff of Association Secretaries, each having a prescribed district, who assist the Associations by their advice and by providing, as far as is required, preachers and deputations for sermons and meetings.

By this system the Associations throughout the country are brought into immediate connexion with the Parent Committee through the Association Secretaries and various other zealous friends, who visit the Associations as representatives of the Parent Committee, − that is to say, through friends who are attached to the principles and work of the Society, and therefore well able to kindle the interest of others in the cause.

The proposal in the Diocese of Salisbury would place the management of the Church Missionary Associations and all other voluntary associations of Churchmen under the charge of a Synod elected for a variety of Church purposes, thereby superseding, more or less, the agency of the Parent Committee and the voluntary action of attached friends by an official Board, of whom there can be no security that they will be specially interested in the Church Missionary Society or acquainted with its principles or its work.

It seems to the Committee obvious that the two systems could not be combined, and that to supersede the present system by the action of the proposed Synod would be greatly to the detriment of the interests of the Society, and endanger the permanence of its income.

The Committee are able also to appeal to experience as a guide in the matter. Thirty years ago a somewhat analogous proposal was put forward, that all Church Societies should be placed under a common Board of Management called a Church Union, and that the different Societies should join in a common meeting, the profits to be divided among them severally. The latter particular is not specified on the present occasion, but the analogy consists in the transfer of the management of the Associations from the Committee and zealous friends of the Society to other parties acting for several other Societies. It was soon found by experience that these Church Unions tended to check the exertions of zealous friends and otherwise to injure the interests of the Missionary cause, which led the Committee to adopt the following Resolutions (1841): −

"That it is expedient to the welfare of the Society that it should prosecute its objects distinct and separate from all other Societies."

"That it is important that all the different Associations of the Church Missionary Society should maintain their independent existence without merging in any Church Union."

The Committee are convinced by the experience of the last thirty years of the importance of these principles. In a few special instances, the influence of the Clergyman of a parish may keep up a flourishing "Union", but in the great majority of instances these Unions have proved signal failures.

The Committee do not presume to dictate to parochial Clergymen, but they are persuaded that after this candid statement of their matured convictions they cannot be expected to accept the offer of the Salisbury Conference, or to relax their exertions for the support of their Associations, or to furnish deputations in support of a system which appears to them detrimental to the interests of the Missionary cause.

The Committee, therefore, feel compelled to adhere to their long established practice and principles, and very respectfully to decline the proposal of the Salisbury Conference of August 9, 1871 . . .

THE VOLUNTARY SOCIETY[11]

. . . The Committee do not lose sight of the fact that many of the operations of the Society are so nearly related to spiritual questions that they require for their due settlement the mutual confidence of ecclesiastical and lay authorities. The *principles* on which such settlement is to be arrived at are laid down in detail in the document referred to; and to this was added a proviso proposed by Archbishop Howley and Bishop Blomfield for adoption by the Society, to the effect that any new questions of ecclesiastical order and discipline which might arise between the Society and a colonial Bishop should be referred by the Committee to the Archbishop and Bishops of the United Church of England and Ireland; but such reference was not to affect "the principles and practice of the Society as they are contained in the laws and regulations, and explained in Appendix II of the Thirty-ninth Report". The acceptance of this rule by the Society, and the subsequent adhesion of the Archbishops and Bishops to the Society, form a permanent and mutual pledge of adherence to the principles as then laid down. A controlling Board of Missions would therefore be an interference with the fundamental principles of the Society.

It must also be borne in mind that the constitution of the Church Missionary Society has been from its very cradle that of a *voluntary society,* receiving in its early years no support from persons of high position in the Church, that its supporters were attracted to it by the declaration of the principles on which it was to be conducted, that its Committees have been annually elected on the faith of their adherence to these principles, – and must therefore regard themselves as trustees of a fund which is to be disbursed with scrupulous regard to the terms of their trust. Such an interference with the Society as the proposed measure would introduce would be regarded, at the present day, as inconsistent with its principles and character as a voluntary society; and the agitation of the question would give rise to conflicts most disastrous to the Missions of the Church of England . . .

THE CONTRIBUTION OF A MISSIONARY SOCIETY TO THE PARISH[12]

... I have been greatly interested by your letter. Your receipts on the Jubilee day appear to me very encouraging. And I cannot doubt but that it is at once a proof that your labours are blessed of the Lord and a means whereby your people will receive still richer blessings.

A vigorous Church Missionary Association has often proved the greatest spiritual blessing to a parish. It teaches us what real conversion is — illustrates the power of the Gospel — enlarges the heart and identifies us with our Master's cause. But to reply to your enquiries.

1. I am strongly in favour of a complete organization of the C.M. Association — so that if you were removed, it might still go on, or draw in (as is very often the case) even a reluctant successor. By organization I mean a Committee, a Treasurer and Secretary — The President would most naturally be yourself — The Treasurer some Layman of standing — the Secretary some active young Layman if possible. But then you must remember that quarterly or monthly meetings for giving Missionary lectures or information are the life blood of our cause. Without this all languishes.

2. In answer to your 2nd enquiry about having a public meeting before the next Annual Meeting I should think such quarterly or monthly meetings preferable. In many cases a Missionary *Lecture* is most attractive and useful. It is a meeting without being supposed to be such. Take the history of the Society — or of any particular Mission, and you will be sure to interest the people.

3. Upon your 3rd enquiry — what means can be adopted to place the C.M.S. and the S.P.G. relatively upon a proper footing, I can only advise making the C.M.S. fully known without approaching to invidious comparisons, meeting objections as they arise — and circulating our publications.

I think it very important for the sake of both Societies that their home agency should be kept distinct — a union is always found a failure in the long run. Each Society has its distinctive character, which will soon be appreciated, and persons will accordingly give their hearts to the one or the other.

The notion of supporting the extension of the church, by giving without partiality to particular societies, is a mere abstraction, a cold abstraction which produces nothing ...

MISSIONARY ADMINISTRATION OVERSEAS[13]

A Corresponding Committee consists of a limited number of friends, lay and Clerical appointed by the Parent Committee, to whom is delegated the administration of the temporal affairs of a Mission. Such a body is formed in every Mission in which there are found friends to whom the Committee can satisfactorily confide this trust. Where formed the Corresponding Committee holds the absolute control of the expenditure of the Mission, and directs and regulates all its details, subject only to the regulations and final supervision of the Parent Committee. Corresponding Committees are formed at Calcutta, for the North India Mission; Madras, for the South India Mission; Bombay, for the Western India Mission; and at George Town, Demerera, for the British Guiana Mission. Where means are not available for the promotion of a Corresponding Committee, the Missionaries themselves are formed into an administrative body for directing the details of the expenditure of the Mission, subject of course to the Parent Committee. Missionary Committees regulate the expenditure of the West Africa, the Egypt, East Africa, the Ceylon, the New Zealand, and the North West America Missions. In Greece and in Asia Minor, in each of which missions only one Missionary is placed, the Missionary regulates the detail of his own expenditure, subject, as in other cases to the Parent Committee.

LETTER TO THE BISHOP OF CALCUTTA[14]

... I seem to perceive, in most of our advanced Missions the rising of peculiar difficulties, from the attempts on the part of Chaplains and Archdeacons to entangle the Missionaries in certain supposed Church regulations: and from the tendency of our Missionaries to settle down upon a kind of Missionary incumbency: instead of aiming to bring the multitudes of the heathen into the fold; and leaving the ecclesiastical settlement of a Native Church to the time when a Native Ministry shall be prepared for it ...

ON THE QUALIFICATIONS OF A MISSIONARY[15]

The Committee have desired me to explain to you the qualifications which they look for in every agent of the Society whether lay or clerical.

A supreme desire to become an instrument of spreading the knowledge of the Gospel of the Lord Jesus Christ, for the salvation of souls, is, in the judgement of the Committee, a prerequisite qualification. To satisfy themselves on this point the Committee require that the candidate should by letter fully explain his views and motives in desiring a connexion with the Society – and also that he should give references to two or three clergymen being members of the Society with whom he is personally acquainted. The Committee do not wish for testimonials, but make their own enquiries from such References.

ON THE OFFICE OF A MISSIONARY[16]

... It occurs to me as very important that you should bring the case before your Father in the most distinct and prudent form. Many persons who are not well acquainted with Missionary subjects have very incorrect views of the office of a Missionary — regarding it as one below the rank of a clergyman: whereas in point of emoluments it is much above curacies in this country; and in point of means and opportunities of usefulness, both to the heathen and to our countrymen abroad, it is far above the greater part of the Incumbencies in this country. Thus the influence, in other words, the position in Society of a Missionary, is I am well persuaded superior to that of an ordinary clergyman.

Several clergymen of high academical standing have gone out as Missionaries — Martyn, Tucker, Chapman, Haslam, Fox, Ragland, etc. In no instance have I heard any disappointment expressed, any doubt whether their talents would have full scope and employment, but on the other hand unfeigned satisfaction in the course they had chosen.

It is sometimes thought that a Missionary has only to explain the elements of Christian truth to ignorant heathen: but there are posts of very great importance as training establishments for educated Christian Natives for which we need persons of superior education and attainment. Such an Institution or College is greatly needed for Krishnaghar, to prepare a native Ministry. We are waiting for an University Missionary before we can commence it. Other similar posts are also open and if your offer were before the Society we should make it a matter of mutual consultation in what particular Mission and department of labour you should be employed.

Many parents regard a son given up to Missionary work as given up for ever: as one who sacrifices not only his own prospects in the Church at home but also those of his children after him, if he should have a family. But such notions are altogether erroneous. Many Missionaries after labouring for a far less period than the Civil and Military Services abroad require, return home and obtain useful and honourable situations at home. Fenn, Mayor, Knight, Squires and many others occur to me at once. I remember on one occasion visiting 17 sons of our Missionaries at Cambridge at one time.

These are a few of the hints which occur to me in the prospect of your communications with your Father on this subject: but after all my dependence is upon the Lord making his way clear by his own and often to us unexpected interpositions. If life has called you to the work, his counsel should stand — a delightful and encouraging thought! Let us remember his presence with ourselves and with those whom we desire to influence — an ever-present friend — far better able than any earthly friend to negotiate (to speak after the manner of men) any delicate affair. To this I commend you and the matter before us.

THE RECRUITMENT OF MISSIONARIES[17]

. . . I now return you the Ms. which I have read with much interest: yet I fear that it would not meet with general approbation. In one word it is too much in advance of the times. The Church of Christ is not prepared to respond to the duty of evangelizing the world as one of the same obligation as that of evangelizing our own population.

Hence we need publications which work out the case in a more elementary way than you have done.

Another remark which I will venture to make upon your Tract is that experience has proved it to be unadvisable to appeal to particular congregations or parishes to supply us with *men.*

Friends at a distance have little knowledge of the peculiar qualifications required to make an efficient missionary to the heathen – many excellent men have been sent out who have been lost to the Church from their inability to discharge the special duties of a Missionary, or to learn the language, etc.

Now if a parish or congregation should respond to your appeal and send to the parent Committee a truly pious but unsuitable man, and the Parent Committee should decline to receive him: experience has shown in several cases, that the zeal of our disappointed friends is damped, and their interest in Missions alas! checked.

We find it necessary therefore to make only a general call to the Church at large.

The offers we receive are more numerous than it is generally supposed – 60 or 70 offer themselves each year, of whom not more than 1 in 10 are accepted.

I have thus freely remarked upon your Tract as you have requested me to do, and I am glad to do so because I thank God that you are enabled to take so enlarged a view of Missionary Duty – I should rejoice to hear that you had the opportunity of advocating the cause in a wider sphere than you describe – as the Lord appears to have inclined your heart towards the subject, He will, no doubt, in his good time give you the scope suited to your desires . . .

SPECIAL APPEAL FOR RECRUITS[18]

Men are needed not only of deep, sound and enlightened piety, nor merely of vigorous mental constitution, but whose minds are formed for intellectual expansion. They must be capable of exercising an influence over others, especially over Native Teachers, who are many of them acute and well educated. They must be fitted to stand in posts of observation and to act upon emergencies. They must be thus strong in the grace which is in Christ Jesus,

It may be asked whether there be not inferior positions in a Mission which humble but pious Catechists or Scripture Readers may fill. The reply is, that though the Society did at one time send out such, the advanced state of the Missions has compelled the Committee to raise their standard. The Missions themselves now supply Native Cathechists, to fill these positions. The Committee therefore no longer send out Catechists, except in a few special cases. They are anxious indeed to engage efficient Training Masters for Native Schools. But as Missionaries they send forth only Clergymen.

SPECIAL APPEAL FOR RECRUITS[19]

. . . none can be regarded as fitted for this work without the possession of at least these two qualifications. There must be evidence of clear and decided personal piety; and there must be enough mental power and resolution to master a difficult spoken language. Only those who have been themselves converted to God can understand how to seek the conversion of others; or, in the words of the Rule laid down by the Society for the selection of its Native Catechists, *"None but spiritual agents can do spiritual work"*. Young men promising but irresolute, of whom the best may be hoped, but nothing definite can be said, are not the men for Missionary Students. And no man will be able to bear up against the trials with which the Missionary life is encompassed, without a clear conviction that God is his reconciled Father in Christ Jesus, and that he may come in perfect assurance and cast his burden on Him. A man, moreover, whom the Lord is calling into the Mission-field, will have manifested his Missionary spirit at home, by earnest and self-denying labours of love for the souls of those around him . . .

THE NEED FOR MISSIONARIES, THE CALL TO PRAYER[20]

Would to God that we were able to supply men in any degree commensurate with the pressing demands of our various Mission Stations. We have at this time Educational Establishments — languishing for the want of Principals — Stations in our oldest Missions calling out for two or four additional Missionaries — and the most promising new fields, as Japan, East Africa, and the Country of the Godavery in South India inviting our entrance. The Committee give their most anxious Consideration and their most earnest prayers for guidance to the question of location, when they have men at their disposal: but alas too many of our Missionaries are disappointed because their particular Stations are, as they suppose, overlooked. Within the last few months several friends have reported to us sentiments of this kind expressed in letters from yourself and Mrs. Hinderer, and complaints that we have no sympathy with you. Dear Brother you grievously wrong us.

It is one of the remarkable signs of the times that everywhere there is a cry for Missionaries. Had we 1,000 men ready to go forth and the means to support them we could not satisfy the demand – the cry would still prevail. We thank God that it is so – we must suffer with patience the reproaches of our unsupplied friends.

Notes

1   M.P.M., Vol. VI, No. 8. A sermon preached in the parish church of St. Mary, Islington, on Sunday, October 2, 1844, on occasion of the death of the Rev. Josiah Pratt, B.D., late Vicar of St. Peter, Coleman Street, London, and formerly Secretary of the Church Missionary Society.
2   He was soon succeeded by Zachary Macaulay. See Eugene Stock, *The History of the Church Missionary Society*, Vol. I, p. 63.
3   See Owen's *History of the Bible Society*, Vol. I, p. 54.
4   M.P.M., Vol. II, No. 9. The substance of an address at the Islington Clerical Meeting, Jan. 10, 1865. Retrospect and prospect of the operation of the Church Missionary Society.
5   A few days after this address was delivered the zealous friend of the Society here alluded to, the Rev. Henry Venn Elliott, of St. Mary's Chapel, Brighton, was suddenly called to his rest.
6   G/ACI/5, July 9, 1846, pp. 148-150. To the Rev. J. Macleane.
7   G/ACI/6, pp. 418-419, Nov. 30, 1848. Letter to a friend.
8   *C.M.I.*, April 1873, p. 144. The above passage occurs in a letter from Henry Venn dated Dec. 7, 1872, acknowledging the Minute on his resignation passed by the Committee on Nov. 27, 1872. It can be recorded, as of more than passing interest, that the principles of equality of responsibility between the Secretaries, the method of arriving at decisions, and the spirit of mutual trust between Secretaries and Committee have remained a tradition of the Society which continues to operate today.
9   G/ACI/5, March 26, 1846, pp. 106-108. Extract from a letter to Rev. J. Mules.
10 M.P., Vol. I, No. 52, Autumn 1871. Extract from a Minute of the committee of the Church Missionary Society describing the operations of a voluntary society and their peculiar advantages.
11 G/AZI/1, No. 165, Oct. 1871. Extract from a letter of Henry Venn to the Archbishop of York.
12 G/ACI/7, pp. 15-17, Dec. 30, 1848. Extract from a letter to the Rev. W. J. Pierson.
13 G/C1, Committee Minutes, May 1843–April 1844, p. 332. Dec. 11, 1843, on Corresponding Committees Overseas.
14 CI.1/L3, pp. 455-456, September 19, 1849. Extract from a letter to the Bishop of Calcutta.
15 G/ACI/5, Nov. 26, 1845, pp. 67-68. Letter to Mr. G. McHenry.
16 G/ACI/5, April 28, 1847, pp. 397-399. A letter written to a prospective recruit, Mr. Frederick Gough, who in a letter addressed to Henry Venn had expressed anxiety as to his father's probable reactions to his becoming a missionary. The happy issue of this correspondence was that Mr. Gough's father offered no hindrance to his son becoming a missionary. Frederick Gough gave thirty-four years of distinguished service in China.

17 G/ACI/7, pp. 54-55, Jan. 24, 1849. Extract from a letter to Rev. Thomas Millington.
18 G/AZI/1, No. 109, May 8, 1854. Extract from a special appeal for an enlargement or the Society's means: the need of men, and the men needed.
19 G/AZI/1, No. 108, Feb. 23, 1859, pp. 3 and 4. Extract from a circular appealing for recruits.
20 CA2/L2, pp. 303-304, Dec. 21, 1859. Extract from letter to Rev. D. Hinderer, missionary at Ibadan.

Chapter IV

A VOLUNTARY SOCIETY AND ITS RELATIONS WITH ECCLESIASTICAL AUTHORITY

INTRODUCTION

Readers who are not in the Episcopalian tradition will need some explanation of Venn's views of the Episcopate and of the relations of the Church Missionary Society with the Episcopate at home and abroad.

Venn's own view of the essentials of the office of a bishop can perhaps be illustrated best by a sermon preached by him on the occasion of the consecration of a bishop. This sermon comes first in this chapter. There follows a long, closely argued statement of the relations of a voluntary society with the ecclesiastical authorities. This represents one of the most important documents produced by Venn; in essentials it determined the subsequent practice of the Society in this respect.

For a full understanding of the importance of this whole subject for Venn's secretariat it has to be remembered that it was his task to define the proper relations of a voluntary society with the ecclesiastical organization of the church of which he was a loyal and devoted member. Some readers may find the legalism in this document, and in some others in this volume, uncongenial. Venn did not always succeed in avoiding a certain pedantry in his arguments. What has to be understood in his handling of such ecclesiastical minutiae is that, in an uncertain ecclesiastical situation, he was concerned to secure for a missionary society that "liberty of prophesying" without which it could not, in his judgment, discharge its evangelistic purpose. This, his primary concern, explains and perhaps excuses the sometimes tortuous course of his argument. As the introductory chapter to this volume sought to make clear, Venn had to lead the Church Missionary Society through a period of acute religious controversy within his own church. And not the least significant factor, about which there was so much controversy, was the nature as well as the proper exercise of the office of a bishop.

On the extension of the Episcopate overseas Venn's own ideas developed rapidly with his practical experience of administration. In 1842 he could still hope that the Society would not have to budget for the support of bishops overseas. By 1844 he had accepted the necessity for such budgeting.

Venn's statesmanship emerges very clearly in regard to the extension of the Episcopate in India. The reader must read between the lines Venn's anxiety lest a certain interpretation of the episcopal office, itself a fierce subject of controversy, might come to prevail overseas after such a fashion, as he saw it, as to stifle the initiative of a missionary society, and more particularly of the missionaries. In insisting that the office of a bishop must be precisely defined and his responsibilities legally delimited before the Episcopate was itself increased in numbers, he was contending for a principle he believed was necessary for spiritual freedom, a principle he saw admirably set forth in the actual ecclesiastical Establishment in Britain. That he would be greatly misunderstood is hardly surprising. The long letter to a friend, dated April 12, 1858, shows him well able to deal with misunderstandings (pp. 164-167).

A SERMON ON II CORINTHIANS 4:7[1]

We have this treasure in earthen vessels, that the excellency of the power may be of God, and not of us.

Assembled, on this occasion, to witness the setting apart and consecration of a parochial minister to the office of a ruling minister of the Church of Christ, in the presence of the people among whom he has discharged his pastoral duties, we are reminded that the Christian ministry, throughout all its ranks, is one and the same in its principles. And we receive from our brother a tacit pledge that the same great aim and springs of action, which have signalised his administration of your parochial affairs, will guide him in his new and higher functions.

I have chosen, therefore, a text, which presents to us the general duties, powers, and responsibilities of the Christian ministry: and I purpose to offer, first, a few plain remarks upon its import, and then such observations arising out of it as the peculiarity of this occasion suggests.

May God the Holy Spirit be with us all, to make this season one of profit to our souls, and of increase to His own glory through Jesus Christ!

I. The text speaks of a divine treasure. This treasure is not dispensed directly from heaven. It is put into an earthen vessel, to be conveyed through that channel to the recipient.

This truth is called a treasure, because of the inestimable benefits, temporal and eternal, which accompany its reception. "It is the power of God unto salvation to every one that believeth".

The verses which precede the text sufficiently explain what is *the treasure.* It is described in the previous verse to be, "the light of the knowledge of the glory of God in the face of Jesus Christ." In the fourth verse it is set forth as "the light of the glorious gospel of Christ." In the second verse it is simply termed "the truth". I need not detain you by proving what is emphatically called "the truth of the gospel" in the writings of St. Paul. It is the grand central truth of man's acceptance with God through faith in the atoning blood of Jesus Christ.

The figure of an *earthen vessel* to contain this treasure may be explained by another passage in the writings of St. Paul, the only one in which the same expression occurs (2 Tim.ii.20): "In a great house there are not only vessels of gold and of silver, but also of wood and of earth". The earthen vessels are of least worth. So that while the idea of a vessel, conveying a treasure, indicates the supreme value of that which is so conveyed, the comparison is heightened by supposing the vessel to be in itself of mean and fragile materials.

And why, it may be asked, is not the treasure presented to us in vessels of gold or silver? The text replies — "That *the excellency of the power* may be of God, and not of us." Power is here spoken of as attached to the Christian ministry. There is a certain power and authority, with which both the law of God and the law of every Christian community invest the ministers of religion. But the text uses the remarkable expression, "the excellency of the power". This carries our thoughts higher than all ecclesiastical power, even to that which reaches the consciences and saves the souls of men. The whole tenor of the passage shows us for what ends and purposes the excellency of the power is imparted. It is to give entrance to the light of the Gospel into minds which the god of this world has blinded. It is to establish the kingdom of Christ in the whole earth. The comprehensive declaration of St. Paul at the conclusion of the next chapter well illustrates the text: "All things are of God, who hath reconciled us to himself by Jesus Christ, and hath given unto us the ministry of reconciliation. To wit, that God was in Christ, reconciling the world unto himself, not imputing their trespasses unto them; and hath committed unto us the word of reconciliation." How exact a comment on the words of the text — "God in Christ, reconciling the world unto himself! " Here is the excellency of the power. "He has committed unto us the word of reconciliation." Here is the treasure put into earthen vessels.

The excellency of this Divine power is exercised over the hearts of those who dispense, and of those who receive, the treasure, by the indwelling of God the Holy Ghost. "They that are in the flesh cannot please God. But ye are not in the flesh, but in the Spirit, if so be that the Spirit of God dwell in you." The indwelling of the Spirit gives life to the soul. It invests the minister of Christ with power, giving light and fortitude, and every Christian grace requisite for dispensing the treasure to others. It accompanies the word spoken to other hearts, and worketh in them "that whereunto it is sent." Yet the excellency of the power, in other words, the gift of the Holy Spirit, is not tied to the ordinances of the Christian ministry; so that it must always accompany the dispensing of the treasure. God hath reserved it to himself as his prerogative. He withholds or gives it according to his divine wisdom. Sometimes the power is withheld, though the treasure is faithfully dispensed. Sometimes it is given contrary to human expectation. The man of faith discerns in these things the exercise of sovereign grace. He recognises the excellency of the power in the very disproportion between the human instrumentality and the effects produced through the excellency of the power.

Thus the text has resolved ministerial success into these essential elements, – the earthen vessel, the treasure, the excellency of the power. The qualifications of the minister constitute the human element. The truth of the gospel is the divine instrument. The success of the instrument, shrouded in this earthly element, is a sovereign act of grace, the work of the Holy Spirit, the great distributor of grace.

By the combination of these three elements Christianity was first propagated, and triumphed over Paganism. Fishermen from the Lake of Gennesareth, and a young man, at whose feet the executioners of the protomartyr laid down their clothes, were the first earthen vessels. The treasure made them Apostles. They dispensed it to the world. Their ministry was effectual, through the Spirit, to the conversion of souls, and to the establishment of Christian Churches in many lands. And wherever Christianity has been since propagated, and whenever true religion has been revived, after a period of lapse and darkness, the same three elements have combined to effect it.

Yet when we speak of the rise and fall of true Christianity as dependent upon the combination of these three elements, we must observe that one only has been liable to alteration. The earthen vessels are the same. They are already the lowest class in the furniture of a great house. The excellency of the power is also the same, yesterday, today, and for ever. The treasure alone can be tampered with. If that treasure be adulterated, or if it be wanting, all fails. It is the presence of the treasure, in its reality and purity, which connects the Divine blessing with the earthen vessel; because the Spirit of Truth will give effect only to the Word of Truth. Hence the extreme jealousy displayed by St. Paul in this and in his other epistles of any tampering with the treasure. "We are not of them that corrupt the word." "Though we, or an angel from heaven, preach any other gospel, let him be accursed." "To whom we gave place by subjection, no not for an hour, that the truth of the gospel might continue with you."

In the foregoing remarks we have distinguished between the ordinary powers of the Christian ministry, and the excellency of the power. We are not unmindful of the many social and civil benefits which are conferred upon a land by the ministry of a Christian Church, and by a well-ordered ecclesiastical constitution. But these were evidently not within the scope of the text. They are of an inferior kind, compared with the spiritual results comprehended under the term "the ministry of reconciliation." These results commence with the individual work of gathering souls to Christ. When men are brought, each one individually, from a state of spiritual deadness and condemnation to be partakers of spiritual and everlasting life, and when such living members of Christ are multiplied throughout the Church at home, and in foreign lands, the kingdom of Christ is advancing. And so it shall advance, in an ever-widening circle, till all nations be brought to the knowledge of the truth. To the parochial minister, who is possessed of the treasure, belongs the work of watching over the souls of his people, to bring each one to Christ. To the rulers of the Church, who have the treasure, it belongs to watch over the souls of ministers, that ministers may save themselves and those that hear them. And their office specially qualifies them for aiding the extension of Christ's kingdom. It is an ancient ecclesiastical maxim, that every bishop is a bishop of the universal Church of Christ. Should not each diocese, therefore, be regarded as a nursery and seed-plot for the barren portions of the earth, to which may be sent from time to time such vessels as seem best fitted for carrying the treasure to a people perishing for lack of knowledge.

For the accomplishment of these great spiritual results the Christian ministry was instituted, and its gradations of authority established, and power given to it adequate to its great undertaking.

II. Having thus discharged the first part of my undertaking, to open out the meaning of the text, I proceed to offer a few remarks arising from it, and suitable to the present occasion.

It may seem like presumption to expatiate upon the duties and responsibilities of the Christian ministry, before those who sustain the chief administration of the Church, and before brethren in the ministry better qualified and more accustomed than myself to claim public attention. I retire, however, within that humble sphere which is allowed by courtesy to every working man, whether in spiritual or temporal things, of speaking such thoughts, on any subject, as his personal experience or post of observation may have suggested to his mind: especially if the thoughts shall not be those of a passing day, but such as have been often revolved in the course of a varied and somewhat lengthened experience. The remarks which I thus venture to offer belong to the subject before us, — the efficiency of the Christian ministry. They cannot, therefore, be deemed out of place on such an occasion as the present.

1. The first remark which I will offer is, that as the power of the ministry in any Church depends upon the purity of the treasure, the preservation of that purity is our first duty as ministers of Christ.

We are surrounded in an established Church by influences which blunt our perceptions of this truth: such as a desire for union amongst those who hold the same office, and the duty of rendering honour to whom honour is due, when those in authority over us do not hold the truth of the gospel. It is often painful to maintain the essential distinction, among authorised teachers, between those who have and those who have not the "TREASURE". Still more difficult and painful it is to maintain this distinction in the face of instances where those having the treasure seem to be inefficient in their ministry, and exhibit little fruit of it in their lives. Our better judgement is warped by the comparison of an earnest, affectionate, interesting preacher of ethics, with one who delivers the truth of the gospel in a cold, dull, or repulsive manner.

Yet let it be ever borne in mind, that the treasure is more than the vessel. A treasure in a very imperfect vessel may be, and often is, of some value. The Master of the House may use its agency for the conversion of souls in many other and indirect ways of ministerial labour besides preaching. A vessel of gold or silver without the treasure is of no value in the house of God. When the conscience of a hearer is awakened, when the salvation of his soul is at stake, all thought of the vessel is lost; as a dying man needing a medicine, and knowing its specific quality, cares not for the vessel from which he drinks his cure.

It is undoubtedly a part of the episcopal office to take all right methods of promoting ministerial efficiency, that every minister may be "fitted and prepared for the Master's use". Let sound learning be maintained. Let the art of composition and of the delivery of sermons be cultivated. Let the study of pastoral theology and of parochial organisation be promoted. Let every effort be made to stir up the spirit of men to energy, activity, and perseverance. Let every means be used to promote harmony, love and co-operation among fellow-workmen. But let all be done under the solemn conviction that everything depends upon the purity of the treasure. Where that is, there alone is the excellency of the power. Without the treasure, eloquence, earnestness, church-order, union, can effect comparatively nothing. These may exist where a Church is dead. "The spirit is life". Where the treasure is, there is the Spirit of Christ: his promised presence with his Church.

2. To strengthen the remark just made, let us refer to the great religious improvement which has been everywhere manifested in our Church and nation since the commencement of the present century. No one can doubt that the ministry of the Word has been one influential instrument of this improvement. And what class of ministers have put the stamp of their spirit

upon the age? If we look back to the season of universal apathy and worldliness which afflicted our Church in the early part of the eighteenth century, though no age was more fertile in learned, earnest, and interesting preachers, it will be seen that a few men appeared in our parochial pulpits who were marked as maintainers of the peculiar doctrines of the gospel. A name of ridicule was soon attached to them, derived from this peculiarity. They were scorned by the world, and opposed by the authorities of the Church. All the tendencies of the age were against them. Yet these men had the treasure. As preachers of the truth of the gospel, they succeeded in gaining the ear of the people; and gradually the whole style of preaching in our Church has assumed a near approach to the preaching of these men. And their spirit has been diffused throughout the Church. Their once distinctive doctrines have become the most approved. Various schemes of benevolence which they devised, and practices of which they long bore the *reproach*, are now sanctioned by authority, and have given a character to our Church – such as missions to the heathen, free Bible distribution, supplemental services in cottages and barns, in Bible-classes, in Sunday-schools, and in open-air preaching.

Of the early leaders of this religious revolution, as it may be well termed, I may be permitted to speak with some confidence, on the ground of the courtesy which I have claimed. Their strength was in the truth they held and taught, often amidst much of human infirmity and weakness. It has been sometimes said that they formed a party, and, as an active minority, rose to notoriety. Nothing can be more contrary to fact. The men of note amongst them received the treasure, not from hand to hand, but by the independent study of God's word, often after years of struggle against the force of truth. Each one watched with as much godly jealousy over the treasure he had found, as if no other vessel possessed it. Each one valued his brother as the possessor of the same treasure. But in various other points they widely differed, and were too often at variance. They lacked the very condition of party – combined action. One of the most celebrated members of the body emphatically and prophetically declared, that "the evangelical clergy ever were and ever would be a rope of sand." True: because each one exercises an independent judgment, and acts upon his conscience. All attempts to organise a party among such men must fail. Unity of action only arises from all dispensing the same treasure.

Fathers of the Church! and you, my brethren, who are entitled to lead the public mind! I would remind you this day, that the great religious improvement of which I have spoken, worked its way up from below to the higher ranks. What may we not expect under God, if rulers and leading men in our Church act out the same spiritual principles; if they exalt only Christ crucified before the world; and make it their chief aim to bring souls – especially the souls of the clergy – into vital union with Christ through faith; and if the extension of Christ's kingdom be thoroughly taken in hand as a duty we owe to him, who still waits to see of the travail of his soul? Thus would the treasure be brought to multitudes whom more humble ministrations cannot reach! We do not forget in these anticipations that an earthen vessel will still hold the treasure; we do not forget that the Lord is jealous of his own glory, and that we of the lower ranks cannot do a worse service to our superiors than to exalt them above measure. Still we know, that if the excellency of the power be given, all is safe, and success is sure: and in the Divine dispensations it has ever been evident that the Lord does specially honour rulers who honour him.

3. Permit me to add another remark, suggested by the subject before us, and suitable to this occasion; namely, that an episcopate characterised by these spiritual principles will possess a weight of authority not at variance with, but additional to and far surpassing, all the power which ecclesiastical principles or law can confer. But if spiritual principles be contravened, the episcopate becomes powerless for good. We live in days when we are compelled to distinguish between spiritual and ecclesiastical principles, and to remind each other that the only real value of the latter is their subserviency to the former. God forbid that spiritual and ecclesiastical principles should ever be brought into conflict; but if the alternative unhappily arise of choosing between the two, there must be no hesitation as to which shall have the pre-eminence.

These considerations have a special weight in a Church in which ecclesiastical law is confessedly very defective, and in which Colonial Bishops are destitute of the power of coercion. But yet this legislative defectiveness may serve to show the world, that where the relation between ministers and their spiritual rulers is based upon a common zeal for the maintenance of the truth of the gospel, such rulers are invested with a power more potent for good than the Canons of the Church; and that their influence over hearts, bound to them by spiritual sympathy, far transcends the exactions of canonical obedience. Long has our Church stood foremost amidst the Churches of the Reformation, as a bulwark of the truth. Its ecclesiastical constitution, whenever put to the test, has been proved to be thoroughly Protestant and Evangelical. It attracts the admiration of other churches by its ministry in each well-ordered parish. Greatly will that admiration be heightened by its exhibiting also in its Diocesan government such a paternal sway of faithful bishops, and such a cordial subordination, or rather co-operation, of their attached clergy.

4. Allow me to add one concluding remark. I have spoken of the possible conflict between spiritual and ecclesiastical principles. I will venture also to indicate what will be the battle-ground of this conflict. It will be, as it seems to me, the question, – In what way can a sinner obtain pardon and peace with God? Other great questions agitate the minds of the few; this is

the great personal question with every man whose conscience is awake. Every church and every minister of a church must give a distinct answer to this inquiry: in seasons of religious conflict this question is sure to be uppermost, and by the answer given every church or minister will stand or fall. Men cannot unite upon other points while they disagree on this. The true answer to the inquiry constitutes, as we trust we have shown, *the Treasure.* By whatever variety of expression the truth of the Gospel may be indicated; whether as the doctrine of the cross of Christ, whether as justification by faith only, whether as the atonement, whether as redemption through the blood of Christ, it has ever encountered opposition. It was "to the Jews a stumbling-block and to the Greeks foolishness." In the earliest ages of the Church, and ever since, the struggle has been going on within the Church, to tear from this blessed truth its significancy or its simplicity; to substitute a way of salvation more in accordance with natural reason and human prejudices. Popery worships the shadow but denies the substance of the truth, by setting up the doctrine of human merit, of works of supererogation, and of the mediation of saints. Superstition substitutes sacramental grace. Yet this truth, though ridiculed by the profane, though cavilled at by others, is cherished as the life of the soul by all who receive it. When received, it frees a man from the slavery of the world; it gives him power; it is accompanied by a change in the moral character which cannot be mistaken. This cardinal truth wrought the Reformation. It has revived our Church. If its enemies are now mustering their forces, so are its friends. Its influence, blessed be God! daily increases. Presuming only to speak from personal experience, I hesitate not to say, that where one heart was swayed by its influence when I first entered the ministry of this metropolis, thirty-seven years ago, hundreds might now be counted. At home it is becoming more and more the rallying-point for all who are zealous on the Lord's side. It is the line of advance of all our social improvements. Abroad it is evangelising the world. It is easily apprehended and cordially embraced by thousands of the negroes of Africa, of the Hindoos of India, and of the islanders of the Pacific. It has raised them into the brotherhood of Christendom.

> *Parent of Hope, immortal Truth make known,*
> *Thy deathless wreaths, and triumphs all thine own;*
> *The silent progress of thy power is such,*
> *Thy means so feeble and despised so much,*
> *That few believe the wonders thou hast wrought,*
> *And none can teach thee but whom thou hast taught.*

They on whom is laid the chief charge to guard the interests of the Church are, as we have presumed to suggest, specially responsible for providing "that the truth of the gospel may continue with us". But let all of us, my Christian brethren, to whom that truth is dear, aid them by its faithful maintenance, each within his own sphere. Let us also strengthen their hands by intercessory prayer for them, such as the present service will now put into our lips; and such as the recollection of the present occasion will, it may be hoped, prompt us frequently to renew, in times to come, before the throne of grace.

REMARKS ON THE CONSTITUTION AND PRACTICE OF THE
CHURCH MISSIONARY SOCIETY, WITH REFERENCE TO ITS
ECCLESIASTICAL RELATIONS

In the *Thirty-ninth Report* of the Church Missionary Society (1838-1839) there is a paragraph headed "Principles and Proceedings of the Society" which reads as follows:

> Inquiries having frequently been made respecting the relations of the Society's Missionaries to the Bishop, when located within the diocese of a Bishop of our Church, a Clerical Member of the Committee was induced to draw up a statement on that and Analogous topics, illustrative of the principles and operations of the Society. This Paper so correctly exhibits the views of the Committee on the points to which it refers, that, with the consent of the writer, they have printed it as an Appendix to the Report (p. 34).

Henry Venn, who became a member of the Committee in 1822, was the clerical member who produced this major declaration of the Society's principles and policies. The first part of the document consists of a careful distinction between the lay and spiritual functions in the Church of England. Henry Venn was concerned to establish the "lay" character of the Church Missionary Society while insisting upon the Society's loyalty to the order of the Church of England. After noting the role of the Society in the collection of the home revenue and its disbursement abroad, and the selecting and educating of candidates for missionary employment, the argument of this document[2] proceeds as follows:

The Sending Forth, to Particular Stations the Missionaries Thus Ordained, or Other Clergymen Who Have Been Previously Ordained

Now, here an objection against the Society has been founded on the use of the term "sending forth": it sounds like an exercise of Ecclesiastical power. But, Ecclesiastically speaking, the Bishop of London "sends forth" every Missionary ordained by him. The Law of the Land has sanctioned the two Archbishops, and the Bishop of London, in ordaining persons to officiate abroad. The Secretary of the Church Missionary Society requests, by letter, the Bishop of London to ordain in conformity with the provisions of the Act of Parliament, such and such persons, whom the Society is willing to support in some Foreign Station. The Bishop, by the imposition of hands, gives them authority to preach the Gospel, with a view to their foreign location. — In the case of persons already in Holy Orders, who may join the Society, they may be said to go forth by their own voluntary act; but their letters of Orders, given by a Bishop of our Church, are their mission and commission, ecclesiastically speaking.

Hence, to call the acts of the Church Missionary Society — in selecting the station, paying the passage-money and agreeing to provide the Missionary's salary — to call these acts a *sending forth* of Preachers, in an Ecclesiastical sense, is to confound names with things, and to lose sight of all true Church principles.

The Fourth general head under which the proceedings of the Church Missionary Society may be arranged, is, THE SUPERINTENDENCE OF MISSIONARIES IN THEIR LABOURS AMONG THE HEATHEN.

Here a distinction must be made between the case of those Foreign Nations which lie within the jurisdiction of a Colonial Bishop, and other stations, which are not so situated, and may therefore be termed Extra-Diocesan.

In the first case the Church Missionary Society has expressly determined, that all its ordained Missionaries shall be submitted for licence to the Bishop of the Diocese in which they may be stationed; and that no Missionary shall exercise his spiritual functions in such Diocese without a licence. The Society has further recognised the uncontrolled discretion of the Bishop to grant or withhold his licence, and the propriety of specifying in such licence a particular district as the field of labour; so that a Missionary cannot be removed from one district to another without the sanction of the Bishop.

Those principles were stated in a letter from the Society to the Bishop of Calcutta, signed by the Right Honourable the President (December 17, 1835), in a manner so satisfactory to the Bishop, that he embodied them in the four following Rules, expressed for the most part in the words of the Society's letter: which were, at the Bishop's request, entered upon the Minutes of the Calcutta Corresponding Committee, as the recognised Rules of this practice: —

1. The Bishop expresses — by granting or withholding his Licence, in which the sphere of the Missionary's labour is mentioned — his approbation or otherwise of the location.

2. The Bishop superintends the Missionaries afterward, as other Clergy in the discharge of their Ecclesiastical duties.

3. The Bishop receives from those (the Committee and Secretary) who still stand in the relation of Lay-Patrons to the Missionary, such communications respecting his Ecclesiastical duties as may enable the Bishop to discharge that paternal superintendence to the best advantage. – The Archdeacon of Calcutta or Bombay acting under the Bishop's immediate directions, when he happens to be absent.

4. If the Bishop[3] or Archdeacon fills, at the request of the Society, the offices of Patron, President, Vice-President, Treasurer, Secretary, etc., he receives, further, all such confidential information, on all topics, as the Bishops officially neither could wish nor properly ask (to receive).

The Bishop also wrote to the Parent Society in the following terms: "You seem to me to lay down the principle most correctly . . . This is to me perfectly satisfactory, as I shall instantly inform the Archbishop of Canterbury, to whom I report all the proceedings of the diocese". – (9th June, 1836)

It will be perceived that the Missionaries, thus licensed, stand toward the Bishop in the relation rather of Stipendiary Curates, than of Beneficed Clergymen. For a Bishop in England cannot refuse a Licence or institution to a benefice without assigning a reason which will bear investigation before a Court of Common Law; nor can he deprive a Clergyman of his benefice without a judicial process. But no law has provided any such check in the case of Missionaries: the Bishop has the power of withholding a Licence, or of withdrawing it, at his sole discretion, without assigning any cause, as in the case of Stipendiary Curates in this country.

If it be asked, what are the checks and safeguards against the undue exercise of this discretionary power of the Bishops? – it may be replied, in the words of the Bishop of Calcutta, in a letter to the Parent Society, April 12, 1837: –

> We are not to take for granted that discretionary power will be abused; but, on the contrary, to provide, by a cheerful and friendly spirit and conduct, against the likelihood of such an occurrence. If the event of arbitrary conduct should arise, or be supposed to arise, the remedies are – public opinion – an appeal to the Archbishop – and the Society's refusing to make other appointments and locations than those unreasonably objected to. Nothing is the least likely (and probability is the guide of life) to arise to impede or cramp the Committee, since they unquestionably and avowedly possess, the choice of men – the appointment of spheres of labour – the temporal power including pecuniary support.

But though the Bishop's Licence is at once the pledge and proof that the

Society's Missionaries are under Episcopal superintendence and jurisdiction, and that the spiritual oversight rests altogether with the Bishop; yet the Society may seem to some persons, to keep up a kind of spiritual jurisdiction and oversight, by requiring accounts from the Missionaries of all their proceedings, and by giving them direction, from time to time, which may bear upon their spiritual duties. And it must be remembered, that the Society stands towards its Missionaries in the relation of trustees of the fund out of which their salaries are paid. In the case of a beneficed Clergyman in this country, the Minister is the guardian and possessor of the temporalities of the benefice, because the benefice is an endowment; and the Patron has no further connexion with the Minister whom he has once presented to the Bishop. In our case, the office of Patron is in a sense perpetuated by the payment of the salary, and the possession of all the temporalities of the Mission.

This matter has been well explained by the Bishop of Calcutta, in a letter to the Calcutta Corresponding Committee, May 26, 1837: —

> The Missionary Committees (says his Lordship) have a far greater latitude in India than any lay-Patrons at home. Upon presenting his Clerk to the Bishop, the Patron at home is *functus officio*. The Clergyman is removed, on being once instituted and licensed, totally and for ever from the Patron, and is transferred to the superintendence of the Bishop.

> The Patron has nothing whatever more to do with him. But in India, the Committee is (i) the continued paymaster of the Missionary, after he is duly Licensed; — for institution and induction there are none. (2) They correspond with him. (3) They supply him with Catechists. (4) They report his chief proceedings home. (5) They propose removals and changes of station to the Bishop. (6) They exercise, unavoidably, an influence which does not belong to the mere Lay-Patron; and are aiding, in a variety of ways, to the comfortable and honourable discharge of the Missionary's most exalted and most spiritual duties.

It remains to consider the case of those stations which are Extra-Diocesan; i.e. Where there is no Colonial Bishop of the Church of England having jurisdiction over them.

In these cases, the Society has endeavoured to procure for such stations the benefits of the Episcopal office from the nearest Bishop of the Church of England. Application was made by the Committee both to the late and to the present Bishop of Madras, to extend, as far as circumstances would admit, these benefits to the Mission in Travancore; which, as an independent state, not forming a part of the British Dominions, was not included in the Diocese of Madras. A similar application was made on behalf of the New Zealand Mission to the Bishop of Australia, who at once acceded to the request, and kindly promised to visit New Zealand as soon as his office duties would permit; stating in a letter to the Society's representative at Sydney, "It is highly satisfactory to me, that our friends at home are taking a view of these things, which proves them to belong not only to a *Missionary,* but also to a Church Society". (See *Annual Report,* 1838).

Such is a General View of the Constitution and Proceedings of the Church Missionary Society.

It is not intended to assert, that errors are not sometimes committed in the application of these principles to matters of detail. It must be remembered that Missionary operations are, alas! new and anomalous in the system of the Church of England, and that it is not always easy to draw a definite line between the two provinces which belong respectively to the Bishop and the Committee. It has been observed by the Bishop of Calcutta (letter, May 26, 1837): "The boundaries of the power of Committees, as they approach to those of the Bishop, can be ascertained, in many points, only by time and observation." Perplexities have consequently occurred; and, unhappily, misunderstandings have sometimes arisen between the Representatives of the Society abroad and Ecclesiastical authorities. But these are the principles by which the Home Committee have endeavoured to guide the proceedings of the Society, and they confidently respond to a sentiment expressed by the Bishop of Calcutta – "The principles of our new relations are now fully recognised: the details will soon find their level." – (Letter, 9 June 1836).

In reviewing the Ecclesiastical relations of the Church Missionary Society, there are two or three points which it seems very important to notice.

1. Missionary operations, as they are conducted by the Church Missionary Society, though apparently anomalous in the system of the Church of England, are yet in strict conformity with its constitution and principles; they are analogous to many other instances of voluntary exertion for the extension of true religion within the Church, in which Ecclesiastical authority and lay co-operation unite for the accomplishment of the same end: so that these operations may be regarded as the acts of the Church of England, putting forth its energy for the conversion of the Heathen World. For it has been shown, that the Bishops of the Church, under the authority of the law of the land, ordain and send forth our missionaries – that these missionaries are Licensed and superintended abroad, in every case where it is practicable, by Colonial Bishops of the Church of England; as are the other Clergymen of the Church officiating in the same colony. The Services which the Missionaries perform are in strict conformity with the ritual and discipline of the Church. Even in the few cases in which Lutheran Clergymen are employed, this rule is observed; and all the congregations which are gathered into the fold of Christ are trained up as members of the Church established in this land.

And here it may be observed, that nothing less than the sanction of a duly assembled Convocation can more fully identify the acts of any

Missionary Society, within the Church of England, with the Church.[4] Without such sanction, all associations of Churchmen must stand in the same position. Still further, not to notice the present abeyance of Convocations, it may be asserted, that even if the Church were to assemble in her provincial Convocations, and to decree and to regulate missionary operations, such proceedings could not essentially add to, or alter, those important particulars which, under present circumstances, entitle the operations of the Church Missionary Society to be regarded as missionary operations of the United Church of England, and Ireland.

2. It must be ever borne in mind, that missionary operations are, in their very nature, temporary and preparative; that they are to be gradually but eventually superseded by a different order of things, when the Heathen Nations shall have become Christianized. In some cases, as in the West Indies, this change is further advanced than in others. Now, it must be expected that in proportion as this change advances, difficulties and perplexities will arise in our Ecclesiastical relations, peculiar to this *transition state* – from Missionary operations, to that happy consummation when there shall be an endowed and established system of Christian Instruction, and a territorial division of ministerial labour. This consummation the Church Missionary Society has ever kept in view and devoutly desired; and, as far as possible, has prepared for its approach. – In an interview with the Bishop of Barbadoes (April 1835), this point was expressly alluded to; and it was stated by the Committee to his Lordship, "that whenever a district should be brought into the state of an organized Christian Community, it should assume entirely the Parochial form, and cease to be occupied as a Missionary Station. – The Bishop entirely acquiesced in this view; and only expressed his anxiety that it should not be so acted upon as prematurely to deprive a district of the Missionary's services."[5]

3. Lastly, it must be evident, from a review of the whole subject, that our Ecclesiastical relations depend, in many important respects, upon a mutual confidence and good understanding between the Committee and its representatives, and the Ecclesiastical Authorities both at home and abroad. This must be the case, to argue upon no higher grounds, while those relations are governed by Ecclesiastical laws and canons made without reference to Missionary operations for an Established Church in a Christian country, and where so much is also necessarily left to the discretion of both parties. If we look to our Home operations, the Committee places confidence in the Bishop of London, that he will continue to ordain the Missionary Candidates introduced to his Lordship by the Society according to the provisions of the Act; and the Lord Bishop of London relies upon the Committee's using every means to select, train, and duly qualify proper candidates to be thus introduced to him.

So, also, in its Foreign operations, the Society places confidence in the

Colonial Bishops (as it has already shown, in a quotation from the letter of Bishop Wilson), that they will not exercise an unreasonable or arbitrary discretion, in withholding or withdrawing licences from our missionaries, or in refusing ordination to our Candidates. And the Bishops, by granting Licences and ordination to the missionaries of a voluntary Society, whose income is liable to fluctuations, and whose agents are constantly changing, manifestly place confidence in the Committees that they will use every endeavour to keep up the Missions once established; and that they will not, on their part, act in an unreasonable or arbitrary manner, or withdraw the salary from a Licensed Missionary, without reason sufficient to prove to the licensing Bishop the necessity of the proceeding.

It seems impossible to supersede this Conventional understanding (as it may be termed), till missions are supported by endowments, or till a code of Missionary canons be established by competent authority.

This mutual confidence and good understanding now exists, it may be thankfully asserted, between the Committee of the Society and the Ecclesiastical Authorities of every Colonial Diocese in which Missionaries are labouring. And may He, Who is the God "not of confusion, but of peace", and "the Great Shepherd and Bishop of Souls" unite together the hearts and hands of those who are labouring in this Holy Cause – "that all and every of these may, *in their several callings,* serve truly and faithfully, to the glory of His Name! "

ON THE RELATIONS OF THE SOCIETY WITH ECCLESIASTICAL AUTHORITIES[6]

I beg to offer the following reply to your Excellency's enquiry respecting the relations which generally exist between a Colonial Bishop and the direction of the Society's Missionary operations in his diocese.

Throughout the system of the Church of England there is a recognised distinction between *lay* and *clerical* functions in matters ecclesiastical. Though the laity cannot discharge spiritual functions yet their cooperation is often necessary for the accomplishment of Ecclesiastical acts.

The principle of a distinction between the lay and clerical provinces, is that upon which the ecclesiastical relations of the Church Missionary Society are regulated.

The direction of the Spiritual duties of the Missions rests solely with the Bishop. The direction of the temporal affairs of the Mission rests wholly with the Committee of the Society: and in this the Bishop only takes part as a member of the Committee.

The management of the temporal affairs of a Mission is generally vested in a Committee composed of Missionaries of the Society, or of laymen and clergymen unconnected with the Society. Such committees are always appointed by the Parent Committee at home and all their minutes are subject to the revision and confirmation of the Parent Committee.

In general cases the Colonial Bishop is the President of such foreign Committees.

But in no case has the Church Missionary Society committed the directions of the temporal affairs of a Mission into the hands of a Bishop alone, from the conviction that the harmonious co-operation between the laity and the Ecclesiastical authorities will be best preserved; and the efficiency of both Departments best promoted, by keeping distinct the spiritual and temporal affairs of the Missions.

OVERSEAS EPISCOPATE[7]

Resolution of Committee of Feb. 14, 1842, Confirmed March 14, 1842.

> Resolved that it be stated to Mr. Moule for the information of the friends who signed the memorial that the Committee do not intend to make any other grant in aid of the salary of a colonial Bishop connected with a Mission of the Society.

The Committee had felt for some time that the New Zealand Mission was in a most critical state: – that it was absolutely necessary that some person invested with ecclesiastical authority should proceed thither, to set many things in order. The Bishop of Australia had kindly attempted to exercise that authority, but had found it incompatible with his other duties. He advised the sending out an Archdeacon or Commissary, but practical difficulties prevented this scheme. We therefore regard the proposal of a Bishop for New Zealand as a providential interference for the removal of many of our difficulties. And by our offer of assistance we secured the immediate appointment of a Bishop. Subsequent events have proved that if it had not been for our offer there would have been little probability of an early appointment . . .

Allow me also to state in answer to the objection which you urge, namely, that the grant to the New Zealand Bishopric will cripple the operations of the Society in other operations, my conviction that the outlay will save more than its amount to the Society's treasury, by facilitating the adjustment of the affairs of that Mission and by hastening the period when the Society shall have accomplished, thro' the infinite mercy of God the evangelization of the interesting tribes of New Zealand, and may therefore withdraw its expenditure from that spot, in order to carry the Gospel to other lands.

OVERSEAS EPISCOPATE[8]

The situation of the Church of England in the Colony of Sierra Leone and on the West Coast of Africa seems peculiarly to demand, if it can possibly be obtained, the superintendence and other important benefits of the Episcopal office. This want has long been felt by the Committee of the Church Missionary Society, and the subject was brought by them under the notice of your Lordship and of Lord John Russell, then Colonial Secretary, in 1840. The reasons for such a measure have gained additional strength since that period.

In Sierra Leone there are at present 14 distinct Christian Congregations, comprising 7,000 worshippers. The Communicants amount to above 1,400. The Mission numbers 15 Missionaries in Holy Orders and numerous Native Teachers. When the state of the settlement is taken in connexion with the Settlements at the Gambia and at Cape Coast, at both which there are Chaplains and the boundless Missionary prospects opening from these points and from Abbeokouta, as well as from Sierra Leone itself, the importance of a Bishop in such a sphere of ministerial labour is apparent.

But there are some special circumstances which I beg to submit to your Lordship's consideration:

(1) A very considerable body of Christians are now growing up who were baptized in their infancy – who are receiving a good education – and whose minds are opening to the various sources of European knowledge – and who, under God's blessing, may be the nucleus of light and civilization to their country. The importance of the rite of confirmation to such an interesting Community cannot be too highly estimated.

(2) There are also in the Colony many Native Teachers – men who have long maintained a consistent Christian character: some twenty years, some less, as Teachers in the Schools and Congregations – and who in the point of knowledge are as much advanced above the rest of the Community, as the Clergy of any Christian society with relation to that society. Many of them now act with much advantage as Catechists. It would be most important that some of these should be admitted to Holy Orders; but the risk to their health and character would be too great to justify their being brought to England, and their attainments would be perhaps scarcely sufficient to warrant their Ordination in this country. But if there were a Bishop on the spot to admit them to Holy Orders and to superintend them, the Advantage to the cause of Christianity would be very great . . .

. . . With regard to the funds for the support of a Bishop, the Chaplaincy, which is now vacant, would afford £500 a year. The Colonial Council have also voted £300 a year for a Bishop, out of the Colonial Chest; so that an income of £800 might probably be obtained for a Bishop, if he undertook the duties of the Chaplaincy. But if it is thought that this would not be sufficient to found a Bishoprick, or if no one suitable for the office can be found to go to Africa, I would submit to your Lordship whether in any way the occasional visit of a Bishop to the West Coast of Africa could be procured, either by the erection of a Bishoprick of St. Helena, according to a plan formerly submitted to your Lordship, or by a visit from one of the West Indian Bishops.

If it be impracticable to appoint a Bishop to Sierra Leone, I would next submit to your Lordship whether at least an Archdeacon might not be appointed as Chaplain, who I presume would be under your Lordship, and who might perhaps, after his constitution had been seasoned to the climate of Africa, be consecrated as a Bishop. And if an Archdeacon could not be procured to go from England, I would suggest whether the senior Missionary of the Society, who has been there 16 years might not be made Archdeacon; so that there might be some Ecclesiastical Head to the Church which has already, through God's blessing, been firmly established in that interesting field of Missionary labour.

A BISHOPRIC FOR PRINCE RUPERT'S LAND, CANADA[9]

Allow me to address you as Secretary of the Colonial Bishopric Fund in the expectation that the proposition for a Bishop of Prince Rupert's Land in North West America will be brought before the Archbishops and Bishops at their next meeting by the Archbishop of Canterbury.

The Church Missionary Society have felt the importance of this measure, and the Committee has made efforts for its accomplishment. They were willing to have borne a part of the salary could a Bishop have immediately been appointed. This proposal was some time since laid before His Grace the Primate and the Bishop of London.

Lord Chichester, our President, with his Grace's concurrence has had a communication with Lord Stanley upon the case from which source we have learned that no opposition will be made by Her Majesty's Government to the establishment of the see, if a sufficient sum can be raised as an Endowment. Mr. Harrison, a leading member of the Hudson's Bay Company has assured us of the willingness of the Company to grant a residence for the Bishop with a sufficient quantity of land for his use . . .

Allow me to remind you of some of the special reasons which may be urged for the full organization of this distant branch of our Episcopal Church.

The territory of the Hudson's Bay Company is of vast extent, comprehending nearly 4,000 miles from East to West and from one to two thousand miles from South to North. In this vast extent of country the Company has isolated Posts connected with the Fur Trade, though only one principal settlement of Europeans, namely at the Red River.

The Red River Settlement contains a population of 5,000; one half being Protestants, the rest Roman Catholics. There has long been a Roman Catholic Bishop at this Settlement.

It should be remembered that the Church residing in this remote territory is more secluded from the benefits and encouragement of the Church at home than is the case in any other part of the British Empire: for there is only twice a year regular communication with England – one by ship proceeding through Hudson's Bay, and once by an Express through Canada. At all other times the communication between the territory and Great Britain through the United States is most uncertain and rare.

The appointment of a Bishop is also most important in relation to the Missionary prospects of the country. The Missionary operations already attempted have been very successful. In a letter of the Bishop of Montreal, written immediately after his return from the Red River, he states:

> It is impossible that I can write to you after my visit, without paying at least a passing tribute to the invaluable labours of those faithful men whom the Society has employed in that field of its extensive operations: and the opportunity which was afforded to me, of contrasting the conditions of the Indians who are under their training and direction, with that of the unhappy heathens with whom I came in contact on the route, signally enabled me to appreciate the blessings of which the Society is the instrument, and did indeed yield a beautiful testimony to the power and reality of the Gospel of Christ.

The Society already has three Missionary Stations, at the first of which on the Red River, a village of converted Indians contains a population of about 300 souls, of whom 200 were confirmed by the Bishop of Montreal in his late visit. Another Station is at Cumberland House, 500 miles distant where a converted Indian was settled four years ago. So successful has this Native Teacher been, that when the station was visited two years afterward by a Missionary, he found 100 Indians under Christian instruction, of whom after examination 85 were admitted to baptism. A third Station has been commenced at Manitoba Lake, 120 miles from the Red River . . . I need not remind you that in such a territory as Rupert's Land, Missionary labours can only be effectually prosecuted by a Native Indian Ministry, and that a resident Bishop is therefore urgently required to direct the preparation for Holy Orders – to ordain – and afterward to superintend and govern Native Ministers.

THE EXTENSION OF THE EPISCOPATE OVERSEAS[10]

1. The Church Missionary Society has been engaged for more than forty years in supporting Missions in India. They have now more than ninety Ordained European Missionaries, together with twenty Ordained Natives, labouring in the three Residencies and Ceylon.

2. Viewing the vast extent of the Indian Dioceses, and the rapid increase of the Ministry of the Word among the Native population in connexion with the United Church of England and Ireland, the Committee feel the importance of an increase of the Episcopate in India, and especially the appointment of a Bishop of Agra.

3. At the same time the Committee are deeply convinced of the necessity of a due regulation of the Episcopal office, and of the adoption of more certain arrangements than now exist for the maintenance of ecclesiastical discipline, under competent authority and adapted to the peculiar circumstances of the Church in India, before such extension of the Episcopate can safely take place: lest the exercise of an undefined, and, therefore, so far, an arbitrary power by the Episcopate, should seriously compromise the interests of the Church, and of Missionary Societies, in the present condition of India.

4. In making the foregoing remarks, the Committee thankfully acknowledge the wise, mild and paternal way in which the Episcopate has hitherto been exercised in India, and the freedom of action which has been very properly allowed to Missionaries. But at the same time they must as frankly declare, that difficulties of a serious kind have even in this early stage of their operations arisen, by occasional attempts to transfer regulations existing in England, and adapted to the parochial and territorial divisions in a Christian Church at home to ministerial labours in the midst of the unevangelised populations of India.

5. The Committee refer also to the very uncertain state of the question, what ecclesiastical laws and canons are of force in any foreign country, more especially in the territories of the East India Company, and in those dependent provinces which retain a Native Sovereignty. This uncertainty being rendered still greater by the provisions of Acts of Parliament (53 Geo. III, c. 155, 3 & 4; Will. IV. c. 85) which make the jurisdiction of the Bishops in India dependent upon the Royal Letters Patent, countersigned by the President of the Board of Control.

6. The Committee refer also to the impossibility of applying the injunctions, rubrics, and canons provided for an Established Church in a Christian Country to the elementary Christian instruction of Native Enquirers, and Catechumens scattered throughout Heathen and Mahomedan communities, and to the evils which must result from attempting to enforce these canons and rubrics in their entirety upon a native Christian Church.

7. They refer also to the uncertain status and position of Missionary and other Clergymen in India who are not Chaplains to the Company, to the undefined power of Bishops, in withholding or withdrawing licences, to the absence of any known law which would afford protection against an abuse of authority, and to the need of some opportunity for the laity of India to take part in the affairs of the Church.

8. The Committee conceive that the circumstances of the Indian Dioceses are favourable to the adjustment of the matters alluded to, in consequence of the Acts of Parliament already cited, and also because the East India Company has long recognised an ecclesiastical department in its administration of the affairs of India; and, further, because there are as yet no vested interests or endowments, but the stipends of the Clergy are paid either by the Company or by Voluntary Societies.

9. The Committee would, therefore, humbly submit to the authorities who have the control of India affairs, an earnest request that this subject may be taken into consideration, and that measures may be adopted for better defining the Episcopal powers, and the relative ecclesiastical position of the Clergy and laity, previously to the establishment of any new Bishoprics in India.

EXTENSION OF EPISCOPATE OVERSEAS[11]

I lament with you the various misapprehensions which have occurred respecting a "Memorial" and "Statement" of the Committee of the Church Missionary Society on the Extension of the Episcopate in India. They have been chiefly, however, echoes of a most unfair critique in the columns of a newspaper, which has long been hostile to the Society, alleging that the Committee had repudiated Episcopal superintendence over its Missions, and had needlessly placed the Church Missionary Society in opposition to the Society for the Propagation of the Gospel, and especially to the late revered Bishop of Calcutta, whose statements had been put forth by the Society in the forefront of their appeals for an extension of the Indian Episcopate.

The facts of the case, as explained in the recent "Minutes" of the Committee of the Church Missionary Society, dated March 30, 1858, negative many of these aspersions. But there are a few points on which I may offer further remarks for your satisfaction.

I. It will be satisfactory to you, and to many other friends, to know what was the judgment of the late Bishop of Calcutta upon the "Memorial" and "Statement" of which offence is taken. His son, the Vicar of Islington, has presented me with the following extract from one of the Bishop's late letters, which will set this matter at rest.

"There is a valuable paper of the Church Missionary Society in our

(Calcutta) 'Christian Intelligencer' on the subject of Missionary Bishops, Canons, Rubrics, etc.; very well done. I concur with it fully". *(Extract from a letter of the Bishop of Calcutta to the Rev. Daniel Wilson, dated Serampore, October 10, 1857.)*

No one had better opportunities of knowing the relations between an Indian Bishop and a Mission than the late Metropolitan of India, who had made frequent visitations of the Dioceses of Madras, Bombay and Ceylon; and whose metropolitan superintendence once extended over the Bishop of Australia and New Zealand. His earlier opinions were in favour of a Bishop's taking a leading part in Missionary work. He commenced the Cathedral Mission upon this principle. But his lengthened and practical experience gradually brought him to another conclusion; and I have the best means of knowing, from other sources as well as from the words of the above quotation, that the statement of the Church Missionary Society is the true exponent of his mature judgment. Yet the Bishop never changed his opinion of the desirableness of the extension of the Episcopate in what I will venture to call the legitimate sense of the term. Surely this is a proof that the Documents of the Society now objected to are not opposed to the *principle* of the extension of the Indian Episcopate, but only to the new scheme which is introduced under the name of "Extension".

II. Let me notice also, another misapprehension of the true question at issue, which has prejudiced the minds of many. The Committee has not opposed the extension of the *Colonial* Episcopate. Its remarks are strictly confined to *Mission fields* in the transition state from heathenism to Christianity, and not yet ripe for the establishment of a settled Ecclesiastical system. It is said, for instance, that additional Bishops have always led to an increase of the Clergy. But in a Colony of Christian settlers a Bishop is able to stimulate a Christian people to build Churches and to support additional Clergymen: whilst a Bishop among the Heathen is dependent upon the voluntary agency of Missionary Societies at a distance to supply the means and the men for the work of the Ministry. As soon as "the Mission" has, through God's blessing, raised up a self-supporting Native Church, with its Native Pastors, so that the Missionary action of a Society in England may be withdrawn, then will be the time for giving the Native Church a Bishop of its own. In the mean time let the Missionaries labour as at present, under a recognised Church-of-England Episcopacy.

There is an equally manifest distinction between pastoral ministrations in a Settled Christian Community and Missionary work among the Heathen. In a Christian colony the Church may be guided generally by the laws and constitution of the Church at home. But in Missions the precedent of the Church at home is inapplicable; and the attempt to establish an analogy between the two cases has only led to confusion. Hence the necessity of Ecclesiastical regulations before the extension of the Episcopate.

III. The Scheme against which the strictures of the Committee are directed is not that which would be generally understood by the extension of the Episcopate: but it is an innovation upon the Episcopate, as it has been established in India for the last forty years; and which, as the Committee believes, has worked well for the Mission cause. It is a scheme which would disturb the present relations between a Bishop and the Missionaries, and would introduce a new, and, as yet, undefined form of Episcopacy. The real question at issue is one which those only partially acquainted with the details of Missions have, in many instances, failed to appreciate. But the Committee regard it as one of such vital importance to the progress of evangelization in heathen lands, that no amount of misconception, or of outcry, or of prejudice, will deter them from urging their views upon it before the proper authorities. Differences of judgment, instead of exciting opposition and jealousy, should rather secure a more thorough investigation of the question, and the firmer establishment of the right system.

The question of the proper relations between a Bishop and Missionaries labouring to evangelise a heathen population, and supported in that work by a voluntary Society, appears to have come upon many of our friends as a new and speculative one. It has, however, been constantly before the Committee of the Church Missionary Society for the last forty years, since it was discussed with Bishop Middleton, at Calcutta, who, at first, refused to notice Missionaries, nor accept the superintendence over them, but greatly modified his views towards the close of his life, and re-opened communications with the Society upon the subject. It was discussed with the late Archbishop of Canterbury and the late Bishop of London, when they joined the Society upon the basis of the "Explanatory Statement of the Ecclesiastical Relations," which was published in the year 1839. It has been the subject of personal conference with many of the Indian and Colonial Bishops. The very same principles which the "Statements, April 11, 1857" contains, have been constantly maintained by the Committee, have been regarded by all the Bishops alluded to, and by other experienced persons, as fair subjects of discussions, and have been cordially supported by many other Bishops, besides the Bishop of Calcutta. You may judge, therefore, of our surprise and regret at the outcry which some parties are attempting to raise against these very principles, as if they had been recently adopted by the Committee.

I need not remind you that the Committee of the Church Missionary Society comprises men of long experience in India, — men who have been the chief supporters of the Church of England while they occupied the highest posts of Government, and who have been otherwise identified for twenty, thirty, or forty years with all the good works carried on in India. It may give you some idea of the amount of Indian experience in our Committee, when I state that the aggregate of time spent in India by seventeen members of the Committee amounts to 363 years. Such a body of men may surely claim the credit of knowing what they are about.

These remarks may enable you to remove some of the objections to which you refer.

The Committee are ready to discuss the principles they have put forth with any parties who are sufficiently acquainted with the subject, and who are willing to be guided by practical experience; but they cannot deal with mere theories, whether Indian or homespun, or answer writers who seize upon detached sentences of an argument in order to make up a hostile article against the Church Missionary Society. To such attacks this Society can only oppose its long-tried and approved principles, which have gained for it all the confidence and support which it enjoys from Christian friends. Its ecclesiastical principles are dear to it, but its spiritual principles are far more precious. Let me borrow from our sister Society its venerable title, and say that we cannot separate the propagation of the Gospel from the discussion of the extension of the Episcopate. It is not merely a question, How can the Indian Episcopate be most rapidly extended and subdivided? but, what system will be best adapted to prepare the Native Converts in their transition from heathenism to Christianity, for the euthanasia of the mission in the establishment of a native Church under native pastors and a native Episcopate? What system will shield a necessarily complicated agency, in a foreign land, from those jars and obstructions which beset every human undertaking? What system will give the freest scope to the pious zeal of those, whether laity or clergy, who know and love the truth, and who desire to be fellow-helpers of the truth? All these questions necessarily involve the relations between the Episcopate and the action of Missionary Societies. And the Committee have gone no further than to state the result of their long study and experience upon this delicate but all-important subject.

I know not whether you or I would take precisely the same view of many of the details of the subject of this letter, but I am sure that we shall cordially unite in the words of the prayer with which our Committee Meetings are opened – that God may unite as one man all who are truly labouring for Him; disappoint the designs of Satan; make all Christian Societies live in harmony and love; give them wisdom in all their plans; perfect His strength in their weakness; and direct their labours to His glory.

THE LAY MINISTRY[12]

My Dear Lord Bishop,

As one of your Commissaries engaged in selecting Clergymen for your Diocese, I share in your difficulties of finding a sufficient number of suitable men in the Church at home willing to go to Australia. You assure me, also, that it will be many years before theological colleges can be established to supply a well qualified ministry within the Colony. In consequence of this deficiency of ministers, a large part of the scattered and outlying population of your Diocese must be destitute of any regular Christian instruction or public worship, on the Lord's day, in connexion with our Church.

Under these circumstances, your thoughts have been turned to the consideration of some auxiliary agency for meeting the want, such as that of Scripture Readers, of City Missionaries, or of District Visitors. These auxiliaries, at home, are of two classes, some receiving salaries, and some acting gratuitously.

There would be almost as much difficulty in obtaining a supply of well qualified agents of the former class as in the case of Ministers, and a great difficulty in raising funds for their support. In a fixed and dense population, paid Lay Agents might succeed. But the people scattered over large districts, and especially those living a migratory life, in the bush or gold fields, would not be likely to support such an agency.

In respect of the second, the unpaid class of Christian Instructors, I have, at your request, made enquiries as to the working of the system of Local Preachers amongst the Wesleyan Methodists, and I now report to you the result of those enquiries.

1. The chief characteristic of the system is that it is an unpaid agency. In this respect Local Preachers differ from Scripture Readers and City Missionaries. They have their own means of livelihood, and give up their Sundays to preaching gratuitously. Many are persons of property, but they mostly belong to the middle classes. Now, apart from the saving of salaries, there is this advantage in an unpaid agency, that none but men whose hearts yearn after the salvation of souls will give up Sunday after Sunday to work; and the addresses of such persons have an additional influence, from the very fact of their labours being voluntary.

2. Another characteristic of the Wesleyan system of Local Preachers, is that of complete organization and subordination to ministerial control. The Local Preachers form a body amongst themselves. They have Quarterly Meetings, at which the Circuit Minister presides. He proposes persons as Local Preachers on trial, and the Quarterly Meeting, after due probation, must confirm the appointment. At these Quarterly Meetings enquiry is made into the progress of the work. If any complaints have arisen respecting the conduct or efficiency of any ministrations, they are freely spoken of and discussed. A plan is subsequently arranged for the next quarter, by the Circuit Minister, in which each Preacher has his assigned preaching-place on each Sunday. Should it be the opinion of the meeting that any one of their body is unsuitable for the work, his name is omitted from the list. The Circuit Minister endeavours to hear each Local Preacher occasionally, so as to judge of his qualifications; at other times he takes the service himself at each of the Local preaching-places or chapels.

It has been found, by the experience of a century, that the Local Preachers afford a great help and benefit to the ministrations of the regular ministers. It is calculated that the number brought by their means to public worship, and under the supervision of the regular ministers, is nearly double the number which could be gathered and held together by regular ministers, without their aid; and, especially, that they carry instruction to a number of scattered families whom the regular ministers could never reach.

4. The system of Local Preachers forms a nursery for regular ministers. The talent of edifying others is thus drawn out, tested and exercised. Many local Preachers are, after a few years' successful labour, received into a theological seminary, where they are supported during a course of three years' study. Some exceptional cases occur in which a Local Preacher is admitted at once as a Probationer for the regular ministry.

It appears to me that such an organized system within the Church would be well adapted to meet the wants of such a population as I have referred to in your Diocese. You have described to me many instances in which settlers have expressed to you their desire for a church and a minister. You visit such parties, and encourage them to collect the requisite funds. You appoint some distant minister to visit them occasionally. The more pious will perhaps assemble by themselves for social worship. But the less zealous and worldly-minded become indifferent to religion and callous, and when, after a year or two, a church and minister are provided for them, habits of non-attendance at public worship have been unhappily, rooted amongst them. Contrasted with this picture, let me give a statement made to me by an eminent Wesleyan Minister, long connected with the foreign labours of that body. He said, "If one hundred emigrants of any rank of life in the Wesleyan Connexion were to arrive in a new country, there would probably be six or eight who are Local Preachers. These, with the nearest regular minister, if any such were within reach, would at once meet together, and organize plans for preaching at different spots for the Sunday after their arrival. The whole district would soon be laid out, so as to meet the wants of the surrounding population, and when a regular minister should come amongst them, he would find his way prepared, and the religious habits of the people sustained, and probably many accessions to the original number."

The question, however, arises, whether the system of Local Preachers can be adopted in our church, in conformity with its principles and system. You have had the advantage, by your visit to this country, of consulting your Episcopal Brethren on this point: but as you have also permitted me to give you my own humble opinion upon the question, I will frankly state that I can see no valid objection, upon our church principles, to the adoption of the system either at home or abroad: and that I think it would prove a great benefit, especially to the Church in the Colonies. At the same time, I must as frankly state, that experienced Wesleyan Ministers have stated to me that there are incidental disadvantages in the system, which in some, although a very small degree, counter-balance the benefit, and which are sufficient to suggest great caution in the appointment of preachers, and in their superintendence on the part of the presiding minister. He must be a man of sufficient standing, experience, and sympathy with the work, to secure the confidence of the Local Preachers.

It appears to me, therefore, essential to the success of the system, in our Church, that the superintendence of such an agency should not necessarily devolve upon the minister of the district in which the preachers labour, but should be committed only to ministers of proved weight, piety, and influence. It would be an additional advantage if such a person were invested with some official designation. I apprehend that what we call the "parochial system" would be far too cramped and confined for the successful working of the proposed plan, though, if wisely superintended, it would throw life and vigour into the parochial system, and supply its deficiencies, without interfering with its essential advantages.

The Quarterly Meetings are, I conceive, an essential part of the plan. These insure regularity in all the arrangements, keep up the mutual dependency of the Local Preachers upon each other, and enable the presiding minister to correct incidental evils, and to remove inefficient or unsuitable individuals by the concurrence of the body, instead of the invidious exercise of official authority. Such meetings would also prove most valuable for the discussion of all questions connected with the general religious interests of the country, and for interesting the laity in their promotion to the remotest limits of the population.

It cannot be doubted that there is in the laity of the Church of England, a large amount of talent for imparting religious instruction, which is now wholly unemployed. In proportion as it has of late years been called into exercise in open-air preaching, many who have had opportunity of judging are astonished at the results.

The proposed system would, I think, fairly come under the sanction of the 23rd Article of our Church, if the Local Preachers be "chosen and called to this work by men who have public authority in the congregation."

The last Session of Parliament has happily swept away the objections which might have been formerly raised under the Conventicle — Acts, which, however, would scarcely have applied to the Colonies.

On the whole, therefore, I venture to express my strong conviction that such a system of voluntary lay agency, under ecclesiastical control, as I have described, might be properly and beneficially introduced into our Church system; and that there would be every prospect of our obtaining a class of local Preachers even superior to that which the limited numbers of the Wesleyan body can furnish. Also, that our Church would afford additional safeguards against contingent evils, so that we might look, under the blessing of God, for a result such as that which the Wesleyans have experienced, namely, that the efficiency of the regular ministers would be largely increased. This prospect is, at least, worth the experiment.

May the great Head of the Church guide you in all your arduous duties, and give you an abundant fulfilment of your heart's desire and prayer to God that souls may be brought to Christ and that all true Christians may be united in the unity of the Spirit.

ON THE USE OF THE BOOK OF COMMON PRAYER, AND OF THE LAYMAN IN MISSION[13]

I thank you for sending me so frankly the objections and difficulties felt by Mrs. Cobbold in respect of the practice of the Church Missionary Society.

The facts of the case are the very reverse of the representations which have been made to her.

The Church Missionary Society uniformly sends out the prayer book with the Bible, wherever a Christian Church exists and has done more to extend the use of the prayer book in different languages than has been done by any other society or agency since the prayer book existed.

The Society has translated and used it in Tamil, Telegu, Malayalam, Singhalese, New Zealand, Hindi, Bengali, Mahratta, Maltese, one of the dialects of Abyssinia, and of several of the American Indians.

The prayers of the church are used in Abbeokuta to this day.

But the prayer book is intended for an established Christian congregation, and it is necessary to train up new converts by shorter and more elementary forms of worship. As soon as the prayer book can be introduced it is introduced.

Upon the other subject to which you allude, I will also add a word of explanation. It was a great disappointment to us that Mr. Van Cooten could not obtain holy orders before going to Africa. It was not in our power to accomplish it. Till he obtains orders he will by no means be able to exercise all the functions of the Ministry.

He will only be able to exercise those functions of a Christian Teacher which have been exercised and recognised in the Church of Christ since the days of the Apostles as belonging to a Lay Teacher.

These functions have a most important place in the work of Missions — whole nations have of old been converted to the faith of Christ by such Lay ministrations: and I trust that Mr. Van Cooten will be so blessed and prospered in his labours, until it shall please God in his providence to open the way for the appointment of a West African Bishop; who would I am well persuaded be ready at once to admit Mr. Van Cooten into the Ministry.

THE SOCIETY'S POLICY RE CHURCH BUILDINGS[14]

The attention of the Committee has been called to the subject of the Consecration of Buildings for Public Worship belonging to the Society in the India Dioceses by the legal difficulties which have been pointed out, as connected with a Trust Deed to secure the property and right of patronage to the Society.

The opinion of the Standing Counsel of the East India Company and an eminent Civilian, was taken upon this subject; but the course which they advised would have had such collateral effects as have induced the Committee to pause and to state to the Bishops of Calcutta, Madras and Bombay, the difficulties in which they feel themselves placed in reference to this subject.

It is presumed that the Consecration of a Building having the effect of setting it apart in perpetuity as a Church should be accompanied by some provision for future repairs and the services of a Minister. But there are many buildings now used as Churches which in point of construction or locality may be found unsuitable as permanent Churches, though very serviceable for temporary use, during the continuance of Missionary operations. The Committee in such cases would be unwilling to involve themselves in any lasting obligation to maintain or provide for such Churches. And it would therefore seem more advisable to defer, on this ground, the Consecration of buildings used by the Society as places of worship till the Missionary operations have reached that point at which they may give place to some more permanent system of ministerial provision.

A second difficulty arises from the consideration that while it is essential that the Society should retain the control of its Places of Worship as long as their Missionaries remain on the spot, yet on the other hand it is inexpedient that a voluntary Association, and especially one like the Church Missionary Society, whose avowed intention it is to quit the field as soon as it ceases to be a proper sphere of Missionary operations, should be possessed of extensive rights of patronage in perpetuity. In what way it may be advisable ultimately to arrange this matter the Committee are not prepared at the present time to determine. And therefore it appears to them that on this ground also the consecration of their buildings for Public Worship should be deferred.

The Committee are aware that many of their Churches have been already consecrated but they have not been able to ascertain what legal securities or obligations have been provided for.

The Committee however having been applied to by their friends in India to devise some general Trust by which their property in India may be held the question of the Consecration of Churches has become collaterally connected with it.

The Committee would lay this statement of their difficulties and their view of the adviseableness of deferring consecration, before the Bishops of India; and they will be very thankful to receive from their Lordships the advice and information which the case may require.

Notes

1 M.P.M., Vol. VII, No. 10. A sermon preached in the parish church of St. Marylebone, June 11, 1857, at the consecration of the Hon. and Rt. Rev. John Thomas Pelham, D.D., Lord Bishop of Norwich.
2 *Thirty-ninth Report,* pp. 136-139.
3 The three Bishops of India, and the Bishop of Australia, are the presidents of the Corresponding Committees in their respective dioceses.
4 The American Episcopal Church has, in Convention, thus identified itself with a missionary society.
5 Extract from Committee's Minute.
6 G/ACI/5, June 5, 1846, pp. 131-132. To Chevalier Bunsen.
7 G/ACI/3, March 15, 1842, pp. 480-482. Letter to the Rev. H. Moule.
8 G/ACI/4, Nov. 19, 1844, pp. 299-303. To the Bishop of London proposing the creation of a bishopric of Sierra Leone.
9 G/ACI/5, July 10, 1845, pp. 1-5. Letter to the Rev. E. Hawkins.
10 G/ACI/1, No. 92, April 14, 1856. A memorial by the Church Missionary Society upon the extension of the Episcopate in India, addressed to the authorities of the East India Company.
11 M.P., Vol. I, April 12, 1858, No. 23. Letter to a friend on the views of the Committee of the Church Missionary Society on the Extension of the Episcopate in India.
12 P.M.E., No. 3. Letter to the Bishop of Melbourne, the Right Rev. C. Perry, on the employment of unpaid lay preachers, Jan. 1, 1856.
13 G/ACI/7, pp. 188-190, Sept. 28, 1849. Letter to Miss Primrose.
14 G/C1, Vol. 22, Committee Minutes, pp. 405-406, Jan. 23, 1844. Resolution of the Committee.

Chapter V

TOWARDS ECUMENICITY

INTRODUCTION

Venn's secretariat covered a period during which there was a determined assault on the privileged position of the Church of England. In large measure this assault was mounted by the dissenters who had suffered many and various forms of discrimination since the Act of Uniformity in 1662. Their increasing numbers and material prosperity, and their signal contribution to the general sobriety of society as a whole, combined to make their challenge to the established order of things successful. Meanwhile the politics of England's relations with Ireland had hastened Roman Catholic emancipation. But the bitterness involved in these attacks on the Establishment of the Church of England were hardly contributory to an ecumenical temper.

As a matter of history, at least as far as Britain was concerned, the ecumenical spirit was first fostered by those who had a deep concern for the proclamation of the gospel throughout the world. This in turn was assisted by all who were concerned with such philanthropic enterprises as the abolition of the slave-trade, and the improvement of conditions among the sufferers from the industrial revolution.

The extracts that form this chapter show the operation of the missionary movement in invoking an ecumenical temper. In the previous chapter, in his letter to the Bishop of Melbourne on the value of a lay ministry, Venn writes with obvious sympathy about what he had learnt of the lay ministry as that existed among the Methodists.

In its own way the *Life of Francis Xavier,* which Venn published in 1862, is an ecumenical document of some importance. Sternly critical as

175

Venn often showed himself to be of Roman Catholic doctrines and practices as he understood or misunderstood them, the extracts taken here from his study of Francis Xavier are notable for their generous appreciation of a great missionary of a tradition so different from his own. We who read these extracts do well to remember that they were written one hundred years before Pope John XXIII and the Second Vatican Council, at a time when deep suspicion of all things Roman Catholic was still second nature to most Englishmen.

TOWARDS ECUMENICITY[1]

... The third and only other great principle which the Committee would this day remind you of, as specially suited to these times, is that which is embodied in one of the fundamental laws of our Society. "A friendly intercourse shall be maintained with other *Protestant* Societies engaged in the same benevolent design of propagating the Gospel of Jesus Christ". We shall shortly allude to circumstances which peculiarly suggest this reference in the case of the Punjab. In Ceylon a union monthly meeting of the Missionaries of the American, Wesleyan and Church Societies has been long kept with happy effects. In Syria the American missionaries have nobly led the way in a vigour of operations and enlargement of views, and a liberal working of the press, from which all other Missions will largely profit – and one of their leading Missionaries lately appeared before the Committee and pleaded for the Church of England to take up its position in the mustering armies for the Evangelization of Syria and the East. The union in foreign Missions is more easy than at home. But may a blessed reflex also return into our bosoms . . .

TOWARDS ECUMENICITY[2]

... I will notice, as a third prominent feature of this Missionary Episcopate, that the Bishop's zeal for Missions was not confined to his own communion. In his early ministry at home his large-heartedness was conspicuous. In the Anniversary Sermon which he preached for the Church Missionary Society in the year 1817, he bore a noble Testimony to the blessing of the Lord which had rested upon the labours of other Societies dissenting from our Church. As a Chief Bishop in India he acted in the same spirit. He encouraged their work, he invited them often to join with his own clergy in prayer. A few years ago he presided at a public meeting of fifty Missionaries of nearly all the Protestant Societies labouring in Bengal. In his very last sermon, preached a very few months ago, on the day of humiliation on account of the mutiny, these golden words occur: "Unity and love prevail amongst the different divisions of the Protestant family; we no longer maintain the old and fatal mistake, that Christian men are not to co-operate for *any* thing, till they agree in *every* thing. We now hold the antagonistic and true maxim that Christian men should act together as far as they are agreed." This candour and largeness of spirit was the result of the ruling principle of his life. The testimony to the Gospel of the grace of God was dearer to his heart than any ecclesiastical forms; without this testimony, that which he regarded as apostolic discipline lost its value; and in respect of Missions, his favourite saying was that of Gericke — "Nothing is so graceless as a Mission without the spirit of Christ . . ."

TOWARDS ECUMENICITY[3]

. . . Thank God the Dissenters stand with us in that declaration: and while all denominations are united their power is almost irresistible in the House of Commons. Lord Stanley tried in our deputation, and many others have made the attempt, to divide us, and to play the Maynooth question against us. But I trust we know each other too well. It is a providential circumstance that the Secretaries of the great Missionary Societies have long thoroughly understood each other and meet monthly in friendly and devotional intercourse. We commence the new year by a united prayer meeting for India . . .

TOWARDS ECUMENICITY[4]

. . . In the early years of the alliance between the two Societies the supply of English missionaries was very scanty; but stirred up in a measure by the zeal of the Churches of Germany, the Church of England has at length awakened to a sense of its duty, and the supply of English Missionaries has proved nearly equal to its resources, while the Basle Missions have so expanded as now to absorb a large proportion of their students; hence few German brethren have of late joined the Church Missionary Society. But the Church Missionary Society has not abated its interest in the welfare of the Basle Missions, and cherishes the confident hope that the two Societies will carry on their respective labours, ever united by fraternal affection in the Lord, mutually strengthening each other in maintaining the truth of the Gospel, and helping each other by counsel, and by intercessory prayer before a common throne of Grace . . .

LESSONS FROM THE MISSIONARY EXPERIENCE OF FRANCIS XAVIER[5]

No. 1

. . . Upon reviewing Xavier's character it will appear that he possessed in a very high degree some of the essential qualities of the leader of a great enterprise. He was of a generous, noble, and loving disposition, calculated to gather followers, and to attach them firmly to his leadership. But in respect of Missions Xavier was little fitted to direct others. Of the peculiar duties of an evangelist to the heathen he had no conception. His directions to his Missionaries are wholly addressed to their conduct as pastors of Christian communities. In his voluminous "Instructions", all that can be gathered of Missionary directions amounts to little beyond the general relations of the clergy with their flocks, with each other, and with their ecclesiastical superiors.

Even if Xavier had better understood the work of Missions, there was one great fault in his system which would have proved fatal to success. He attempted to carry every thing by authority. He constantly inculcated the supreme merit and advantage of implicit obedience to himself. The sequel of his history will show how completely this system failed to form an efficient body of coadjutors. Xavier's history will, therefore, afford a useful caution against a notion, too much countenanced at the present day, that an ecclesiastical head of a Mission is needed to secure efficiency by uniformity of action, and to counteract the evils which may arise within a Mission from the contrariety of individual opinions. Such absolute power may consist with the government of a settled Christian Church, where the relation between ecclesiastical authority and the pastoral function has been defined by canons, and by experience. But no canons or regulations have been yet laid down for Missions to the heathen. That work is so varied, and its emergencies so sudden, that the evangelist must be left to act mainly on his own responsibility and judgement. It pre-eminently requires independence of mind, fertility of resource, a quick observance of the footsteps of Divine Providence, a readiness to push forward in that direction, an abiding sense in the mind of the Missionary of personal responsibility to extend the kingdom of Christ, and a lively conviction that the Lord is at his "right hand". These qualifications are, like all the finer sentiments of Christianity, of delicate texture; they are often united with a natural sensitiveness; they are to be cherished and counselled rather than ruled; they are easily checked and discouraged if "headed" by authority. Yet these are the qualities which have ever distinguished the Missionaries who win the richest trophies, and advance the borders of the Redeemer's kingdom. Among such a body of workmen no formidable difficulties will arise from the contrariety of individual opinions; and such as do arise will be easily composed by affectionate, Christian, and wise counsels, whether offered on the spot, or transmitted from Europe . . .

No. 2

... The following features may be studied with great advantage by all who are engaged in Missions to the Heathen.

1. Francis Xavier affords an admirable example of *energy in his calling;* setting at once to work, from the first moment he placed his foot on a heathen soil, as at Melinda, Socotra, and on his arrival at Goa, before his particular field of labour was designated. The same energy never ceased till the day of his death. This was manifest even in the island of Sancian, amidst the intervals of his last fatal disease. All his letters show that the man was alive in every part, that nothing bearing upon his great object escaped his eye or his ear, and that he was ever ready to spend and be spent in his work. Having devoted himself to India for life and for death, the idea of a return to Europe, even to plead for fellow-labourers, was regarded by him as a simple impossibility. Where there is spiritual power in such a character the results are glorious. These men of persevering energy have been the most illustrious Missionaries in Protestant annals. Such men live two lives in one. If faithful to the Truth, God honours them by giving them great success in winning souls to Him.

2. Another point of view in which Xavier may be proposed as an example to Protestant Missionaries is the maintaining a *bold position as a Christian Missionary*. It will, indeed, have been seen that he carried this conduct to an extravagant extent, and stretched the bow till it broke in his hand. He had also special worldly advantages for maintaining such boldness. But still there is much which may be imitated under better regulation, and in a more Christian spirit. Xavier was everywhere the Missionary. In the suite of an Ambassador, in the palace of a King, among the crew of a ship, in the busy sea-port while waiting for a passage, among civil and military officers, in the neighbourhood of native Kings, and even in their courts, Xavier was the Missionary, known and read of all men as such, and therefore enforcing attention, and exercising an important influence in favour of Missions. More especially in respect of the native races he acted the part of a true Missionary, maintaining their rights against the oppression and injustice of his own countrymen, and treating them as possessing the same feelings and capacities as their more civilized fellow-men.

3. Xavier's example is equally striking in *his sympathy for* all his fellow-labourers in the Mission field. Though placed by his political and ecclesiastical status prodigiously above all of them, and also invested with autocratical power over all the Jesuit Missionaries, he yet manifested in all his communications the most delicate attention to the feelings of a Missionary, and a prompt zeal in ministering to their wants. The secret of this bright feature in his character was perhaps in the experience which he had gained by his first year's personal labours on the Fishery Coast. The section which is devoted to an account of his management of a Mission, affords many valuable

hints to all Missionary Committees, and to the Bishops and other ecclesiastical authorities presiding over a Mission field. There is indeed much to avoid in the practice of Xavier, but also much to imitate.

4. An eminent and bright feature in Xavier's character was also his zeal as a *peace-maker.* He regarded it as a part of his office, wherever he was, to compose quarrels. His energetic remonstrances, affectionate entreaties, and sound, practical counsels, by which he strove to make his brethren dwell together in unity, deserve the highest praise. He knew, as he tells us, the peculiar irritability of Europeans in a tropical climate, and he spared no pains to secure the preservation of harmonious co-operation and brotherly love amongst all fellow-workers in the Christian ministry.

5. One more excellency in Xavier's Missionary example may be pointed out, namely, *the fulness and frequency of his communications with the Church at home.* In his day, letters to India were only sent and received once a year by the annual fleet: he had also renounced Europe for ever. Yet he continued to write to the last year of his life with all the freshness and fullness of his first impressions. He stood between the Church at home and the Church abroad as the representative of both. He wrote with all the confidence and authority of one who was still identified with his old University at Paris, with the Missionary College at Coimbra, which he had never seen and with Rome as the metropolis of his Church. Much as we must lament the "dressing" which his letters to Europe received at his hands, yet we cannot but wish to receive from those Missionaries to whom God has given the pen of a ready writer, letters as full and as fresh, though more consistent, than those written by Francis Xavier . . .

No. 3[7]

. . . It may be permitted to one who has had large opportunities and long experience in the supervision of Missions to state his firm conviction, that all attempts to lay the foundations of a Protestant Mission, without true conversions and spiritual life in individual souls, will be as unsatisfactory and as transient as those of Xavier and his followers. Christian education may be extended; a visible Church, in all its completeness, may be established; civilization may be promoted by Industrial Institutions; but there may be no "living" Church. For a season, especially in the early days of freshness and hope, the Mission may appear to flourish; but if the spiritual "substance" be wanting, the end will be disappointment, failure, and, too often, the apostasy of converts. The conversion of the heathen is hard work, even when the word is accompanied with power and demonstration of the Spirit. It is the testimony of every Missionary of spiritual discernment, even of the most soberminded, that Satan has a power in heathen lands, of which we in the Church at home have little conception. If the spirit of Christ be not with the Missionary, he will be baffled at all points, and wear out his strength in continuous and incessant, but profitless labour.

The compilation of these pages has served to deepen the conviction, in the mind of the compiler, of the truth and importance of these cardinal Missionary principles; and he will esteem his labour well repaid if his work serve to uphold these principles in the Missionary efforts.

The faithful Missionary, whose aims all culminate in the exaltation of "Christ crucified", will receive generally a few seals to his ministry; and if they stand fast in the Lord, he lives. His chief employment should thenceforth be to cherish them, as a nurse cherishes her children, to stir up the grace that is in them, to set them to work in gathering into the fold fresh converts, to make them the pivot upon which his Missionary operations turn. Their example of holiness and liberality will give a tone to the whole Mission which nothing else can supply: as their numbers increase, the strength of the Mission increases; its stability, its self-support, and its self-extension are secured. An open Bible keeps open the stream of the waters of life. Thus a Native Church is formed, from which the Word of God is "sounded out". God giveth the increase to the labour of the planters and waterers. Against such a living branch of the true Church the gates of hell shall never prevail; like the vine brought out of Egypt, it takes deep root, and fills the land.

To those who long for the day when Jesus "shall have dominion from sea to sea, and from the river to the ends of the earth", I confidently point, in the history of Protestant Missions, to the abundant evidence that the spirit of Christ is with them; that under His influences a native agency is in preparation which will have power and grace to carry on the work without foreign assistance. I point, also, to the providential removal of hindrances to the extension of Christianity, which has become a sign of the times, since Missions have been prosecuted in the spirit of the Gospel — to the gradual preparation of the nations for the living Word of God, and to its multiplication in all languages. In these things we see the way of the Lord prepared, and may anticipate His predicted and universal dominion; when "all nations shall call Him blessed . . ."

Notes

1   CI.1/L4, pp. 8-9, June 21, 1851. Extract from letter of instruction to missionaries proceeding to open a new mission in the Punjab.

2   P.M.E., No. 6. Extract from a sermon preached by Henry Venn on Sunday, Feb. 14, 1858, on the occasion of the death of the Rt. Rev. Daniel Wilson, D.D., Bishop of Calcutta, Metropolitan of India.

3   CI.1/L5, p. 88, Dec. 24, 1858. Extract from a letter to the Rev. J. Long, a missionary in North India, with special reference to a "national declaration" about Christian responsibility in India, following upon the Queen's declaration.

4   G/AZI/1, No. 143, May 8, 1865. Extract from a Minute of the Committee of the Church Missionary Society, May 8, 1865, with reference to the Jubilee of the Basle Evangelical Missionary Society.

5   Extract from *The Missionary Life and Labours of Francis Xavier,* by Henry Venn (London: Longman, Green, Longman, Roberts & Green, 1862), pp. 145-147.

6   *Ibia.,* pp. 251-254.

7   *Ibid.,* pp. 324-326.

Chapter VI

THE ROLE OF A MISSIONARY SOCIETY
IN PROMOTING
WELFARE AND EDUCATION

INTRODUCTION

The extracts that form the first section of this chapter have been arranged in order of date. They show the consistency with which Venn prosecuted the, for him, subsidiary activities of the missionary enterprise. Always seeking to safeguard the primary purpose of proclaiming the gospel of the grace of God, he was never afraid to give the most careful thought to the secondary activities of the Christian mission, even if thereby he might sometimes be accused of "secularity" (see Introduction to Ch. 3).

This chapter shows how practical was Venn's appreciation of the need for special methods to be applied in an area that had been ravaged by the slave trade. Venn, in common with many others, had been alerted to the fact that the long-fought campaign for the ending of the slave trade had not yielded the expected results. Britain's own action, treaties with other powers to outlaw slavery, a British squadron on the west coast of Africa, all these measures had failed to stop the trade in slaves. Some other remedy was called for. The facts about the slave trade were presented in 1839 by Thomas Fowell Buxton in his book *The African Slave Trade*. A year later, in 1840, he published *The Remedy*. [1]

Venn would quite certainly have read these books, though I have not, as yet, identified any statement that he had done so. But in passage after passage Buxton outlined ideas and proposals for action that we find echoed in Venn's letters to Africans and to missionaries. Buxton was essentially a propagandist concerned to enlist the widest possible public support for a great campaign to deliver Africa from the curse of slavery. Time was fully to justify his vision and the broad principles of action that he proposed. Immediately, however, his advocacy of an expedition up the Niger River proved premature and was a disaster. For the time being his vision and his ideas were discounted, but not entirely. Venn, more practical than Buxton, set to work to apply Buxton's ideas in a number of local situations. Content to start in a small way Venn was able to record a modest degree of success. Later, others were to prove how far-sighted Buxton had been, how practical Venn. Indeed, perhaps in no other aspect of his missionary vision and statesmanship is Venn more surely a contemporary of our own than in his insistence that the whole duty of man involves a stewardship that includes man's relation with his material environment.

In the second part of this chapter a number of extracts from Venn's correspondence illustrate his views on education. It is clear that his views of this important element in missionary work failed of a synthesis in his own thinking. He was clear that education was indispensable for the Christian community. He was much less certain that missionary resources in manpower and money should play any significant part in the education of those who were not members of the Christian church. Yet it is clear that he had hopes, in West Africa at any rate, that Christian education would lead to the creation of African leaders in the state no less than in the church. The logic of his whole policy in West Africa pointed towards a very widely diffused system of education.

In regard to India it would appear that he was an opportunist. He did not share Alexander Duff's vision of what Western education, given to those who were not Christians, might achieve in changing the minds of Indians and preparing them for the gospel. It is almost as though he allowed the pressure of events to force him in a direction, of the wisdom of which he was less than fully assured. But the extracts in this chapter show how carefully he planned even when he was most in doubt.

I

SOCIAL WELFARE[2]

... Another point briefly referred to in the Instructions is the introduction among the natives of useful arts and elementary general knowledge calculated to improve their social condition. Three means may be pointed out as of powerful efficacy in improving the condition of man. 1. The first and chiefest, and that beyond all comparison of the most potent influence, is the Gospel of the grace of God. In proportion, therefore, as that part of the Committee's Instructions which relates to the preaching of the Gospel is carried out with faithfulness, affection, zeal and diligence, will you be laying the foundation on solid grounds of the improvement of the Social condition of the Natives, while you are imparting to them spiritual blessings. 2. Agriculture. This secures a due supply of the necessaries of life — fosters habits of industry — leads to fixed habitation — creates property — and consequently operates as a preventive of wars and rapine. 3. Commerce. For this agriculture lays the basis and supplies the means of carrying it on. Commerce brings in from abroad necessaries, conveniences, and comforts, which are diffused through the Community. It also expands the minds of those engaged in it from the intercourse which they are brought into with foreigners and foreign lands. Commerce also is promotive of peace, for in peace only can it prosper and advance. But while we speak thus we do not overlook the difficulties and dangers of missionaries dealing with these things. They must not engage in commerce themselves, nor in agriculture, except to a very limited extent. They must not give an undue proportion of their time to matters of a secular nature, not indispensable to the working of the Mission; and especially must they be watchful against having their own minds secularised or the tone of them lowered by these things. Much prudence and caution will therefore be requisite on the part of the Missionaries while stimulating the Natives to agriculture and Commerce. It is, however, the elements of these things only which we conceive that part of Africa wherein you are about to be located is at present susceptible of. With regard to commerce, one other remark is necessary. Fire-arms, powder, ardent spirits — these are generally articles above all others coveted by an uncivilized people. With these, however, and suchlike as articles of barter or for sale the Missionary must on no account whatever have anything to do ...

MISSIONS AND COMMERCE[3]

... A great change has taken place since you left England in the price and demand for Cotton. The manufacturers of Manchester have become most eager for the encouragement of African cotton. This has already become a powerful argument in favour of the Squadron. One manufacturer has given Mr. Peyton £100 to be laid out in Africa for the purchase of Cotton and Cleaning Machines, and we could easily procure the same offer for Abbeokuta if there were any prospect of a supply. We will suggest that you should immediately collect specimens (the larger the quantity the better) of the different Cottons used in the Native manufacturers, being very particular to keep them separate, and to procure if possible an account of the localities in which they are grown, together with a few dried specimens of the leaf, pod, etc. Let them be sent home with an account of the quantity which could be supplied, especially referring to the importance in that view of opening the communication between Lagos and the sea. Such samples should be turned to your purpose in this country, and would show to Earl Grey that your interview with him at the Colonial Office was not forgotten. We are authorized by private friends to say that you may go to an expense of £20 or £30 to do the thing effectually for which you may draw separately, from us.

If the Cotton Gin which you took out, is in working order, it will double the chance of success if the Cotton is sent home clean and well packed. We remember your speaking of a fine, silky Cotton. This may be useful as a specimen, but the Cotton which is grown in most abundance will be the chief thing . . .

THE ROLE OF THE SOCIETY IN SOCIAL WELFARE

Suggestions for the Improvement of the Social and Intellectual Condition of the Native Africans at Sierra Leone[4]

1. The population of Sierra Leone amounts to more than 40,000, about one-half of whom have embraced Christianity. Christian instruction has been widely diffused, and the greater part of the converts have been well instructed in the Truths of the Bible; but hitherto very little has been done to promote the subsequent improvement of their minds or to initiate them into modes of obtaining an honest livelihood.

2. The inducements and opportunities for the profitable employment of their mental or physical powers are very limited. Hence, many who have shown great quickness in acquiring knowledge in reading and writing, as children, afterwards become the victims of a vicious indolence; and the progress of civilization, both within and beyond the Colony is by no means so encouraging as might have been expected.

3. In Freetown some employment is provided by Merchants' Offices, and the general business of a large town; but in the country villages, which comprise nearly three-fourths of the population, the evil of the present state of things is very apparent.

4. The remedy of the evil must be sought in the introduction of such measures into Sierra Leone as have been proved, in other places, effectual for the exciting a spirit of laudable exertion and for the encouragement of industry; such as the institution of prizes for agricultural and mechanical enterprise, and of Model Farms; — the establishment of Savings' Banks, Loan Societies, etc.; — the institution of Public Lectures, Libraries, Reading Rooms, etc.

5. Though such measures might be justly regarded as falling within the province of the Committee of the Church Missionary Society, yet there would be many advantages in their being undertaken by a separate Committee, acting in concurrence with the Society.

6. A separate Committee might also prove a centre of union – combination for the efforts of all other parties desirous of aiding the social and intellectual improvement of the Natives of Africa.

7. The following measures seem to be especially important in the present state of society in Sierra Leone; and to fall within the sphere of an African Industrial Committee.

I. Establishment of a Savings Bank

The want of such an establishment has been long felt. When the Natives obtain a little money they are obliged to hide it in the ground, or to invest it in furniture, or other goods, which are sold at a disadvantage when the money is wanted. The following scheme is suggested for the management of such an establishment:

(i)   To obtain the consent of the Government for depositing the money in the Colonial Chest, and for allowing per cent interest.

(ii) To appoint a Committee of Managers in Sierra Leone, partly European, partly Native, to manage the Bank, under rules to be approved by the Committee in England; one of which Rules should be, that the presence of two managers, a European and a Native, should be necessary for any receipt or re-payment of money.

(iii) The Committee in England to provide books, etc., and to allow for the expenses of Management for three years; in which time it may be hoped that the Bank will be able to pay its own expenses, and the Management of it to be sufficiently established.

(iv) Branch accounts should be opened in the rural parishes of Sierra Leone.

II. The Institution of Industrial or Provident Societies such as,

(i)   A Loan Society, for advancing loans either upon Colonial produce or upon personal security

(ii) Benefit Clubs

(iii) Clothing Clubs

(iv) A Dispensary

The Church Missionary Society has already engaged the Services of a Medical Practitioner of high character and experience who will go to Sierra Leone in the course of a few months – for the double purpose of affording medical aid to the Mission, and of training up a few hopeful native youths in medical knowledge and practice.

III. The Encouragement of Agriculture
  (i)   By establishing and superintending Model Farms. The Improve-
        ment Committee might establish Farms of its own, or undertake
        the direction and superintendence of Farms, and of Agricultural
        Agents belonging to other parties.
  (ii) By sending out agricultural implements; such as ploughs and
        harrows; small carts for oxen, and hand-trucks; steel mills for
        grinding corn, to go by men or wind.
  (iii) By giving agricultural prizes, for the encouragement of native
        industry.

IV. The Establishment of a Free Store-House at Freetown
    for receiving consignments of colonial produce and for negotiating
    for their sale, or transmission to Europe.
    The importance of this measure has been frequently urged by
    Missionaries, to whom complaints are made, by those Natives who
    have cultivated arrow-root, coffee, ground-nuts, etc., of the difficulty
    which they have experienced in disposing, upon fair terms, of their
    produce in Freetown; the merchants, taking advantage of their
    ignorance and poverty to set a very low value upon their produce
    and obliging them to take out the value in goods from their stores,
    which are charged at a high price, and are useless when purchased.

V. The Establishment of Reading Rooms, Lending Libraries, Philo-
   sophical Lectures, etc.

8. If an Industrial Committee be established for the accomplishment of
the objects alluded to, it will be important that the Church Missionary
Society adopt certain concurrent measures, tending to a same end, and suited
to the progress of social improvements; such as:

  (1) To bring over each year two or three promising young men, to
      complete their education in England, and to be trained according to
      their abilities,
      (i)   As Teachers;
      (ii) In practical Sciences;
      (iii) As Agriculturalists.
Two young men, Messrs. Nichol and Maxwell, were brought to England
in the year 1844, and placed in the College of the Church Missionary
Society at Islington for eighteen months. Their health was good; they
entered with spirit and success into the studies of the Institution; their
association with the other students was mutually agreeable and profitable. Since their return to Africa their conduct has been exemplary and

satisfactory in every respect; and they have exhibited a zeal for the conversion and improvement of their countrymen which they had never before felt, immediately commencing the systematic study of the native languages. They are now employed as tutors, the one in the Grammar School, the other in the Fourah Bay Institution.

(2) *To send out an Agricultural Agent, and to establish one or more Model Farms upon the Society's property*
Such farms might ultimately serve for the endowment of the Native Church, and of Educational Establishments.

(3) *To place the Native Catechists in situations of confidence and trust,* by establishing them as Pastors of native flocks, providing them with suitable parsonages and small glebes, and making them partly dependent upon their congregations for their support, thus laying the foundations of a Native Self-Supporting Church.

(4) *To instruct the European Missionaries to regard their office as that of Superintendents of a Native Ministry and Agency*
Hitherto the European Missionaries have been charged with the pastoral duties of the Native Congregations; but the advanced state of many Catechists has justified their being placed in charge of the villages, as already proposed under the preceding head. The European Missionaries, being thus relieved, should devote their energies to the giving the impulse and direction to native machinery – to the fixing native languages, and translating the Scriptures into the same; – to the making missionary tours, with Native missionaries, into the interior of Africa; – to the showing hospitality to Native Chiefs visiting the colony, and keeping up correspondence with them.

MISSIONS AND COMMERCE[5]

Dear Mr. Johnson,
   The African Native Agency Committee, have given you the benefit of a residence of three months in England, in the hope, that upon your return to Africa, you will introduce improvements in agriculture, and also the cultivation of many new and useful plants. By such means the wealth of the colony of Sierra Leone will be increased and its trade will become more valuable.
   You take back with you a very rich collection of plants, which you are to rear on your farm. If they grow and increase, they will in a few years, yield

valuable produce, and you will be able to sell the young plants which you have propagated to other persons; and so, in the course of a few years, there may spring up many plantations of nutmeg, clove, allspice, black pepper, etc., and in future years, ships may be laden with the produce from some of the small plants which you now carry with you in the box from Kew Gardens. Chocolate trees and sago plants may, in like manner, be multiplied and supply your own market with excellent food, and help to swell the exports. The new varieties of oranges and lemons, and the jack fruit, will attract the admiration of the market people at Free-town, and bring many purchasers, both of your produce and of the young trees which you will rear.

Your own observations at Kew Gardens, and the instruction which you have there received, have shewn you how much care and skill are required for the cultivation of valuable plants. Things of most value, require most care and labour. You must carefully study the nature of each particular plant — what it requires in soil, water, pruning, etc., etc., to keep it in health — how it may be propagated, by grafting, or by cuttings, or by division of the roots, or by seeds; so that you may be able to teach your children and others, the art of cultivating trees and shrubs to advantage.

When you first return to Sierra Leone, and look at your own farm, and then recollect Kew Gardens, you may think that your lots are worth little care. But remember, that the ground of Kew Gardens was once of as little value as yours — that it only grew grass and trees without fruit, till cultivation made it what it is; so the value of your farm, if the soil be better tilled, and it be stocked with valuable plants, may become double, or five times its present value.

I hope also that you will take pains to procure from the forest, gums such as you have seen in the Museum at Kew; keeping each sort separate, and send them to us, as soon as you have a box full — always giving the name of the tree from which any product is taken, and in the first instance send a description of it, with leaves and the fruit dried as specimens. Send also such other things, as seeds, and dried plants, for the Museum at Kew.

Lastly, remember the Word of God — the blessing of the Lord maketh rich, and he addeth no sorrow with it (Prov. x. 22). May you enjoy this blessing, then you will be rich, whether you possess much or little, rich to all eternity, as well as for the few years of this life.

MISSIONS AND COMMERCE[6]

The Committee have received with very great satisfaction your carefully prepared Statement of the prospects of the Cotton trade at Abbeokuta, and they agree with you in the conclusion which you draw that it only needs to be wisely encouraged for a few years to acquire such an establishment as to go forward by its own momentum.

In laying out our plans for the future we have had the benefit of personal conference with Messrs. Townsend, Gollmer, and Smith, respecting the proper footing on which the Society's Industrial Institutions at Lagos and Abbeokuta are to be placed; and we now purpose to give you detailed direction for your guidance in connexion with this department of labour.

It is evident that the chief Industrial Institution must be at Ake in Abbeokuta where the Cotton Store has been already erected, this Roller Gin set up, a Printer's Press established, and where our Normal School may be best located in connexion with it.

The preparation of Cotton for European Markets must not be regarded as the only branch of industrial employment. It is hoped that workshops will soon be added for carpentry, joinery, sawing, a smithery for repairing machinery, means for the preparation of indigo, and other branches of profitable labour.

But the Cotton trade will be the most profitable branch at present. It will be a depot for receiving, preparing and sending Cotton to England. It will not be a trading concern in itself, for not one shilling of Society's money must be employed in purchasing Cotton or any other materials. It will only transact the Cotton business on commission for other parties who supply the money. The profit in this and in other branches of industry, such as carpentry, etc., will go, in the first instance, to the payment of the managers and labourers, and to the enlargement of the Institutions by the erection of buildings, and machinery, and supplying tools.

If the Institution prospers so far as to afford any surplus profits, such surplus will be available for Missionary purposes. But this is not the object of the Institution. That object is to train up Natives, especially those educated in our Schools, to industrial employments, and to help the Natives to establish themselves in profitable trade and commerce, to supersede by God's blessings the abominable traffic in each other.

It is hoped also that by keeping up direct intercourse between African Growers of Cotton and other produce and the European markets, the trade may be placed on a more satisfactory and prosperous footing than if it were altogether in the hands of European traders as middle men residing on the Coast.

In order to carry into effect these plans, it is clearly necessary that the Cotton Press now at Lagos should be removed to Abbeokuta, and that Mr. Robbin should make Ake his head quarters. A turning lathe and other machinery and tools, as they may be brought into employment will also be provided if the Institution prospers.

The Industrial Institutions are placed under the management of Messrs. Crowther, Junior and Mr. Robbin, under the general superintendence and authority of the Yoruba Finance Committee and the Parent Committee as

every other branch of the Society's operations. Should any difference of
opinion arise between the managers and the Finance Committee, the
managers must yield to the local Committee pending a reference home.

It must be ever borne in mind and made manifest to others, especially to
European merchants engaged in the Africa trade, that the sole object of the
Institution is to encourage native industry, and to teach Christian converts to
support themselves when by their Christianity they will be cut off from
former associations and employments, either by their connexion with
idolatry, or through the jealousy and opposition of the heathen or Mahomedans. Especially it must be constantly shown that the funds of the Church
Missionary Society do not support the Institution, and are not in any way
implicated in its commercial character; that the Society is only in the position
of landlord of the workshops and warehouses, and the owner of the "plant"
employed in the trades, which are let out to the managers; so that the Society
incurs no risk whatever, while it receives remuneration for the use of its
property.

The duty of the managers will be to carry forward the various branches
of industry and to train and instruct as many natives in industrial works as
can be profitably employed, giving a preference to native converts and the
senior pupils of the Schools. Remuneration must be given to the persons so
employed as soon as their labour is profitable. A few will probably be
retained on full wages; but it must be regarded as most desirable to fit
workmen for supporting themselves elsewhere, and to take in their place fresh
learners of the different trades.

The Managers will for the present receive salaries from the Society; but it
is hoped that in a year or two the prosperity of the Institution will allow of
their receiving a commission upon the foreign shipments of Cotton, etc., and
upon the sale of work done under their management in the workshops; so
that their pay may be transferred to the Institution and their emoluments
become much larger than their present salaries. They will not be debarred
from purchasing Cotton on their own account if they have the means.

It is of the utmost importance that the most exact accounts should be
kept by daily journals and ledgers of every transaction connected with the
Industrial Institution. These Accounts should be submitted to and audited by
the members of the Finance Committee monthly, or copies of them sent
home monthly.

The Managers of the Institutions should also make it their business to
collect all possible information respecting the industry and trade of Abbeokuta and of other Yoruba towns, and to transmit the same to the Parent
Committee. The Committee wish to know the history and working of the
guild or association of traders in palm oil and whether any such other guild
exists.

Finally we remind you of the great object which the Society has in view in Africa, to give full scope to the Word of God to the Gospel of Christ; and they pray that you may ever keep this in view in your management of the Industrial Institutions and in your intercourse with the natives, and that the blessing of God may abundantly rest upon your labours.

MISSIONS AND COMMERCE[7]

... Our object in placing you with Mr. Crowther in charge of the Industrial Institutions is to make them as extensively useful as possible to your countrymen, to enable them to act as Principals in their own commercial transactions, to take them out of the hands of European Traders who try to grind them down to the lowest mark. We hope that by God's blessing on our plans a large body of such Native independent growers of Cotton and traders may spring up, who may form an intelligent and influential class of Society and become the founders of a kingdom which shall render incalculable benefits to Africa and hold a position amongst the States of Europe.

What on the other side is the object of European Traders to Africa? It is to obtain the produces of Africa for the least possible consideration, at the cheapest rate – They prefer to deal with savages whom they can cajole into parting with their goods for beads and rum, rather than to deal with civilized and intelligent races who can compete with them in the markets of Europe. Everywhere the white trader has degraded the Native and kept him down. It is very possible that the planters from South America may attempt to work with slaves on the coast of Africa, instead of transporting the slaves at great cost to another continent. I do not speak of individuals like good Mr. Clegg but I speak of two opposite systems.

Now into which of these systems will you throw your energies, and those acquisitions which you have made in England through the liberality of the friends of Africa? I am sure you cannot hesitate. You will prefer being an independent Patriot to being an Agent of Europeans – you will prefer the benefit of your Countrymen by helping them forward, to the selfish consideration of a better present salary.

I am persuaded that in a very few years you have as good a chance of being well off in one way as in the other – you need not fear our casting you off – we desire to see the Industrial Institutions well established and diffusing their benefits far and wide, and sending out branch Establishments to other Towns – The Superintendents will rise in their emoluments with the Establishments, and while you are allowed also to trade on your own private account, you have every facility for getting forward.

I enclose you a letter from Mr. Walker – I should be glad to hear your opinion of his workmanship both in the lathe and new press – also give your opinion of the next piece of machinery which would be useful for the

Institution. I have thought of a set of circular saws, fixed in a bench and turned by a horse. I have seen such an one at Walkers for £18 and the gear, etc. £18. You will perhaps soon try the horse gear in the roller gin and be able to form an estimate of its applicability . . .

MISSIONS AND COMMERCE[8]

. . . I am happy to inform you that Mr. Edward Gurney put a sum of money into my hands a few days ago for the encouragement of Native Industry in Africa, and especially at your Station. I can therefore authorize you to draw upon the Society for the establishment, if profitable, of a Cotton cleaning store at Ibadan. There must now be natives at Abbeokuta quite capable of cleaning and packing cotton, whom you might hire by a liberal salary: and I suspect there will be both screw presses and gins on sale out of the wreck of Mr. Clegg's imprudent venture.

I am able to authorise the expenditure of £250, two hundred and fifty pounds, for this object, which you can obtain if you want it.

I am able to add that if you should wish to send over to England any Native to be trained to the Cotton business, you are at liberty to do so: and the expense will be defrayed in addition to this grant . . .

MISSIONS AND GOVERNMENTS[9]

Neglect of the Colonial Governments to promote Agriculture and to develop the natural resources of Africa

The Parliamentary Committee of 1842 pointed out the neglect of the Colonial Governments in not promoting agriculture, and especially in not establishing model farms. Nothing has since been effectually attempted in this direction.

The neglect of agriculture in these colonies is the great drawback upon their prosperity, and is often alleged against them as a flagrant reproach. One fact may be stated in proof. Sierra Leone is supplied with rice, the staple article of food, from the surrounding countries. When war breaks out, the supply fails. For the last two or three years, in consequence of internal wars, rice, which had been imported into England from India, has been again sent out from England to supply the market in Sierra Leone, though any quantity might have been grown in the colony itself! This neglect of agriculture arises chiefly from the taint of African slavery. Agriculture in other parts of Africa is carried on by slave labour. The free men of the British Colonies, therefore, prefer any kind of trade or barter to agricultural labour. Here, then, the Colonial Governments should have supplied the remedy by establishing model farms, by prizes to successful producers of agricultural produce, by public warehouses where small farmers might store their goods for shipment, and by various other modes of instruction and encouragement.

A model farm, to be of real service, should also be a botanical garden for ascertaining and cultivating the best specimens of native produce, and for receiving from the Royal Botanical Gardens at Kew specimens of tropical plants which might be introduced into Western Africa. Sir W. Hooker, the Curator of the Kew Gardens, has often urged upon Missionaries the importance of introducing new plants which might become sources of profitable commerce, and he has furnished several boxes of specimens; but for want of a model farm and botanical garden all isolated attempts have hitherto failed. There is no record of any such attempt, on the part of Government, to develop the natural resources of Africa, though the native races are in that stage of civilization in which helps are most needed, and they have proved themselves apt to take immediate advantage of new sources of profit.

It may be said that the enterprise of private European traders would supply the necessary encouragement and direction to profitable industry. But this is not so. The climate prevents the influx of European capital and enterprise into Africa. European merchants upon the coast of Africa seek quick returns and large profits on small consignments, such as gold-dust, ivory, and palm-oil. They have thought it beneath their notice to look out for large consignments with small profits, though such commerce may of course be most beneficial to the native producer. Here, then, the action of a paternal Government might be most properly applied to encourage an infant trade.

For instance, the introduction of cotton as an article of trade was urged upon the Colonial Governments by Sir T. F. Buxton twenty-five years ago, and again by the Parliamentary Committee of 1842. But the first African cotton brought to the English markets, was through the exertions of a private friend of Africa, who sent out a small sum and a few cleaning machines to a native teacher in Africa. That native teacher sent over his first consignments of African cotton in 1852. Thomas Clegg, Esq., of Manchester, a true friend of Africa, then undertook the encouragement of African cotton upon the principle of dealing direct with the native producer, and the result was a rapid increase in the exportation of cotton from Lagos, reaching, in the eighth year, 4000 cwts.; until an unhappy misunderstanding between the Governor of Lagos and the chiefs of Abbeokuta closed the roads to the cotton-growing countries. Governors might have done, twenty or thirty years back, what private individuals have since done to introduce new articles of profitable commerce. There are many branches of trade which might be thus introduced and encouraged, such as indigo, vegetable fibres, gums, etc.

Questionable policy of removing liberated Africans from the African coast

To one of the recommendations of the Parliamentary Committee of

1842 an exception must be taken, namely, the removal of liberated Africans to the West-India Islands, rather than their location in the colonies on the coast. Great numbers of them have also been liberated in St. Helena. It is submitted that this policy has materially checked the civilization of Africa, and so far has retarded the grand scheme of extinguishing the slave-trade by the substitution of native industry. The present advancement of Sierra Leone is wholly due to the liberated Africans located there upon their release from slave-ships. Separated from all their old heathen associations, and brought under civilizing and Christian influences, they have proved, as a body, tractable and industrious. The testimony of Governor Ferguson and of others establishes the truth of this. Bishop Crowther, and many of the most wealthy native merchants, were liberated Africans. Many hundreds of this class, after acquiring the Christian and civilised habits of a British colony, have migrated to different parts of the coast, as traders. The European traders, their rivals, are too often accustomed to speak of them with bitter contempt and vituperation. But the evidence of the naval officers, and of the better class of European traders, gives a very different account of their character, and of their influence with their countrymen, and represents them as a hopeful element in the civilization of Africa. Yet the supply of liberated Africans has been for some years stopped in the African colonies. Ships containing several hundreds of captured slaves have, within the last few years, come into the harbour of Sierra Leone, and, after condemnation by the Mixed Commission, have been taken to the West Indies, without any opportunity being allowed of communicating with their countrymen in the colony. Other slavers have been condemned by the Mixed Commission in St. Helena, and located there, who would otherwise have added to the population of the West-African colonies.

This policy is the more to be regretted, as the colony of Sierra Leone has lately obtained a large accession of territory in the Quiah and Sherbro countries, which would support a far larger agricultural population than these countries supply.

It is hoped that this matter may be a subject of enquiry before the present Parliamentary Committee.

II

EDUCATION[10]

... The Committee of the Church Missionary Society have long felt the importance of training African youths in Sierra Leone for employment as Religious Teachers of their Countrymen. Experience has fully proved that the

European constitution cannot long bear up against the insalubriety of the climate of West Africa. It is therefore plain, that, for the extensive diffusion of the Gospel in that country a Native Agency must be resorted to . . .

. . . While, in accordance with the design of the Institution, the course of study will comprise a good general education, the main object will be the sound Theological training of the Youths and the diligent use of the means best calculated to promote, under the Divine Blessing, personal Religion. It is proposed that the course of study should embrace, (1) English Composition, Geography and History; (2) Arithmetic, Euclid, Algebra, Trigonometry, and the Branches of Natural Philosophy; (3) The Elements of Latin and Greek; (4) the most considerable of the Native Languages of West Africa; (5) Vocal Music; (6) Drawing and Perspective; (7) Scriptural Instruction, including the Holy Scriptures, as the basis of all Religious teaching; (8) Ecclesiastical History, with the Government, Articles, and Formularies of the Church of England; (9) Exposition of Scripture, Composition of Sermons, and the method of communicating knowledge to others. The whole of this course, however, can only be gradually carried out as the capacity and attainments of the Students will admit.

In addition to what has been already stated, it is intended that the students should be encouraged to acquaint themselves with useful Mechanical Arts; the Principles of Gardening and Agriculture; and such other departments of knowledge as may contribute to enlarge their capacity for promoting the social improvement of their countrymen . . .

EDUCATION, AGRICULTURE AND INDUSTRY[11]

It is the desire of the Committee that every endeavour should be used from the first to induce the pupils to pay for their teaching and to make them work at some manual labour for a part of each day with the view of raising food and contributing to the support of the school. The paying a price, however small, for the teaching can alone convince the people that they are not doing us a favour by sending their children, and that we are not bound to provide for those who grew up under our teaching. Industrial employments are also in such an early state of society a most proper department of education independently of the system of self-support. The separation of scholastic life and manual labour is a refinement of advanced civilization. It may be doubted whether even in this case it is desirable, but certainly it is not desirable in Missionary schools, or according to the examples of the Great Apostle to the Gentiles, who gloried in supporting himself by tent-making while he preached the Gospel to some of the Churches he founded.

ON EDUCATION AS A FUNCTION OF A MISSIONARY SOCIETY[12]

My Dear Brother Long,

Your letters of 15 October 1842 and 18 April 1843 have been read by me with very great interest. I can assure you that the Committee have ever regarded education such as you describe as one of the chief branches of missionary work. I will not enter into any comparison of the relative importance of Preaching or Education. It would be wrong to do so. The Lord not only gives to different persons qualifications specially suited to either the one or the other department; but also in his providence directs and opens the way for the more zealous promotion of one or the other branch of labour. He has evidently qualified you for, and called you to the work of education, and given you large opportunities for exercising this talent. May he give the increase, so that you may make it two talents. Knowing how much you valued education I was particularly rejoiced to hear Mr. Sandys say that you had agreed to visit occasionally and look after the villages south of Calcutta Parsonage and because I think that some direct preaching will be necessary to keep up the tone of your own mind. I have known many excellent men Tutors of Colleges, or Masters of schools, but never one who did not find the benefit of having some ministerial work to refresh his own spirit by declaring to an assembled congregation the unsearchable riches and love of Christ.

There is one point connected with your letters to which the attention of the Committee has been directed. You state that you are accustomed to read with your Christian Students Milton's works – and also to other students Pope's works. I presume that you do not mean that either Milton's or Pope's works form what would be called Class-books – though your expressions have not been sufficiently guarded against this interpretation, because it would be most unadvisable to introduce either one or the other – especially the latter to the heathen students. There are so many unobjectionable Christian Poets – upon which their time would be much better employed – and there are so many wrong sentiments in Pope and so many things in Milton which are calculated to lead into erroneous views any one not thoroughly established in the truth. I am aware of the difficulty of judging as to the impression which Milton's work would make upon a heathen – but surely it would be difficult to draw the distinction between truth and fiction – or to guard the heathen against some countenance being given to polytheism.

These hints will be sufficient to show you the apprehensions which have been awakened by the expressions alluded to in your letters. I read with much interest your animated appeal to the Scholars of Cambridge and Oxford. Would that such appeal might meet with a just response. I feel with you the necessity for talent and information of the highest order in the present crisis of India and I will not be wanting on my part in pressing, as I am able, the appeal.

May the Lord abundantly strengthen, direct and comfort your heart.

LETTER TO A MISSIONARY[13]

. . . Such general views as you have sent me are very valuable – I trust that you will continue to write, with the same fulness, on the great Missionary topics which need to be enforced upon the Church at home, to awaken it to a sense of its responsibilities. There cannot be a doubt of the importance of Calcutta having a strong body of Missionaries and that Education with a view to training native Christian Teachers is of unspeakable moment at the present crisis . . . But at the same time we must not forget that it often pleases the Lord to work in a very different way from what we expect. While we aim at a certain end by means which appear to us the most direct, He may choose the foolish things of the world, and the weak things of the world, and base things of the world and things that are despised by us – for the accomplishment of that very aim.

The educational duties in which you are engaged appear to you, justly, of paramount importance – the ministering to the feeble native converts of the villages, a small thing. But what is it which alone can stamp any real value upon your labors? Only the Holy Spirit's operation upon the heart of a sinner – and where that is vouchsafed, through your instrumentality, an infinite value is attached to your work. When I see how abundantly God is blessing the labours of Missionaries amongst the poor palmyra climbers of Tinnevelly – and the liberated "slaves" of West Africa – and how a blessing is withheld from the proud cities of India, I am apt to think that the Gospel will work its way upwards as we should speak: and I dread the idea of exalting education and talent too highly. I have often observed something of the same kind in Christian England – I have known men of the highest talent untouched by the preaching and conversation of talented piety – but sub-dued and won over by simple and illiterate piety. It may be that the talent of "young India" may be ultimately gained to the cause of Christianity through native converts of the "despised" caste instead of through the teaching of European talent . . .

LETTER TO A MISSIONARY[14]

. . . I should be glad to hear from you respecting the comparative importance of Christian education imparted to heathen boys, as in English and vernacular schools – and direct preaching to Adults. The case of Reynolds may illustrate the question. You thought him more usefully employed in the English school than in pastoral work at Lolo. I do not allude to the education of *Christian* children, I think that branch of Missionary work must on no account be neglected — I am aware also that both schools and preaching have their respective advantages, which it may not be easy to compare in importance. But yet I think that it will be of service to obtain the views of different persons on the comparison.

When I speak of preaching to the heathen I do not mean merely delivering a stated address at a stated place — but the following up the work by personal application of the truths of the Gospel wherever attention can be gained — and especially in villages and new places . . .

ON EDUCATION AS A FUNCTION OF A MISSIONARY SOCIETY[15]

. . . In all the Missionary labours of this Society the promoting of the education of the Natives is a principal object, a sufficient proof of which is that, in the various Missions of the Society, there are 800 Schools, comprising 38,007 Children . . .

ON EDUCATION AS A FUNCTION OF A MISSIONARY SOCIETY[16]

My Dear Madam,

Your letter of 26 September should not have remained unanswered so long if I had not felt my great difficulty in giving you advice, and also wished to obtain some further information, for I feel that the matter you have referred to me is one of solemn and important interest. I understand the two points which you refer to me to be (1) the advisableness of devoting a legacy of £600 to the opening of a school at Port Lokkoh for the instruction of Mandingoes in Arabic and their native language, in Scriptural truth.

After much consideration I have come to the conclusion that such a measure could hardly be adopted. The encouragement at Port Lokkoh has hitherto been so small, and the difficulties so many that the Society has thought of removing the Mission to the West into that part of the Timneh country chiefly inhabited by the heathen. Besides which it is very questionable whether Mandingo children could be collected at Port Lokkoh — and if collected and instructed whether they would afterwards return to the Mandingo country with any prospect of exercising a useful influence.

(2) The question is very different with respect to our College at Fourah Bay. In this respect I have no doubt that your intentions with respect to Arabic and to Mandingo scriptures may be fully carried out.

It is not a little remarkable that we have been lately taking measures to carry out the study of Arabic and the native languages of Africa in Fourah

Bay College by the appointment of a Tutor well acquainted with Arabic and oriental languages, whose business it shall be to superintend that department.

Late accounts have shewn us that the Arabic language may be made more effectual than we had supposed for the diffusion of Truth.

I send you an extract from the journal of our Native Missionary, the Rev. Samuel Crowther bearing upon this point.

Now should you be disposed to leave any sum of money for the purpose of promoting Arabic studies by the Natives at Fourah Bay and the Study and translations of the Mandingo language: I believe that your intention would be faithfully and fully carried out.

There are many Mandingoes in Sierra Leone – some of them are connected with our Mission Schools and Churches – and I have a confident hope that we shall soon introduce the study of that language in Fourah Bay.

I heartily respond to your appeals respecting the importance of working while it is day, and of doing what we are able for the spread of the Lord's revealed Truth throughout the world.

An open world lies before us – Oh that the Lord would pour out his Spirit upon our Church – and give the word that great may be the company of Preachers.

MISSIONS AND EDUCATION[17]

1. From the deep interest in the Education question evinced by the Government, and the various witnesses who appeared before the Parliamentary Committees on Indian Affairs last year, it may be presumed that great and comprehensive measures will, before long, be announced on the subject.

2. It can hardly be doubted that the Christian Mission Schools, which have afforded education to fourfold the number of scholars taught by the Government Institutions – which have almost exclusively established Female Schools – and have been almost the only Teachers of the Village-Vernacular Schools of their respective districts – will not be overlooked in the future distribution of funds appropriated for Educational purposes by the several Governments of India.

3. It is, however, equally to be expected, that the mere teaching to read and write will not constitute a claim for public assistance to any School. A standard of examination in useful knowledge will no doubt be established, varying, of course, in subjects and degrees, according to the nature of the School; requiring probably much from the Anglo-Vernacular Schools in towns, but something also of really substantial knowledge in the simplest Village-Vernacular Schools.

4. It may also be reasonably expected, that, in order to insure the

acquisition of the amount of useful knowledge which may be prescribed to each description of School claiming assistance from the public funds, Inspectors will be appointed, as in this country, upon whose certificate alone the aid sought for will be afforded.

5. The probability of measures of this nature being adopted and extended indiscriminately to all Schools desirous of partaking of the benefit contemplated, and willing to observe the prescribed conditions, cannot but excite the liveliest interest and sympathy throughout the Missionary body in India; and the Society anticipates your earnest and cordial co-operation in giving effect to them; if our hopes of their adoption should prove to be well-founded.

6. It need scarcely be observed, that our own interest in the subject is less with reference to the pecuniary aid to be derived from the adoption of the measures referred to — important as that aid must of course be deemed, in the event of any material increase, such as we hope to see, in the number of our Schools — than from the prospect which those measures open to our view of the vast impulse to be given to the native mind by the wide-spread establishment of Schools, in every one of which some knowledge will be acquired of historical and natural truths, while in all the Schools of Christian Missions pure religious truth will be superadded, without interference, much less obstruction, from the public authorities, by whom the pecuniary aid will be administered.

7. The interest attaching to the subject at this time, renders it likely that as little delay as possible will be allowed in carrying into effect the scheme which the Government may order to be introduced. It therefore becomes important, that, from every Station where Schools of any kind are attached to our Missions, we should learn, at the earliest period, what is the nature and extent of learning now afforded in the School or Schools of your Station. We understand that you have already been furnished with forms of return for this purpose.

8. We are more especially anxious to draw your attention to the means of improving your Schools, so as to meet the probable requirements of the Government plan. Where our Missionaries are situated in districts in which conferences are held periodically, we wish that each of the brethren should attend the next conference, carrying with him the fullest particulars relative to his own Schools, and prepared to consider, with his brethren what practical steps can be taken for the improvement of the Schools of the district or Station, and to adopt, in communication with the Corresponding Committee with which they are connected, the most effectual measures for supplying the *desiderata* of the Mission Schools, in order to their being placed on a footing to be presented for examination by the Government Inspector, whenever such an officer may be appointed.

9. It is certain that other Missionary Societies are alive to the vast

importance of the subject, and it would create great disappointment if our Schools were to be found backward, at the proper moment, in the race for extending the benefits of an enlarged Education among the people, and for a share of the Government countenance and support.

10. We are in this country exerting ourselves to obtain duly qualified Training Masters, and with hopeful prospects of success, and we confidently rely on your state of preparation to turn their services to the speediest and best account.

11. Besides various collateral considerations arising out of the subject, there is one, in connection with the progress of Education, to which we desire to draw your particular attention. It is the opening for public employment presented by the progress of Education among the lower castes of the country. We are not without hopes that some amelioration may be afforded, by Government regulations, to the low-caste people (with whom Christians of all conditions are, we regret to think, generally classed) in regard to their admission, either for employment, or as suitors, to the public Courts of Justice and Revenue offices of Government; but the difficulty of asserting their admitted or allowed rights, may, notwithstanding, still be experienced in remote situations under sole native authority. Education presents the most obvious means of relaxing the dominion of caste, now that the Government have, by their answer in the recent instance of the high-caste Memorial from Mangalore, sustained the course adopted by Mr. F. Anderson, in the court of that place, of making admission to official employment to be competed for by the test of public examination in learning. By that test of qualification, sundry low-caste youths have effected their entrance to the Court of Mangalore, and the spell of Caste — as regards public employment, and consequent social position and influence — is there at an end.

We will only further remind you, that the Church Missionary Society, having under its charge the largest number of Native Christians, is both placed on a vantage-ground, and is laid under a special obligation, in respect of this great movement. For if this Christian population be well educated, they must exercise a vast amount of influence over the whole of India.

Commending this Circular to your careful consideration, and the blessing of Almighty God.

THE PLACE OF EDUCATION IN MISSIONARY WORK[18]

. . . The more I contemplate the prospects for India the more I am persuaded that the Societies at home must chiefly work through their central Educational Establishments — and that these Institutions must rise with Missionary work, and out of Missionary work, as at Agra and Benares, not being formed and fashioned too much in advance of the native Church. They will eventually take the form most adapted to the wants of the native population – and for centuries to come the influence of a home Society may continue to benefit the Native Church by feeding these fountains of light . . .

THE IMPORTANCE OF ORTHOGRAPHY FOR LEARNING A LANGUAGE[19]

At length I send you the scheme in print on which we have often conversed and written.

You will be perhaps surprised to find some departure from the last paper which I transmitted to you. Professor Lee has taken great pains with it and I have also had the advantage of speaking with other first rate scholars. All of them have remonstrated against the adoption of (ei) for the English (i) and would urge upon you the use of (ai). The very reason which you and I had thought sufficient, namely the possibility of confounding it with "ai", they think an argument on the other side, as the passing from (ai) to (ai) they think will eventually help to bring out the structure of the language and may lead to other unforeseen results.

I confess that my own mind has been brought over to this opinion, (ei) is clearly a different sound from (ai) and its use for the English (i) violates the fundamental principle of the vowel sounds.

Besides which as (ai) will be adopted in Yoruba and probably in Bornu it will break the analogy of kindred languages if such a difference in orthography be introduced.

Against all this there can only be set the inconvenience of a possible mistake of the printer or the reader.

I cannot but anticipate that upon these grounds you will see the matter in an altered light and exchange your (ei) for (ai).

You will perceive another change in the sh, th, ch. This is not so important as the vowel sounds; yet it seems right to preserve (h) in its independence, and the sh, th, sounds are so evidently *simple* sounds that it spoils the system to represent them by *double consonants*.

MISSION TO EAST AFRICA[20]

. . . The Committee have lately been much encouraged by the conferences which they have held with Dr. Krapf our Missionary from East Africa. The way into the interior of Africa from his station appears to be open by a remarkable combination of providential circumstances. Dr. Krapf's linguistic talents have mastered several of the Dialects upon the Coast and have ascertained also the fact that all the African languages south of the Equator, including the Kaffir, Sechuana etc. are of one stock and character so that a Missionary may easily press on from one tribe to another, adapting his acquirements in one language to the new country. The Committee have determined to send with Dr. Krapf upon his return in January next three Missionaries and three mechanics, all to be German Brethren and to go out upon the footing already established in that Mission, only food and raiment of the simplest kind . . .

Notes

1 These two books by Thomas Fowell Buxton have recently been reprinted in one volume with the title *African Slave Trade and its Remedy.* This volume comes in the Colonial History Series, published by Dawsons of Pall Mall, London, 1968.

2 CA2/L1, Oct. 25, 1844, pp. 5, 6. Extract from letter of instructions to missionaries proceeding to Abbeokuta.

3 CA2/L1, pp. 155-156, Nov. 29, 1850. Extracts from letter to the Rev. H. Townsend, a missionary in Abbeokuta (Nigeria).

4 G/AZI/1, No. 70, undated, probably 1853 or 1854.

5 A.M., Vol. III, No. 5. Some account of the efforts made by the African Native Agency Committee to promote the growth of cotton in Africa, and of other exportable produce by means of native African agency itself. Letter from Henry Venn to Mr. Henry Johnson, an African, Oct. 22, 1853, p. 29.

6 CA2/L2, pp. 45-50, Oct. 21, 1856. Letter to the Rev. Samuel Crowther, Jr., and Mr. H. Robbin, two Africans.

7 CA2/L2, pp. 87-89, Jan. 22, 1857. Extract from letter to Mr. H. Robbin, an African.

8 CA2/L2, pp. 302-303, Dec. 21, 1859. Extract from a letter to the Rev. D. Hinderer, a missionary in Ibadan.

9 A.M., Vol. III, No. 7, pp. 32-35. Extract from pamphlet "West African Colonies," 1865.

10 G/AZI/1, Sept. 29, 1842, No. 34. Fourah-Bay Institution Building Fund.

11 CA2/L2, Jan. 29, 1856, p. 7. Letter to Mr. W. Kirkham, a missionary proceeding to Abbeokuta.

12 CI.1/L3, 11 July 1843, pp. 40-42. Letter to Rev. J. Long.

13 CI.1/L3, pp. 149-150, March 24, 1845. Extract from letter to the Rev. J. Long.

14 CI.1/L3, p. 270, November 24, 1846. Extract from letter to the Rev. G. G. Cuthbert, a missionary in India.

15 G/ACI/5, Sept. 10, 1846, pp. 197-198. Extract from a letter to Mr. B. Hawes.

16 G/ACI/6, pp. 372-374, Oct. 6, 1848. Letter to a Mrs. Hancock.

17 M.P., Vol. I, No. 27, June 27, 1854. Circular to the Society's missionaries in India.

18 CI.1/L4, p. 216, July 10, 1854. Extract from letter to the Rev. T. Valpy French.

19 G/ACI/6, pp. 278-279, June 3, 1848. Letter to the Rev. J. F. Schön, a missionary in West Africa, specializing in translating the Bible into Hausa.

20 CI.1/L3, p. 506, August 24, 1850. Extract from letter to a missionary, the Rev. G. G. Cuthbert.

Chapter VII

MISSIONS AND GOVERNMENTS

INTRODUCTION

One of the documents in this chapter is a letter from Venn to the British Governor of Lagos. In it he remarks that the representatives of the Church Missionary Society have "always been allowed confidential access to the Home Government." In view of the somewhat uneasy relationship of the C.M.S. missionaries with the Governor of Lagos this remark of Venn's may perhaps be interpreted as a warning to the Governor! What is significant and calls for understanding is that it could have been made at all, and with such confidence.

For readers who are accustomed to thinking of a virtually complete separation of church and state, it is not easy to understand the general situation within which Henry Venn worked out his policies in the middle of the nineteenth century. This was a period during which it was still widely assumed in Britain that something, recognizable as at least a quasi-Establishment of the Church of England, could be exported.[1] Venn would have assumed this without making it an essential part of his political *credo*. But in common with most of his contemporaries in the state, no less than in the church, he was deeply convinced as to the obligation of the state to further the interests of the Christian religion whenever it was in a position to do so.

It may be noted, incidentally, that it was because the Church of England Episcopate was traditionally so intimately related, constitutionally, with the state that Venn was always anxious to see that in its extension overseas the Episcopate should operate constitutionally. In practice, in Venn's time, this appeared to involve the nearest possible equivalent to a church Establishment corresponding to that in England (see the long paper on "Colonial Church Legislation," pp. 219-235).

In this general attitude to the state two facts need to be noted. From the discoveries of Columbus and Vasco da Gama onwards, some form of church-state relationship in regard to missions had been the norm, not the exception. Operating as he did within the setting of an established church that was also the established church of an expanding empire, Venn was opportunist enough to enlist the generally accepted pattern of action to advance his missionary aims.

It may be fairly argued that in so doing he was making a direct contribution to the embarrassment being suffered today by the churches of Asia and Africa in so far as they are the legatees of a past imperialism. That is a fair assessment of the present position of these churches. It is not a fair basis upon which to condemn Venn. For while it is clear that Venn believed in using the state, he was uncompromising in his resistance to the state whenever, in his judgment, it was hindering rather than helping the Christian mission. This chapter contains ample evidence to demonstrate Venn's independence of mind and his jealousy on behalf of the true independence of the missionary enterprise and of individual missionaries. Moving evidence of this latter point is to be found in the letter of instructions to two missionaries dated Dec. 19, 1856 (pp. 215-216).

Perhaps it is not too much to claim that more than most missionary thinkers, and more than most missionaries, Venn had discovered in the realities of politics, and in the administration of a missionary society itself inescapably involved in politics, how best to resolve the ambiguities in the dominical order and to "render to Caesar the things that are Caesar's and to God the things that are God's."

MISSIONS AND GOVERNMENT[2]

TO THE HONOURABLE THE COMMONS OF THE UNITED KINGDOM OF GREAT BRITAIN AND IRELAND, in Parliament assembled:

The humble PETITION of the COMMITTEE of the CHURCH MISSIONARY SOCIETY for AFRICA and the EAST —

Sheweth —

That your Petitioners are the managers of a Society which has been employed for above fifty years in the promotion of civilization and Christianity among the Aboriginal and Heathen Tribes of the different countries of the world.

That in this Undertaking the Society has expended above two millions of pounds sterling.

That the efforts of the Society were first and specially directed to the West Coast of Africa.

That your Petitioners therefore humbly claim the attention of Your Honourable House upon questions relating to the social and religious welfare of Heathen and Aboriginal Tribes, especially those of Western Africa; and also pray for protection to an undertaking involving such important interests, moral and commercial, pecuniary as well as religious.

That your Petitioners have heard with great concern and alarm the proposals which have of late years been made for the diminishing or for the removal of the Squadron now employed upon the West Coast of Africa.

That while your Petitioners have never entertained the idea that the cruising system could of itself and singly effect the suppression of the Slave-trade, they are firmly convinced that it is a co-ordinate instrumentality of the greatest possible value, restraining by its presence, and by the chastisements which it inflicts, the injurious operation of the Slave-trade, until the great remedial measures, now in operation, shall have had time and opportunity for affecting the cure of the evil at its source, by eradicating from the native mind the desire to engage in the traffic; so that the African kings and chiefs themselves, under the altered influences and feelings which Christianity and its attendant blessings will introduce, shall become convinced of the impolicy and atrocity of the Slave-trade, and, renouncing its delusive bribes, shall refuse any longer to engage in the Slave-hunts and bloody razzias by which the slave market has been hitherto supplied.

That the remedial measures to which allusion has been made, are in successful operation through the instrumentality of various Missionary Societies of England, Germany, and America; as well as through the extension of lawful commerce; though here your Petitioners will only particularly refer to the labours of the Society which they represent.

That in the year 1824 the Society entered into a formal engagement with the Secretary of State for the Colonies, the Earl Bathurst, to supply religious instruction and pastoral oversight for the large negro population, liberated by the cruising squadron, and located in the Colony of Sierra Leone; and has so faithfully performed its engagement that, at the present time, when such population amounts to about 45,000, the Society not only maintains a resident Clergyman in each of the thirteen parishes of the Colony, but has a staff of twenty European Clergymen and Teachers, together with sixty-four Native Teachers, of whom three are in full orders of the United Church of England and Ireland; that it possesses twenty-six places of worship and school-houses in the numerous villages of the Colony, forty-three schools, with between 5,000 and 6,000 scholars, and in Freetown a grammar-school containing fifty pupils, imparting a general and liberal education, and a females school; as well as a theological college for the training of Native Teachers. That upon the maintenance of these establishments the Society expends nearly £10,000 annually.

That your Petitioners confidently appeal to a chain of documentary evidence, published under the authority of Parliament, which shows that this important scheme for the welfare of Africa has been faithfully and efficiently followed out by the Society, according to its means and to the time allowed for its operation. They will only select two Testimonies in proof of this assertion. Sir George Collier, in 1821, while commanding on the African Station was required by Government to report upon the several settlements on the coast. In his report presented to Parliament, the following testimony is given respecting Sierra Leone, and the labours of the Church Missionary Society –

"The manner in which the public schools are here conducted, reflects the greatest credit on those concerned in their prosperity: and the improvement made by the scholars proves the aptitude of the African, if moderate pains be taken to instruct him. I have attended places of worship in every quarter of the globe, and I do most conscientiously declare, never did I witness the ceremonies of religion more piously performed or more devoutly attended to, than in Sierra Leone".

In the year 1842, a Committee of your Honourable House, of which Lord Sandon was the chairman, inquired into and reported upon the Settlements upon the West Coast of Africa, and the following passage occurs in their Report –

"To (the British) Government, beyond his rescue from the slave-ship and emancipation from future slavery, and a temporary sustenance, and his being placed within the reach of Missionary efforts – to which it has not contributed – the liberated African cannot fairly be said to owe much. To the invaluable exertions of the Church Missionary Society, more especially, and also to a considerable extent, as in all our African Settlements, to the Wesleyan body, the highest praise is due. By their efforts, nearly one-fifth of the whole population – a most unusually high proportion in any country – are at school; and the effects are visible in considerable intellectual, moral and religious improvement – very considerable, under the peculiar circumstances of such a Colony."

That your Petitioners have further to represent that the large expenditure and liberal educational establishments thus formed and cherished in Sierra Leone, were not undertaken merely for the benefit of that small locality, but in order to make that Colony a seed-plot for the whole Western coast of Africa – that the liberated Africans brought in from time to time by the cruising squadron from various points of the West Coast of Africa, and comprising Natives speaking above forty different languages, might be well trained in human and Divine knowledge, and prepared in due time to return to their father-lands, carrying with them the arts of civilization, the Christian religion, and gratitude indelibly stamped upon their hearts towards the British Nation; and thus introducing among their countrymen such improved habits, feelings, and employments, as might tend to counteract the African slave-trade at its sources, to carry the Christian Religion into the interior, and to open out to England the vast resources of Western Africa, as a cotton-growing country, and for the supply of various other productions of a tropical climate; which expectation has been already fulfilled in a very signal manner by the return of considerable numbers of the Yoruba Tribe ten years ago to their native country on the Bight of Benin, 1300 miles east of Sierra Leone, which movement originated entirely with themselves, in reliance upon the protection of British cruisers.

That such returned Natives have retained their Christian knowledge and Christian worship in their Heathen country; that the Society was able to supply them with Missionaries and with Native Teachers trained in Sierra Leone, one of these Native Teachers having received holy orders in this country from the Bishop of London, that there is now a Native Christian community in a large town, called Abbeokuta, sixty miles in the interior of Africa, and containing above fifty thousand souls; that the Native language has been reduced to writing, and that portions of the Bible and Prayer-Book have been printed for their use; that a manifest influence is exerted upon the Heathen population, tending to the counteraction of the Slave trade, and to beget a desire for lawful commerce, and the arts and comforts of civilized life; that one of the Chiefs has sent his son to Sierra Leone for further education; and that the Chief of the Tribe lately sent a letter to Her Majesty expressing their desire to give up the Slave-trade, and to receive the protection of England.

That the situation of Abbeokuta and of the Yoruba Tribe is peculiarly favourable to the introduction of commerce into the heart of Africa — being on a line of communication between the coast and the river Niger, far removed from the unhealthy localities of the delta of that river, and forming a connecting link, by language, between the coast and the interior, with the Hausa and Bornu tribes.

That your Petitioners, relying upon the protective influence of the Squadron, are promoting other migrations from Sierra Leone, to carry with them to other parts of Africa the same elements of civilization and the benefits of Christian knowledge.

That your Petitioners humbly represent, that were the cruising squadron to be removed from the coast, or even were its efforts to be relaxed, the existence of all agencies for the regeneration of Africa would be placed in imminent jeopardy. The agents of the Slave-trade would at once take means for the expulsion of Missionaries, for the exciting of internal wars, and for debasing the population by ardent spirits, and by all the degrading influences which have ever marked the progress of the Slave-trade.

That your Petitioners ground their conviction of this danger upon numerous testimonies which they have received from their Missionaries, and from intelligent Natives; one of which alone they will venture to place before your Honourable House, as speaking the sentiments of many — the writer being himself a liberated African, who was rescued from the hold of a Slave ship, received his education in the schools of this Society, and is now engaged in imparting religious instruction to his countrymen in Sierra Leone, from whence he writes in these words:

"The hearty desire and earnest expression by all throughout the Colony is 'Oh, who will entreat the favour of our Queen for us, that the squadron should not be removed from our coasts? If this should be, we are undone: our peace, our comfort will all be gone. Our fathers' land, or the whole continent of Africa, will be thus given up to ruin by wars and bloodshed. Slavery will increase twenty-fold more than it is now. Were Her Majesty, and the friends of the Africans, to hear the sighs of the people and witness their cries, they might be able to judge how deeply we are sensible of the benefit of Her Majesty's cruisers on the coasts and of the favour conferred on us by the generosity of the British Nation.' "

Your Petitioners humbly and earnestly pray that Your Honourable House will give your full and cordial support to Her Majesty's Government in continuing the services which have been rendered by the squadron on the coast of Africa, to the security of lawful commerce; to the protection of the lives and property of Her Majesty's subjects there, and to the encouragement of the efforts of Christian Missionaries in extending the greatest of all blessings, the light of the Gospel, to our benighted brethren, the Natives of the vast Continent.

MISSIONS AND GOVERNMENT[3]

I much regret that my detention in the Committee room when you did me the favour to call on Tuesday kept you waiting so long and necessarily made our interview a hurried one. I am anxious therefore to assure you that the Committee feel obliged by your call and by the kind expression of your wish that there may be a good understanding between all parties in your future Government of the Colony of Lagos.

I can assure you that the Committee cordially reciprocate these sentiments and that as Her Majesty has been pleased to send you again as her representative they consider it a sacred duty to enjoin upon their Missionaries the honour and respect due to those who bear Her Majesty's Commission and a respectful deference to their authority in all matters which do not appear to them to involve the higher consideration of conscience, justice or humanity.

The Committee also enjoin their Missionaries even in the event of their feeling themselves bound to protest against the policy pursued by the Constituted Authorities, to make the protest in the most respectful form to the Authorities themselves and to transmit a copy of the same to the Committee: at all events to abstain from such public strictures upon the policy of the Authorities as may tend to lower them in public estimation.

The ground on which these injunctions are founded is the fact that Missionaries stand in a very different relation to the Government of a Colony from all other settlers or merchants. They are not only the representatives of a Christian Society at home, which has always been allowed confidential access to the Home Government; but they have also a recognized relation to the native races as their confidential advisers, and in some sort their protectors and representatives with the British Authorities.

This peculiar relation of the Missionaries to the Native races has been on several memorable occasions recognized by the supreme Government of India, as well as by many of the Governors of the British Colonies, especially of late by Sir George Grey in his measures for the pacification of the Cape tribes and the tribes of New Zealand.

The Committee would also suggest, as they have already stated to Captain Glover, that the Governor of Lagos may advantageously address any important Communication which he may wish to make to Missionaries through the Secretary residing at Lagos, and if he see fit such Communication may be addressed to the Missionaries as a body. Communications and replies sent through the Secretary come under the review of the Parent Committee, whereas the direct Communication with a Missionary may be regarded as a private matter over which the Committee of the Society has no supervision.

The open and friendly way in which you referred to your past and future administration emboldens me to add a few words on another topic.

The main objection to your policy felt by a large body of those who have been long interested in the welfare of Africa was that the native races both within the Colony and in the surrounding districts, those at Porto Novo and Efe as well as the Egbas, were treated harshly, and that many of those Europeans who had long been rivals in trade with Native merchants were at once exalted to places of authority and profit, while no steps were taken to bring such advantages within reach of natives.

The Colony of Lagos was taken by Great Britain with the sole professed intention of promoting the social elevation and civilization of the Native tribes and thereby extinguishing the Slave trade at its source. But all experience proves that a British Colony on the Coast of Africa, where European traders have the chief consideration instead of promoting retards the civilization of the surrounding tribes. Better things were hoped of Lagos. That hope you have revived by the tenor of your closing remarks on Tuesday, and I speak in the name of many influential friends when I assure you of the fullest measure of sympathy and support for all efforts in this direction.

MISSIONS AND GOVERNMENT[4]

Sir Herbert Edwardes must now permit the offering of a few parting words to himself from those amongst us who have taken a public part in religious questions connected with India. We avail ourselves of this last opportunity of tendering to him the expression of our Christian sympathy, and of our grateful remembrance of the powerful assistance which he has given to our cause during his sojourn in England.

We offer no formal address, but only the frank and cordial expressions of Christian friendship. The words are read, because they proceed from many hearts and are not the mere utterance of the humble individual who now delivers them.

We look back, Sir Herbert, to the high and responsible positions which you have formerly held in India with so much advantage to the State. We recognise the special goodness of God, which gave you those opportunities, at an early period of your Indian career, of distinguishing yourself; but we recognise more gratefully the grace given to you to dedicate to the glory of God your abilities and influence in military and political employments.

On the eve of our separation, however, we seem to lose sight of the public distinctions you have won, and may yet win, from Her Majesty's Government, in the contemplation of higher and more Christian topics.

We thank God for the noble declaration which proceeded from the chief authorities of the Punjab, that the mutiny had taught a lesson from God to the statesmen of India, touching their Christian duty. We congratulate you upon having been one of that band who, both in word and in deed, exercised a bold but wise and just influence in favour of Christian truth. God has put his signature upon this righteous policy, by making the Punjab, in His providence, the chief stay of India's safety in the hour of peril, and one of the brightest jewels of the Indian Crown afterwards placed upon the head of our most gracious Sovereign.

You are returning to share once more the responsibilities of the administration of the Punjab. We pray that your return may not only strengthen the hearts and hands of colleagues, but bring with it an increase of wisdom, strength, and blessing from above.

Would that we could cheer you, in this parting hour, by the hope that measures are in progress at home for ensuring the safe and legitimate exercise of the influence of a Christian Government on the side of Christian truth among the Indian subjects of a Christian Queen!

But this we cannot do. We must confess that the one Christian measure which it has been attempted to carry at home, since the mutiny, has failed, namely, the removal of the authoritative interdict upon the Bible in Government education.

In the hour of peril, the whole Christian population of Great Britain seemed to recognise the wisdom – not to say the political necessity – of such a public recognition of the only standard of truth and morals; but partly by the slackening of zeal when a providential judgment is removed, and partly by the revival of a traditional policy, this Christian measure was defeated, and the interdict remains. Yet you have been yourself witness to a declaration by Lord Palmerston, as Prime Minister of the Crown, the Secretary of State for India standing by his side, that the principle is admitted, and that the interdict does not prevent a voluntary Bible Class in school-houses, provided it be held half-an-hour before or after school hours.

We are sure that the country is still with us on this great question; and should an occasion arise, the voice of the public would make itself heard. But we are compelled to confess that we see no immediate prospect of such an occasion arising at home; but it may be created by events in India.

Our hopes, under God, rest upon Christian statesmen in India, and especially upon the bold line of Christian policy maintained by the authorities of the Punjab. Any practical measure which may be adopted in India, if wise and legitimate, would be sure of support at home; the Christian feeling of Great Britain has proved, indeed, too weak to carry a practical measure originating *here,* but it would rise with a giant's strength to uphold and vindicate any such measure of Christian policy originating in India.

We wish you, Sir Herbert, farewell, in the name of that Lord who has upheld and will uphold you by His grace in the arduous and honorable position which He has called you to sustain. Our prayers and desires for you are summed up in familiar but comprehensive terms – that you may continue Christ's faithful soldier and servant unto your life's end.

MISSIONS AND GOVERNMENT[5]

. . . It is not a little remarkable that you brethren are each of you going to stations, in which your first dangers may arise from the favour and patronage of Christian friends in high authority who will welcome you upon your arrival. The Bishop of Calcutta has provided for one of you a Church, a residence, and will regard you as in an especial manner connected with his Cathedral. At Peshawur the Chief Commissioner and other public officers have solicited the addition we now make to the Mission – while the generous offer of a free passage in a Queen's ship is our inducement to hasten the departure of a schoolmaster for Western America. Therefore the Committee ventures in a very special manner to remind you of those severer duties, such as self-denial, and self-sacrifice, detachment from the world, taking up the cross to follow Christ, which must be the characteristics of the missionary. These are the genuine *Missionary habits,* which must be cultivated with all diligence. Without these you cannot do the work of an evangelist. The more easy and agreeable the missionary's external circumstances, the stricter watch he must keep upon his own spirit and behaviour lest he give any first cause to the slander of the day, that missionaries have departed from the simplicity and hardness of earlier days, when the office was despised by those who occupied high places in the world . . .

MISSIONS AND GOVERNMENT[6]

. . . I have the honour to acknowledge your letter . . . in which you have requested the Society to inform Earl Grey whether they know of any Gentleman of African descent whom they can recommend for the office of Chaplain at Cape Coast Castle . . . they do not at present know of any person of that description whom they can recommend to his Lordship . . . They have directed me also to express the great satisfaction of the Society at the proposal of Earl Grey as they are persuaded that the appointment of a person of African descent to a Colonial Chaplaincy on the Coast would have a very beneficial influence upon the African race generally . . .

GOVERNMENT AND MISSIONARY EDUCATION[7]

. . . In order to understand the importance of this Order, in its bearing upon the moral improvement of the natives of India, it must be borne in mind that in India ALL OFFICIAL AGENTS, connected with every department of civil and municipal government, whether of justice, police, or public works, are appointed by Government and its responsible servants; and that, consequently, the patronage of Government extends throughout every district of the land, and its influence is immense. This influence being now pledged to the encouragement of the general education and improvement of the people, the most momentous results may be anticipated from the measure.

Attention must also be particularly directed to the expression contained in the Government Order — "In every possible case a preference shall be given, in the selection of candidates for public employment, to those who have been educated in the institutions thus established; and especially to those who have distinguished themselves therein by a more than ordinary degree of MERIT AND ATTAINMENT". These terms evidently include moral conduct as well as literary attainments; and, therefore, afford a countenance and encouragement of the most important character to Christian education. To this circumstance, the Bishop of Calcutta thus refers, in his fourth and farewell Charge just published —

> The happy opening, of late, of all the branches of the Honourable Company's service to native talent, connected with moral character (for such is the express condition laid down by the present Governor General — to whom our warmest thanks are due for this, and other instances, of the interest his Excellency takes in the civilization and moral elevation of India) must have a most salutary effect.
>
> It is further to be observed that the Order places on an equal footing all educational establishments, whether Government or Missionary Institutions, or public or private schools. This is the first public recognition, in immediate connexion with the service of the State, of Missionary and other similar Institutions. The Order recognizes no partialities, no preferences, in favour of young men trained in Government schools and colleges. This is one of the most remarkable features of the measure.
>
> To borrow the words of Dr. Duff, in reference to this document — "Of what mighty and indefinite changes, prospectively, does this Order then contain the seeds! What fresh motives for evangelising labours in the vast realm of India! "

It is requested that the Readers of these papers will communicate to the Secretaries any facts with which they may be acquainted, or any suggestion which may occur to them calculated to assist the Committee in maturing their views on the proposed measure itself, and on the various details connected with it . . .

MISSIONS AND GOVERNMENT[8]

. . . The Committee beg me to send to you their very sincere congratulations on the success of your peace-making endeavours. They entirely concur in the principles which you so ably laid down in your first letter to the Governor and they think that your communications will appear in favourable contrast with the harsh requirement of the exclusion of European Merchants from Abeokuta. The answer of the Chief to this unreasonable demand is admirable. We are well aware of all that you have had to bear in these negotiations, but your success will repay all. At the same time we know the risk of future difficulties, where there is an impulsive will in high authorities and we can only wait and pray that the God of peace may interpose his arm, for the sake of the infant Church of Abeokuta, that it may have rest and that the converts "walking in the fear of the Lord and in the comfort of the Holy Ghost" may be "multiplied".

We can well understand your desire to escape from political complications and you well know how rejoiced we should be to welcome you on a visit to England, and how useful we could make your presence amongst us. You have so long exceeded the term of residence in Africa that you need no vote to sanction your return. But you know even better than we do what is the present pressing necessity for your help to the Mission . . .

MISSIONS AND GOVERNMENT[9]

. . . The Government of India profess to have the real welfare of the country at heart, and one instrument by which they believe that will be effectually promoted is education. Their object may be attained in two ways. They may take the entire education of the country into their own hands, in which case their principle of neutrality in religion must exclude all but voluntary Scriptural instruction, though undoubtedly a considerable amount of Christian truth must necessarily be borne on the tide of European knowledge thus introduced into India, or, secondly, they may in whole or part adopt the course of offering pecuniary aid to the best and most efficient general instructors they can meet with, who are already extensively engaged in the work which the new measures are designed to promote. Such aid they have offered to Missionary Societies. Their assistance, however, being offered to missionary agents, as teachers generally, and not as Christian Teachers, it is clear that the state of the case renders it unavoidable to proffer the same aid to all teachers in common, without respect to their faith, and Hindus, Mahomedans, or Roman Catholics, if good secular teachers, will have an equal claim upon Government grants . . .

. . . The Committee append a few brief remarks by way of suggestion or caution.

1. They are anxious, as a general principle, to point out that their educational work is still *Missionary*. The Society are willing to accept the aid of Government, so far as they will give it. But they consider themselves as doing their own work, and not as standing in the position of Schoolmasters to the Government; and in reference to the fear expressed as to the secularizing tendency of the system, they feel every confidence that their Missionaries will be alive to the paramount importance of maintaining the Missionary principle intact, and that they will watch unto prayer, lest any injurious influences, arising from the encouragement given to the secular branch of their teaching, obtain any advantage over them. The Committee are alive to the difficulty but cannot abandon the line of operation opening before them without a trial. It is one which admits of no remedy but that which is derived from on high; and they are unwilling to believe that it will be withheld.

2. The same principle applies to the salaries of Native Teachers, the scale of which must still be Missionary. If really inadequate, they ought to be

increased; but in good faith to Government, as well as on other grounds, Government aid must not be swallowed up in increasing the incomes of existing agents, instead of enlarging operations by additional schools and scholars.

3. The regulation which requires all the accounts and records to be open to inspection, appears to the Committee to be far too wide, and they trust that upon the first revision it will be modified. But even as it stands, a just principle of interpretation must confine the inspection to such reports and accounts as bear upon the avowed object of inspection, namely, the present state of the *secular* education given in the School, and to none other. On the question of inspection, generally, however, the Committee entertain no fear. They feel persuaded that any improper conduct on the part of a partial and unfair inspector would be promptly noticed on representation to the proper authorities; or, if not, that public opinion in India and England would soon be brought to bear a salutary influence on such a case . . .

COLONIAL CHURCHES AND GOVERNMENT[10]

In the discussions which have taken place upon the subject of Colonial Church Legislation, it has been too often taken for granted that Ecclesiastical Law is the same in all the Colonies of Great Britain; and that one general Church Constitution may be provided for all, by an Act of the Imperial Parliament.

The following observations are intended to show that this is an erroneous view of the subject; and to assist an enquiry into the laws Ecclesiastical, which govern the members of the United Church of England and Ireland, in the different Colonies and Dependencies of Great Britain: — as well as to suggest the mode in which a remedy may be best applied to the difficulties which have arisen in the regulation of Church affairs, in several Colonial Dioceses.

The proposed enquiry will consist of three branches:

1. What legislation, Imperial or Colonial, has already taken place in respect of the Church in the Colonies?

2. What portion of the Ecclesiastical Law of England is of force in the Colonies?

3. What remedies may be applied to the alleged defects of Colonial Ecclesiastical Law?

The first measure of the Imperial Legislature in respect of the Church in the Colonies, appears to have been in the case of *Nova Scotia,* under which name the whole of the North American Colonies, were then comprised, in the year 1791, consequent upon the establishment of a bishopric for that Province. This was the first of the Colonial Sees, and had been erected a few years previously in 1787, by Letters Patent. These Letters Patent recite a local Act of an earlier date, which had established the Church of England in that Province – "Whereas, by an Act passed in the year 1758, by the Governor, Council, and Assembly of the said Province of Nova Scotia, it is enacted that the sacred rites and ceremonies of Divine Worship according to the Liturgy of the Church established by the laws of England, shall be deemed the fixed form of worship within the said Province."

The Act of the Imperial Parliament (31 Geo. III. c. 31, 1791) commonly called, "The Constitutional Act of the Canadas," enables the Governor to form parsonages, rectories, etc., and "to present to every such parsonage or rectory an incumbent or minister of the Church of England, who shall have been duly ordained according to the rites of the said Church, and to supply, from time to time, such vacancies as may happen therein; and that every person so presented to any such parsonage or rectory, shall hold or enjoy the same, and all rights, profits, or emoluments, thereunto belonging, or granted, as fully and amply, and in the same manner, and on the same terms and conditions, and liable to the performance of the same duties as the incumbent of a parsonage or rectory in England." (Sec. 39). "That every such pre-sentation of an incumbent or minister, to any such parsonage or rectory, and also the enjoyment of any such parsonage or rectory, and of the rights, profits, and emoluments thereof, by any such incumbent or minister, shall be subject and liable to all rights of institution, and all other Spiritual and Ecclesiastical jurisdiction and authority, which have been lawfully granted by his Majesty's Royal Letters Patent to the Bishop of Nova Scotia, or which may hereafter by His Majesty's royal authority be lawfully granted, or appointed to be administered and executed within the said provinces, or either of them respectively, by the said bishop of Nova Scotia, or by any other person or persons, according to the laws and canons of the Church of England, which are lawfully made and received in England." (Sec. 40).

The next instance of Imperial Legislation, appears to have been in the case of the *East Indies.* An Act was passed in 1813 (53 Geo. III. c. 155) which recites, that if it shall please His Majesty to constitute a bishopric, the bishop shall not have or use any jurisdiction, or exercise any episcopal functions whatever, either in the East Indies or elsewhere, but only such jurisdiction and functions, as shall or may, from time to time be limited to him by His Majesty by Letters Patent under the Great Seal of the United Kingdom. (Sec. 51).

"That it shall and may be lawful for His Majesty from time to time, if he shall think fit, by his Letters Patent under the Great Seal of the said United Kingdom, to grant to such bishop, so to be nominated and appointed as aforesaid, such ecclesiastical jurisdiction, and the exercise of such episcopal functions within the East Indies and parts aforesaid, as His Majesty shall think necessary for the administering holy ceremonies, and for the superintendence and good government of the ministers of the Church establishment within the East Indies and parts aforesaid, any law, charter, or other matter or thing to the contrary notwithstanding." (Sec. 52)

"That when and as often as it shall please His Majesty to issue any Letters Patent respecting any such bishopric or archdeaconry as aforesaid, or for the nomination or appointment of any person thereto, the warrant for the bill in every such case shall be countersigned by the President of the Board of Commissioners for the affairs of India." (Sec. 53)

In the *West Indies* two bishoprics were erected by Letters Patent in the year 1824, without any previous Act of the Imperial Parliament. But in the next year, 1825, an Act was passed to provide salaries for a certain number of bishops, archdeacons, ministers, and catechists. The first section of this Act (6 Geo. IV. c. 88), recognizes the Letters Patent in these terms, "Whereas His Majesty by his several Royal Letters Patent has been graciously pleased to direct and appoint, that the Island of Jamaica, etc. etc. should be and become a bishopric and the diocese and see of a bishop of the United Church of England and Ireland, as by law established, to be called, etc., etc., be it enacted that the persons who shall from time to time exercise and enjoy the several dignities and offices hereinafter mentioned, under or by virtue of His Majesty's Letters Patent, or authority, shall receive the several salaries, etc. etc."

This Act relates merely to salaries and pensions, and does not define the authority of the bishops, or the status of the clergy.

In the case of one of the West Indian Colonies, the Bahamas, an Imperial Act was passed, prior to the foregoing, (6 Geo. IV. c. 12), giving the Bishop of Jamaica jurisdiction within the Bahamas, and "all laws, ordinances, and canons ecclesiastical, which are now in use and force in England, are to be in force over the clergy in the Bahamas." It is noticeable, that a former Act of Parliament (40 Geo. III. c. 2) had enacted that the Common Law of England, except as to Ecclesiastical affairs, and some other specified matters, should be in force in the Bahamas.

After the erection of the West Indian bishoprics, the Colonial Legislatures in each island passed numerous laws relating to the jurisdiction of the Bishops, and to ecclesiastical affairs. The case is thus referred to by Sir James Stephen: "I hold that all our Colonial Legislatures are already competent to adapt the Ecclesiastical Law to their respective local exigencies. In proof of that conclusion, I refer to the Statute books of the West India Colonies, in which will be found a long series of enactments of that nature, commencing with the year 1825, and continued to the present time." (Letter to the Earl of Harrowby.)

In the case of the *Australian Colonies,* no Imperial Act has been passed in respect of the bishoprics, or of the Ecclesiastical Law. The Act (9 Geo. IV. c. 83) being the Constitutional Act for New South Wales and Van Diemen's

Land, declares, that all the laws and statutes in force within the realm of England, at the time of passing the Act, shall be applied in the administration of justice in the Courts of New South Wales and Van Diemen's Land respectively, so far as the same can be applied within the said Colonies; and if any doubts shall arise as to the application of any such laws or statutes, the Governors and Legislative Councils are to declare by ordinance whether such laws and statutes shall be deemed to extend to such Colonies. (Section 24.) These general terms, even if stretched to apply to Ecclesiastical Law, are only the enunciation of a principle respecting the transfer of British Law into British Colonies, to which reference will be subsequently made.

The Colonial Legislatures in Australia, have passed laws to regulate the temporal affairs of Churches and Chapels of the United Church of England and Ireland, but these acts do not touch the question of what Ecclesiastical Laws are in force in those Colonies.

A question has arisen respecting the power of Royal Letters Patent to convey jurisdiction and legal authority to a Bishop. The care taken in the case of Nova Scotia and of the East Indies, to strengthen the Letters Patent by Acts of Parliament, raises at least a presumption that the royal authority is insufficient in itself to do more than assign territorial limits to a Diocese, and to designate the individual for the See. Dr. Phillimore, indeed, remarks in his edition for Burns' Ecclesiastical Law (Vol. I, p. 415).

"In order to ascertain the authority and jurisdiction which may be exercised by any Diocesan of a Colonial See, the patent of his appointment must be consulted; but, generally speaking, he is empowered to exercise personally, or through his Commissary or Commissaries, the same ecclesiastical jurisdiction and authority as may be exercised according to the Ecclesiastical Laws and Canons of England."

The soundness of this doctrine was brought to the test by the Bishop of Tasmania, who claimed to exercise such jurisdiction, and who pleaded the words of his patent to that effect. The members of the Scotch Presbyterian Church in the Colony, and the Established Church in Scotland, presented Memorials to the Government denying the power of the Queen to grant any such jurisdiction, and prayed that such part of the Letters Patent might be cancelled.

The matter, after much correspondence, was submitted to the Law Officers of the Crown, who gave their opinion that Her Majesty has no authority, by Letters Patent, to create such Ecclesiastical jurisdiction, and the Letters Patent were altered, with the Bishop's consent, to a more general form, which has been since adopted in other patents, giving the Bishop power "to perform, all the functions peculiar and appropriate to the office of a Bishop within the said Diocese . . . And especially to give institution to benefices, to grant licences to officiate, to visit all ministers in holy orders resident within the Diocese; as also to call them before him, and enquire as well concerning their morals as their behaviour in their said offices and stations respectively." (See Parl. Paprs. 175, 25 March 1850).

It seems therefore that the Royal Letters Patent can convey no authority and power to the Bishop beyond that allowed by the Laws Ecclesiastical in force in the Colony.

The foregoing review will show that the Ecclesiastical Laws and Canons of England have been imported by express legislation, to a greater or less extent, into various Colonies. In such cases, the state of the Ecclesiastical Law depends upon the construction of Statutes. But where there has been no Imperial or Colonial Legislation, the question arises, how far the members of the United Church of England and Ireland carry with them their Ecclesiastical Law into the dependencies of Great Britain.

II. In pursuing the proposed enquiry, two points present themselves as involved in the question.

1. How far the Colonists of Great Britain carry with them the Ecclesiastical laws in force in the mother country, which are not expressly restricted to any one part of the United Kingdom.

2. What part of the Ecclesiastical law of England is so restricted.

1. The general principle which regulates the transfer of the law of England into the British Colonies is thus stated by Blackstone in a passage quoted by Dr. Phillimore, in his edition of "Burns' Ecclesiastical Law", under the title, "Church in the Colonies, General Principles relating thereto."

"It hath been held that if an uninhabited country be discovered and planted by English subjects, all the English laws then in being, which are the birthright of every subject, are immediately there in force. But this must be understood with very many and very great restrictions. Such Colonists carry with them only so much of the English law as is applicable to their own situation, and the condition of an infant Colony; such for instance, as the general rules of inheritance, and of protection from personal injuries. The artificial refinements and distinctions incident to the property of a great and commercial people, the laws of police and revenue (such especially as are enforced by penalties), the mode of maintenance for the established Clergy, the jurisdiction of spiritual courts, and a multitude of other provisions, are neither necessary nor convenient to them, and therefore are not in force. What shall be admitted and what rejected, at what times, and under what circumstances, must in case of dispute, be decided in the first instance by their own provincial judicature, subject to the revision and control of the King in council; the whole of their constitution being also liable to be new modelled and reformed by the general superintending power of the legislature in their mother country. But in conquered or ceded countries that have already laws of their own, the King may indeed alter and change these laws, but till he does actually change them, the ancient laws of the country remain, unless such as are against the law of God, as in the case of an infidel country.

Our American plantations are principally of this latter sort, being obtained in the last century, either by right of conquest, and driving out the natives (with what natural justice I shall not at present enquire), or by treaties: and therefore the Common Law of England, as such, has no allowance or authority there, they being no part of the mother country, but distinct (though dependent) dominions. They are subject, however, to the control of the Parliament, though (like Ireland, Man and the rest), not bound by any Acts of Parliament, unless particularly named." – (Blackstone's Com., Introd. iv. p. 190).

The question before us is one of difficulty. The state of Ecclesiastical Law in England is confessedly, in many particulars, imperfect and uncertain; and if the Colonies have further to enquire what part of this law is applicable to their own circumstances, the investigation will become a complicated one. It seems especially questionable how far the Canon Law, and the Canons of 1603, are in force in the Colonies. Upon one part of Blackstone's statement there can, however, be no doubt, namely, that "the jurisdiction of Spiritual Courts" is "not in force" in the Colonies: although in the East Indies Consistorial Courts have been established under the provisions of the Act of Parliament already referred to. Generally speaking, also, no provision has been made to supply the want of Ecclesiastical Courts, in which charges against a clergyman may be judicially enquired into and adjudged. This is a most important requisite in the Colonial Church System. Hitherto it has been less urgent in those Colonies in which most of the clergymen have been supported by Societies which have the purse strings under their control. But as the Colonial Church becomes settled, the need of such means for exercising discipline becomes more and more manifest and imperative.

If the application of Blackstone's doctrine to Ecclesiastical Law, generally, be disputed, yet this need not embarrass the present enquiry, which is instituted upon the supposition that the members of the united Church in any Colony continue such, and desire to carry out their Church system and to retain as close a connexion with the Mother Church as their circumstances will allow of. The Bishops and Clergy have also all entered into solemn declarations and oaths at their consecration and ordination, "always so to minister the doctrine and Sacraments, and the discipline of Christ as the Lord hath commanded, and as this Church and realm hath received the same, according to the commandments of God."

In all practical questions of ritual or discipline, reference should be had to the general tone and spirit of the Church of England as a Protestant and reformed branch of the Church of Christ. There should be no going back to Popish times, or to the scanty and uncertain records of patristic precedents. The Church of the Reformation, as established, and as gradually matured in the reigns of King Edward the Sixth and Queen Elizabeth, will afford the best precedents for an Episcopal Church, which is to win the hearts and cordial co-operation of British subjects, and to perform the great ecclesiastical duty of gathering souls into the fold of Christ, and of building them up in their most holy faith.

2. There is less perplexity in respect of Statute Law: much of which is restricted in terms to England and Wales.

Many statutes have been passed by the Imperial Parliament for the regulation of the Church, which do not extend to the Church in Ireland, and which cannot be regarded as laws of the United Church of England and Ireland, of which every Colonial Church is a branch.

Among these may be mentioned, as important to our present enquiry, the Clergy Discipline Act, under the provisions of which discipline is now exercised in the Church of England, which has no force in the Colonies, being for England and Wales. (3 & 4 Vic. c. 86, A.D. 1840).

Also the Acts which now regulate the status of stipendiary curates in England.

The most important enquiry, however, under this head respects the Acts of Uniformity. Uniformity of Common Prayer, and service in the Church and administration of the Sacraments is enjoined by two Acts – viz., 1 Eliz. c. 2, A.D. 1558; and 13 & 14 Car. II., c. 4, A.D. 1662. The former Act binds "All and singular ministers in any Cathedral or parish Church, or other place within this realm of England, Wales, and the Marches of the same or other the Queen's dominions." – (Clause 3.) – And the last enacts, "That all laws, statutes, and ordinances, wherein or whereby any other service, administration of Sacraments, or Common Prayer, is limited, established, or set forth, to be used within this realm, or any other the Queen's dominions or countries, shall from henceforth be void and of none effect."

The second Act of Uniformity, though it confirms the former Act of Elizabeth, substituting the new Prayerbook in the place of the former edition, yet in respect of certain other particulars, only binds, "All and singular ministers in any Cathedral, Collegiate, or parish Church or Chapel, or other place of public worship within this realm of England, dominion of Wales, and town of Berwick-upon-Tweed." – (Clause 2.) – and in subsequent clauses the provisions of the Act are restricted to ministers and places of worship "within this realm of England, or places aforesaid."

It is easy to point out reasons of this restrictive language: for the Episcopal Church was established by law in Scotland from 1660 to 1668, but encountered so much resistance that it would have been impossible to attempt the introduction of such an Act into that part of the King's dominions. Several of the American Colonies also were the refuge of the Republicans and Non-Conformists, and it was the policy of the Government rather to encourage their emigration than to check it, by introducing the provisions of the Act into those dependencies. Neither were the provisions of this Act transferred to Ireland till three years after it had been adopted in

England, viz., Stat. 17 & 18, Car. II. c. 6. (Ireland), A.D. 1665, and then in a modified form, and after a consultation with the two Houses of Convocation in Ireland. On these grounds it is presumed that the second Act of Uniformity does not necessarily extend to the Colonies, unless imported into them by express legislation.[11]

Now, it is to be observed, that it is only the second Act which enjoins upon the beneficed Clergymen the declaration of "unfeigned assent and consent, to all and everything contained in the Book of Common Prayer", which declaration, though it may be shown to be justly interpreted, as only declaring assent and consent "to the use of the book" yet has been a stumbling-block and hindrance to a large body of conscientious members of the Church of England.

The second Act of Uniformity, also, first declared the necessity of Episcopal ordination to the holding of any benefice or preferment in England, which caused a large body of persons who had received Presbyterian ordination, to be ejected from their preferment.

It is, therefore, a question whether a Bishop of the United Church of England and Ireland, in certain Colonies, has not the power to give a licence to a Presbyterian minister, upon his conformity to the Church without Episcopal ordination; but even if this point be doubtful, a great barrier would be removed against the reception of many who would willingly unite with the Church, if the other requirement of the second Act of Uniformity be removed.

At all events, such Colonies as have not imported into their codes of law, the whole of the Ecclesiastical Law of England, are at liberty to determine how far provisions made in England under the very peculiar state of things in 1662 are "applicable to their own situation:" and whether the Church in the Colonies should not stand in the position which it occupied in England after the Restoration, and before that fatal Feast of St. Bartholomew, in 1662, which unhappily excluded from its pale many of the brightest ornaments, and the most useful ministers of the Church of Christ.

III. The foregoing statements will show that Ecclesiastical Law in the Colonies is uncertain and defective, and that a remedy is needed. It has been shown, also, that the state of things in different Colonies is so varied, that the remedy must be varied according to the existing state of Ecclesiastical Law in each Colony. The same statements will further indicate the mode in which the remedy is to be sought and applied, namely, by the joint action of Imperial and Colonial Legislation: and will suggest an answer to the practical question, How may a remedy be best applied to the defective state of the Church system in the Colonies?

For the resolution of this question, it is necessary, first to notice certain abortive attempts already made in parliament, and then to point out another and safer course, and also to show that the Australian Colonies have in fact made much progress in the course suggested.

(1) It was first proposed to pass an Act of Parliament, to give power to the Bishops, Clergy, and laity of any Colony to meet together, and to make whatever Ecclesiastical regulations they might deem necessary: maintaining, however, the standards of faith and worship, and the supremacy of the Crown.

The chief objection to this course was, that the Regulations made by such an Assembly would have the force, in the Colonies, of Imperial Law, in virtue of the proposed Act; that is, it would confer undefined *legislative power,* in respect of Church affairs, upon these conventions of the Clergy and laity. It will sufficiently appear from the foregoing review that such a course would be at variance with all past legislation, and would over-ride the Colonial Legislatures. Such powers have not been given to any other religious communities. They are not, in fact, possessed by the members of the Church of Scotland, or by the Wesleyan Methodists; they are assumed only by Independents, whose congregations form no part of any organised Church. Such powers are inconsistent in principle with the supremacy of the Crown in all causes Ecclesiastical, as well as with the powers hitherto exercised by the local Legislatures in every British Colony. And it is impossible to predict what changes might be introduced into the constitution of the Church, by such legislative action, notwithstanding the proposed checks. Hence, no less a number than four successive Bills, framed upon this principle, have been rejected by Parliament; having been opposed by those who object to give exclusive privileges to the Church, and by those, on the other hand, who desire to maintain the integrity of the United Church of England and Ireland abroad, and who, therefore, deprecate its dismemberment by opening the door to a variety of local Church constitutions.

(2) In order to avoid these difficulties, a second proposal has been made to give, by an Imperial Act of Parliament, legal sanction to the holding of Diocesan Conventions by the Clergy and Laity, but to deprive their decisions of the force of law. The Bishop of Oxford proposed, in the House of Lords, upon the debate on the Australian Government Bill of 1850, clauses to this effect, providing "that no such Regulations shall have any other force or effect than the Regulations, Laws, or Usages of other Churches or Religious communities in the said Colonies." These clauses were not adopted. In the Session of 1854, a Bill was introduced into the House of Commons by the Solicitor-General, to sanction such meetings, but contains a clause: "Provided always, that such meetings, or the regulations, agreements, or arrangements that may be made thereat, shall not obtain any force or authority from the enactments hereby made." These words being thought ambiguous, since they seemed to contain a lurking meaning that such regulations would have legal force from some other source than the present enactments, it was proposed, by Mr. Dunlop, to add the words, "and shall not have any legal force or

authority other than that which may arise, according to the law of the Colony, from consensual compact express or implied among the members, clerical and lay, of such Churches in the Colonies as aforesaid." This Bill did not reach the stage in which this amendment could be proposed, but it will serve to illustrate the distinction between meetings for mutual agreement, and synods or conventions possessing legislative powers.

The objections to this proposal were, that it was too indefinite, that it might revive old ecclesiastical pretensions, and that it stopped short of the necessity of the case. Such voluntary agreements would not bind dissentients or successive Bishops. Though the Bill professed to provide a remedy for certain acknowledged deficiencies, it would have still left the main defects untouched.

(3) There is, however, a third course open to the Church in the Colonies, clearly indicated by the course of previous legislation, of which the Diocese of Melbourne has set an example, namely, *to obtain a legal sanction for ecclesiastical arrangements through the Colonial Legislatures.* Let the Bishops, Clergy and Laity meet together to prepare such measures as may seem necessary for adapting the laws of the Church to their local necessities, and for perfecting their Church constitution. Let the measures so prepared be proposed *for the adoption of the Colonial Legislatures;* and, ultimately, for the sanction of the authorities at home.

And since doubts have arisen whether such meetings can be properly held by the Bishops and Clergy of the United Church, and also whether Her Majesty will have the power of giving her consent to such measures as may be adopted by the Colonial Legislatures in respect of such Colonial Legislation, an Act of the Imperial Parliament should be obtained, to authorise such meetings, and to enable her Majesty to give her consent to the measures, so sanctioned by the Colonial Legislatures: providing, also, that the measures should be submitted by the Home Government to the Archbishop of Canterbury, for his observations upon them, before they receive the final approval of the Crown.

The objections which have been fatal to former Colonial Church Legislation Bills, would not apply to the course now suggested. It does not propose to give legislative powers to conventions, but only power to propose legislation to the Colonial Legislatures. The Church would have the initiative of the measures. Its consent would be the foundation of the proceeding.

The proposed course would be a safe course for all the interests involved. The Church in the Colonies is best acquainted with its own local exigencies, and best able to suggest a specific remedy. The Colonial Legislature will take care that nothing is done at variance with Colonial policy. The Archbishop and the Home Government will guard Colonial measures against any departure from the essential principles of the Church at home, or the prerogatives of the Crown. It claims for the United Church of England and

Ireland no exclusive legislative advantages; but may be equally followed by other religious communities. The Colonial Legislatures will thus maintain their principle of treating the Churches of England and Scotland, and other Christian societies, upon terms of civil equality.

It may be shown, also, that upon the soundest Ecclesiastical principles a Diocesan Synod can claim no powers of legislation. The functions of a Diocesan Synod are thus described and limited by Johnson, a writer of authority as a Canonist, in his "Clergyman's Vademecum." "Diocesan Synods are the assemblies of the Bishop and his Presbyters to enforce and put in execution Canons made by General Councils, or National and Provincial Synods, and to consult and agree upon rules of discipline for themselves."

Should it be thought right, in any Colony, so far to depart from the principle here laid down as to give the Convention of the Clergy and Laity a measure of Legislative action, it will be at least necessary that this action shall be restricted to the management of the temporal affairs of the Church, and to the exercise of discipline over the Clergy.

It has, indeed, been sometimes asserted, that the Church of England is placed in so disadvantageous a position in the Colonies, relatively to other religious bodies, that it may fairly claim greater legislative privileges. So much misstatement and confusion has existed upon this part of the subject, that it is important to enter into a fuller explanation of the case. The allegation that the Church is in this disadvantageous position, may be traced to the fact that the constitutions of other bodies are more adapted for the circumstances of Colonists than that of the Church of England, especially in respect of the maintenance of discipline. The Church of England in the Colonies has no Ecclesiastical Courts, for enforcing its discipline. Its Ecclesiastical Courts are all at home, its bishops and clergy are dispersed in all parts of the world. Whereas in the Presbyterian Church, and among the Wesleyan Methodists, their means of enforcing discipline lie in Synods, Presbyteries, and Conferences, which can be held wherever a few ministers and laymen of their persuasion meet together.

Again, other religious communities have secured their discipline by vesting their Chapels and other property under Trust Deeds, which insert their doctrines and regulations of discipline in their declarations of trust: and thus, even without express local acts, they are enabled to enforce the ejection of any minister from their churches and houses of residence, by an appeal to the Civil Courts, if he violates their established rules. In this way the whole of the trusteeship of the property of the Wesleyan Methodists, in all parts of the world, is vested in trustees, under the provisions of a Poll-deed, executed by Wesley, bearing date 28th Feb., 1784, enrolled in the High Court of Chancery, reciting the distinctive principles and discipline of Methodism. Thus they have been enabled to keep up their uniformity of doctrine and discipline, throughout all the Colonies of Great Britain; and have frequently had recourse to the civil courts of the Colonies where any resistance has been made to their exercise of such discipline.

A similar course is open to the members of the Church of England, of vesting their property under Trusts. Such a scheme was drawn out by the Church Missionary Society, under legal advice, in respect of their property in Sierra Leone, which was approved by the late Bishop of Sierra Leone, by the Archbishop of Canterbury and by the Bishop of London, and will be shortly carried into effect. And so, whenever in the Colonies property either in churches, houses, or glebes, is conveyed to trustees, which is the usual tenure, a Declaration of Trust might be adopted, declaring the conditions under which ministers hold the same.

Still further, it remains to be shown that the Church in the Colonies of Australia has already taken some important steps in the course which it is the object of these Observations to recommend. The facts to be adduced in confirmation of this remark will throw light upon the whole subject under consideration.

In New South Wales, a Local Act was passed in 1836, entitled — "An Act to promote the Building of Churches and Chapels, and to provide for the maintenance of ministers of religion in New South Wales." (7 Will. IV. No. 3). This Act equally applies to all denominations of Christians. It provides for making grants of money to places of worship and houses of residence on certain specified terms, whenever one hundred or more adults shall subscribe a declaration of their desire to attend the place of worship, and "to give stipends towards the support of the ministers of religion, duly appointed to officiate in any Churches or Chapels to be erected in the manner aforesaid." (Clause 2.) Stipends to be withheld, "if it shall appear to the said Governor and Council that the said duties have been culpably and wilfully neglected." The property to be vested in not less than three or five trustees approved of by the Governor.

Consequent upon the passing of this Act, all the chief religious communities in the Colony procured separate Local Acts for the regulation of their affairs, in conformity with the provisions of the general Act.

(1) An Act for the United Church of England and Ireland, was passed, 6th September 1837, entitled "An Act to regulate the Temporal affairs of Churches and Chapels of the United Church of England and Ireland in New South Wales. (8. Will. IV. No. 5.)

This Act makes various provisions for the election of trustees and of churchwardens, and allows the Bishop to be elected as a sole trustee. It also enacts that no person shall be allowed to officiate in any consecrated Church or Chapel, unless he be first approved, and thereunto licensed by the Archbishop of the province, or the Bishop of the Diocese. (Clause 19.)

"And it shall be lawful for the clergyman in holy orders of the United Church of England and Ireland, who shall be duly licensed by the Bishop to officiate in any Church or Chapel under this Act, to have free access to the church, to exercise his spiritual functions therein, and to have possessions of the house and glebe; provided that he shall have no such rights after the licence of such clergyman shall have been withdrawn, cancelled, or revoked by the Bishop of the Diocese, upon cause shown." (Clause 20.)

(2) An Act was passed 9th September, 1837, entitled "An Act to regulate the Temporal affairs of Presbyterian Churches and Chapels connected with the Church of Scotland in the Colony of New South Wales." (8. Will. 14. No. 7). This Act makes provision for the election and duties of trustees, and enacts that a clergyman duly inducted by the Presbytery into any church or chapel under this Act, shall have free access to the chapel and enjoy the dwelling-house; and shall have no such rights "after he shall have been removed from his office by the decision of the Presbytery."

This Act was amended 4 Vic. No. 17, 7th October, 1840, by an Act constituting a Synod in the said Colony, which was to have the powers granted to the Presbytery by the former Act. "Provided always that the several powers, privileges, and advantages conferred by this Act upon the said Synod of Australia, shall cease and determine, unless the said Synod shall continue its adherence to the doctrines of the confession of faith, and to the other standards and formularies of the established Church of Scotland, and in the exercise of discipline shall follow the laws of that church."

(3) An Act was passed 17th August 1838, entitled "An Act to regulate the Temporal affairs of the Religious Societies, denominated Wesleyan Methodists, Independents, and Baptists." (2 Vic. No. 7). This authorises the trustees appointed under the former Act to transfer the property to other trustees to hold the real estate "to the use of such Society, upon the trusts stated and set forth in a Model Deed of such Society, to be enrolled in the Supreme Court of New South Wales within two years after the passing of this Act, after the same shall have been proved to the satisfaction of his Excellency the Governor and the Executive Council, to be a deed recognized and established by the usages of the religious society to which it professes to belong."

These Colonial Acts place the question of the relative freedom of action possessed by the Church and by other religious communities in a clear light. We here find that they all had the same opportunity of making regulations for their temporal affairs, including their Ecclesiastical discipline, provided that such discipline should be presented to the Legislature in some recognised form and substance, as in a Model Deed.

It has been reserved for this stage in our observations, to remark upon a very common but erroneous notion, that the British Colonies have generally cast off all connexion between Church and State, and have therefore precluded themselves from all claim to legislate for the Church. The history of the New South Wales, Tasmania, and Melbourne Acts, shows that in some of the most important Colonies the local governments have pursued a very different course. They have not cast off their connexion with the Church, but they have entered into the same relations with other Christian bodies whose principles and constitution they can approve of. They have conferred inestimable benefits upon those countries, by the encouragement and pecuniary support they have given to religious teachers, as well as to education. They have therefore not forfeited their inherent claim to be, within their respective governments, the sole source of legislation.

We may now advance a step further in the investigation of the subject, and show that the alleged difficulties of the Church in one special case, has been owing to an error in Colonial Legislation, to which it was itself a party. It is a common assertion that the clergy of the Church of England in the Colonies are necessarily under the arbitrary power of the Bishops, and therefore require the protection of legislative Synods. In confirmation of the assertion, reference has been generally made to the case of Tasmania, as illustrated in a mass of Parliamentary Papers (25th March, 1850, 174, 5.) A reference to these documents will show that the alleged arbitrary power of the bishop, was based upon the terms of a Colonial enactment. An Act similar to the general Act of New South Wales was passed by the Legislature of Van Diemen's Land, making the clergymen of certain churches dependent upon the bishop's licence. A bishop's licence is a vague term. In the Church of England, the licence of the bishop has a very different legal quality, according as it is a licence to a stipendiary curacy, or a licence to a perpetual curacy. In the one case, the licence may be refused by the bishop without cause assigned, and may be cancelled with an appeal only to the archbishop. In the other case, it cannot be refused or withdrawn without a cause assigned, the validity of which may be enquired into by the Civil and Ecclesiastical Courts.

The Bishop of Tasmania withdrew his licence from one of the clergy of the Colony, and refused to assign the cause. The clergyman appealed to the Supreme Court, to compel the bishop to restore the licence. The question at once arose as to the nature of the bishop's licence, and the status of the clergy; and the two judges differed widely in their opinion. It turned out at last that the clergyman had never been actually licensed, and that his Church did not come under the Act, so the Supreme Court dismissed the application.

The history shows the error of the Legislature of Van Diemen's Land in making the status of the clergyman depend upon the naked assertion of a licence from the bishop, which led the bishop to act arbitrarily. The Colonial Act should have more fully explained the nature of the licence or have required also the assent of a Church Commission, or Committee, as in the case of the recent Melbourne Act: or it might in many other ways have given protection to the clergyman, and laid restraints upon the bishop.

It is clearly the part of the Church in Tasmania to seek a remedy, by submitting to the Colonial Legislature an amended Church Act, as the Scotch

Church did when they needed a Synod in Australia. But let them also follow the example of those loyal sons of a Mother Church, who declared that their powers should cease if they should deviate from the principles of the Church at home.

Reverting to the course of proceeding which has been suggested, namely, of an Act of Parliament, authorizing the Bishop, Clergy, and laity of any Colony, to meet together and prepare Ecclesiastical regulations, to be submitted for approval to the Colonial Legislatures, and ultimately to the authorities at home: – it is conceived that such an Act would confer great and immediate advantages upon the Church in the Colonies, by enlisting the co-operation of the laity, and by giving encouragement, direction, and confidence, to the efforts of its zealous and energetic friends for perfecting its system. There will be much work of a preparative kind, before measures can be sufficiently matured for procuring legislative sanction. Plans may be tried, and improved: they may be acted upon by mutual consent, and their adaptation to the wants of the Colony may be thus tested. If they should prove satisfactory to the members of the Church generally, no Colonial Legislature could long withhold the legislative sanction required to make them effectual and permanent, after an Imperial Act has been passed in favour of this course of proceeding.

In all meetings for the regulation of Church affairs, care should be taken to secure a full and bona-fide representation of the laity. It is very desirable that the deliberations, should be conducted by the clergy and laity conjointly, though they may vote separately. The division of votes should not go beyond this. In the United Church of England and Ireland there is no precedent for giving the bishop of a diocese a separate vote, on questions in which the whole Church is interested. In the Convocation, there is a House of Bishops as well as a Lower House: but this can form no precedent for giving a veto to a single Bishop. The power of dissolving such assembly should rest with the whole body, for if given to any one party, it gives, in effect, a veto to that party. In the Episcopal Church of America, the bishop has no separate vote. The matter is thus described in a work of authority: "The right which existed in former ages of a full negative upon the act of any Diocesan Synod or Council has been by the consent of the Bishops of our Church, in almost all the Dioceses, renounced. I know but of one partial exception to this. By the constitution of Kentucky, should the Bishop express his disapprobation of any canon, regulation, or resolution, it shall be returned to the Convention for re-consideration, when a majority of two-thirds of both orders shall be necessary for its adoption. The same was the regulation in Missouri, but it is changed, as appears in the Constitution of 1847."[12]

The most pressing need in every Colony is the institution of some standing Ecclesiastical Committee or Council, for the correction or removal of clergymen who offend against law, or neglect their duties, in the place of

Ecclesiastical Courts in the Church at home. Such a Council should also have some power analogous to that of Courts at home, of inquiring into the reasons and legality of a bishop's refusal to admit a clergyman to any church to which he may have been duly appointed. It is most important that in any provision made for judicial proceedings, there should be an Assessor or Judge, skilled in law. This provision is the great safeguard of the rights and liberties of the Church of England. In all matters of evidence, as well as of interpretation of documents, a lawyer has the advantage of a professional education, which gives the best security for right decisions. The clergy may properly take the chief part in drawing up Articles of faith and formularies of devotion; but when these are once adopted by any church as the recognized standard of faith and worship, then it is the proper province of men skilled in the law to decide upon the true interpretation of those formularies, upon the general principles applied to the interpretation of all written documents.

The Church Council or Committee which may have to decide upon cases of discipline, must decide according to the Ecclesiastical laws in force in each Colony. And if, in those Colonies in which conventions of the Clergy and Laity may be empowered to make local regulations, the range of such Regulations be restricted to the two heads of the management of the temporal affairs of the Church, and the exercise of discipline over the clergy, there can be no departure from the standards of faith and worship, as established in the Articles and Formularies of the United Church of England and Ireland. All questions of interpretation also can be decided *authoritatively* only in constituted Ecclesiastical Courts, with an appeal to Her Majesty in Council. It would not, therefore, be competent in any such Church Council or by any regulations under the proposed Act, to put such authoritative interpretation upon the declared doctrines of the Church.

These observations cannot be closed without noticing a fact which must have struck all who are fully informed of the religious circumstances of the Colonies of Great Britain. There is a great variety in respect of the influence and numbers of the members of the Church in different Colonies, and in the disposition manifested by the Local Legislatures to protect and assist the interests of the Church. The advantage in these respects has been in proportion as the genuine spiritual Protestant and evangelical principles of our Church are manifested in the ministrations of the Bishops and Clergy. In such cases there is no lack of local support or encouragement, either from the community at large, or the Legislatures. But should there be presented unhappily in any Colony the predominance of Ecclesiastical assumptions, above zeal for the truth of the Gospel, and for the salvation of souls, there distrust ensues, the Church is watched with jealousy by the authorities, and local pecuniary support is withholden. It is not surprising if in such cases an outcry should be raised for independent synodical action, and for a free Episcopal Chapel in the Colonies, at the same time that there is a sincere desire to retain all titles and prestige of a State Church in England. It is earnestly hoped that the authorities at home, may never be induced to legislate upon such cases, but to adhere to the principles of constitutional law as they have been heretofore applied to Colonial Church Legislation, and to the preservation of the integrity of the United Church of England and Ireland, throughout the Colonies and Dependencies of Great Britain.

Notes

1 See Max Warren, *Social History and Christian Mission* (London: S.C.M., 1967), ch. I, "Church and State in the British Colonial Empire from Palmerston to Macmillan."

2 G/AZI/1, No. 56, March 18, 1850. West African squadron. Petition of the committee of the Church Missionary Society deprecating the diminishing or removal of the squadron.

3 CA2/L3, pp. 306-309, Oct. 23, 1863. Letter to H. S. Freeman, Esq., Governor of Lagos.

4 M.P.M., Vol. III, No. 1. An address to Colonel Sir Herbert B. Edwardes, K.C.B., Commissioner of the Cis-Sutlej States, Punjab, on occasion of his return to India. Presented on January 3, 1862.

5 CI.1/L4, Dec. 19, 1856, pp. 421-422. Extract from the letter of instructions to two missionaries proceeding to North India.

6 G/ACI/5, Oct. 3, 1846, pp. 211-212. An extract from a letter to the Hon. H. Grey.

7 G/AZI/2, Sept. 1845, No. 257, pp. 15-16. Papers relating to the education of the natives of India through the medium of the English language including government orders issued by the Rt. Hon. Sir Henry Hardinge, Governor-General of India, on the education of the natives of that country, 1844, with comments.

8 CA2/L3, pp. 432-433, Sept. 22, 1865. Extract from letter to Rev. H. Townsend in Abeokuta.

9 G/AZI/1, No. 89. Extract from Minute adopted by the Committee of Correspondence, Tuesday, Dec. 4, 1855.

10 P.M.E., No. 4. Colonial church legislation – an enquiry into the ecclesiastical law of the colonies and dependencies of Great Britain; and into the best means of remedying its defects. 1856.

11 An extensive note on pages 12, 13 and 14 is not included.

12 *Treatise on the Law of the Protestant Episcopal Church in the United States, by M. Hoffman, Esq.,* New York, 1850.

INDEX

Abbeokuta 41, 53, 160, 185, 190, 191, 192, 194, 195, 205n, 211, 217, 235n
Abyssinia 171
Acheson, Alexander 104n
Afghans 123
Africa 23, 32, 53, 60, 69, 72, 96, 126, 127, 161, 171, 183, 193, 205n, 218
Africans 11, 15, 29, 30, 32, 41, 43, 52, 54, 57, 58, 60, 61, 151, 183, 195
The African Churches among the Yoruba, 1882-1922, by James Bertin Webster 33n
African Native Agency Committee 38, 189, 205n
African Outline, by Paul Bohanan 15, 33n
The African Seminary (*see* Fourah Bay College)
The Age of Equipoise, by W. L. Burn 21, 33n
Agra 77, 163, 203
Agriculture 38, 185, 188, 189, 194-196, 197
Ajayi, J. F. A. 12, 15, 16, 23
American Baptist missionaries 68
American Board of Commissioners for Foreign Missions 11, 51
American Episcopal Church 173n, 233, 235n
American missionaries 118, 176
Amritsar (Umritsur) 123
Anderson, Bishop D. 37
Anderson, F. 203
Anderson, Rufus 7, 23, 36, 51
Annals of a Clerical Family, by John Venn 18, 33n, 48
Annual letters from missionaries 27, 38, 93, 98-103, 180
Apocrypha, The 31, 34n, 36

Arabic 200, 201
Arctic Circle 124
Armenians 68
Arrians 123
Asia Minor 68, 136
Asians 52
Associations 41, 42, 94, 122, 127, 132-134, 135
Aurangabad 123
Australia 23, 78, 155, 159, 165, 167, 173n, 221, 222, 227, 230, 233
Ayandele, E. A. 33n

Bahamas 221
Baptism 48, 52, 57, 67, 79, 80, 81
Barbadoes, Bishop of 157
Basil, St. 80
Basle Evangelical Missionary Society 39, 45, 177, 181n
Beaver, Pierce 8, 11, 82n
Bedagary (Badagry) 41, 82n
Benares (Varanasi) 203
Bengal 38, 43, 122
Bengali 171
Benin, Bight of 211
Bezwada 123
Bhagalpore (Bhagalpur) 94
Bible (Scriptures) 20, 27, 31, 39, 52, 61, 69, 71, 73, 74, 75, 80, 83n, 88, 90, 98, 100, 127, 139, 171, 205n, 218
Birmingham, St. Mary's Church 114
Blomfield, Bishop 134
Bohanan, Paul 15, 33n
Bombay 115, 123, 165, 172
Book of Common Prayer 171, 225, 226
Bornu, 204, 211
Bowen, Bishop J. 52
Brighton, St. Mary's Chapel 140n
British and Foreign Bible Society 31, 34n, 36, 113, 124, 127

237

*British and Foreign Bible Society, History
    of,* by John Owen 140n
British Guiana 135
Budd, H. 65
Bunsen, Chevalier 173n
Burmah (Burma) 68
Burn, W. L. 33n
Buxton, Thomas Fowell 23, 183, 184,
    195, 205n

Cairo 123
Calcutta 30, 45, 77, 94
Calcutta, Bishop of 18, 23, 41, 47, 90,
    136, 140n, 153-156, 164, 165,
    166, 172, 181n, 199, 215, 217
Cambridge University 13, 86, 97, 137,
    198
Canada 23, 53, 115, 124, 161, 220
Canterbury, Archbishop of 24, 28, 116,
    166, 228, 230
Cape Coast 160, 216
Cashmere 123
Catechists 64, 65, 66, 67, 68, 73, 75, 89,
    96, 115, 139, 160, 189
Cecil, R. 95, 114
Central Asia 123
Ceylon 16, 23, 40, 47, 64, 115, 123, 163,
    165, 176
Chapman, J. 137
Chichester, Lord (President of C.M.S.)
    161
China 23, 41, 46, 53, 118, 121, 124, 141n
Christian "Companies" 69, 70
Christian love 72, 86, 87, 88, 180
*Christian Missions in Nigeria, 1841-1891
    – The Making of a New Élite,* by
    J. F. A. Ajayi 12
The Christian Observer 13, 39, 41, 49, 51,
    56, 82n, 113
Church buildings 172-173
Church Establishment in Britain 20, 22,
    26, 28 (*see also* Ecclesiastical author-
    ities 143-173)
Church Missionary Intelligencer 35, 48
Church Missionary Record 18, 49
Clapham and the "Clapham Sect" 13, 18,
    32, 56, 57
Clegg, T. 193, 194, 195
Coimbra 180
Colonial bishops 150, 153, 156, 158, 165,
    166
Colonial church legislation 38, 40, 208,

    219-235
Columbus 208
Commerce 32, 48, 55, 185-186, 189-196
Commission on Clerical Subscription 48
Committees, Corresponding 39, 44, 45,
    75, 94, 95, 135-136, 140n, 202
Committee, Parent 24, 38, 39, 41, 42, 43,
    53, 62, 64, 65, 71, 73, 75, 76, 77,
    83n, 89, 90, 93, 95, 96, 98-103,
    105-141, 154, 158, 163, 164, 172,
    173n, 186, 191, 196, 212-213,
    218-219, 235n
Constantinople 123
Constitution of the Society 28, 152-158
Consecration of churches 41, 47
Cotton 32, 38, 185, 190, 191, 192, 194,
    205n
Crimean War 21
Crowther, Bishop Samuel 29, 30, 32, 34n,
    45, 65, 73, 126, 196, 201
Crowther, Samuel, Jr. 191, 193, 205n
Cumberland House (Canada) 162
Cuthbert, G. G. 104n, 205n

Deccan 123
Demerara, George Town (*see* British Gui-
    ana)
Deputations 131, 132
Derajat 123
Dewasaygan, John 65
Dissenters 17, 68, 77, 177, 225, 231
Duff, Alexander 184, 217
Droese, E. 94
Drypool 13

East Africa 40, 46, 53, 124, 139, 204
East India Company 115, 163, 172, 173n
East Indies 220, 221, 222
Ecclesiastical authorities (*see also* Episco-
    pate) 24, 28, 44, 143-173
Ecumenicity, Ecumenical Movement 30,
    31, 175-181
Education 38, 39, 41, 43, 44, 47, 91, 92,
    127, 139, 184, 196-204, 210,
    216-217, 218-219, 235n
Edwardes, Sir Herbert 39, 126, 214-215,
    235n
Efe 213
Egbas 213
Egypt 136
Elliott, Henry Venn 39, 140n
Ellore 123

The Episcopate 21, 25, 29, 143-173, 176
Episcopate, Extension of 20, 24, 25, 26,
    29, 30, 38, 39, 40, 42, 44, 46, 47,
    48, 68, 70, 86, 126, 143-173, 207
The "Euthanasia of a Mission" 11, 28, 29,
    63, 85
Evangelicals and Evangelicalism 16, 18,
    21, 22, 23, 29, 39, 119-120, 150
Evangelism 23, 65, 66, 67, 68, 69, 71,
    113, 143, 151, 166, 176, 216

Farm, Model 186
Fenn, C. C. 137
Finance 40, 41, 42, 43, 44, 45, 46, 47,
    82n, 94-97, 141n
Founders of Church Missionary Society
    47, 48, 113-114, 116
Fourah Bay College 41, 56, 57, 59, 73, 74,
    82n, 196-197, 200-201, 205n
Fox, H. W. 130-131, 137
Freeman, H. S. 235n
French, T. Valpy 205n
Fuh-Chau (Foochow) 124
Fyzabad 123

Galilee 123
da Gama, Vasco 208
Gambia 160
Gambier, Lord 57
German missionaries 23, 53, 57, 177, 205
Godavery River 123, 139
Gollmer, C. A. 191
Gorruckpore (Gorakhpur) 92, 94
The Gospel 11, 19, 22, 25, 28, 33, 51, 54,
    67, 72, 74, 85, 91, 93, 98, 100,
    101, 105, 106, 122, 123, 128, 130,
    135, 136, 149, 151, 162, 175, 177,
    184, 193, 197, 200, 234
Gough, Frederick 140n
Government 31, 38, 39, 40, 41, 42, 43,
    44, 46, 47, 55, 91, 127, 161, 166,
    194-196, 201, 202, 203, 207-235
Grant, Charles 18
Grants-in-Aid 38
Greaves, William 56, 57
Greece 136
Grey, Earl 186, 216
Grey, Sir George 213
Grimshaw of Haworth 57
Gurney, E. 194

Hancock, Mrs. 205n

Hardinge, Sir Henry 235n
Hartwig, P. 57
Hasel, J. 104n
Haslam, J. F. 137
Hausa 205n, 211
Hawes, B. 205n
Hawkins, E. 173n
Haworth 57
Hennell, Michael 33n
Hinderer, D. and Mrs. 139, 141n, 205n
Hindi 171
Hindus 45, 151, 218
History of the Church Missionary Society,
    by Eugene Stock 11, 140n
History of the British and Foreign Bible
    Society, by John Owen 114, 140n
History of the Ecumenical Movement,
    The, by Ruth Rouse and Stephen Neill
    31, 34n
Hodgson, George 128
Holloway, St. John's Church 13, 24
Holy Spirit 61, 64, 86, 88, 98, 99, 144,
    145, 146, 148, 180, 199, 201, 217
Hong Kong 26, 37, 43, 124
Hooker, Sir W. 195
Horne, Melville 54
Howley, Archbishop 134
Howse, Ernest Marshall 32, 33n, 34n
Huddersfield 57, 113
Hudson Bay Company, 161
Humanitarianism 23
Humphrey, W. J. 24

Ibo 61
India 16, 20, 23, 24, 25, 38, 39, 40, 43,
    44, 47, 48, 53, 89, 91, 92, 93, 96,
    104n, 115, 126, 127, 144, 151,
    163, 166, 173n, 176, 181n, 198,
    201, 205n, 214-215, 218-219,
    221, 235n
India, North 93, 98, 115, 121, 123, 235n
India, South 37, 45, 98, 115, 122, 123,
    139
India, West 98, 123
Indian Mutiny, 21, 39, 44, 121, 126
Industrial institutions 191, 197
Innes, J. 104n
Instructions, Letters of 27, 38, 47, 83n,
    85, 87-88, 92, 98-103, 104n, 176,
    181n, 184-185, 205n, 235n
Ireland 43, 94
Islam 123

Islington Clerical Meeting 117, 140n
Islington College 42, 73, 91-98, 188
Islington, St. Mary's Church 140n

Jamaica 40, 45, 55, 78, 83n
Japan 139
Jerusalem 123
Johnson, E. 104n
Johnson, G. and Mrs. 104n
Johnson, H. 32, 38, 189-190, 205n
Jonas, Simon 61
Jubilee, C. M. S. 37
Jubilee, Sierra Leone 45
Judaea 123
Juggernauth, Temple of 122
Junir 123

Kaffir 119, 204
Kandeish 123
Kangra 123
Karens 68
Kenya 25
Kew Gardens 190, 195
Kingston (Jamaica), Bishop of 40, 45, 83n
Kirkham, W. 205n
Knight, J. L. 137
Knight, William 11, 48
Kois 123
Krapf, J. L. 204, 205
Krishnaghar 93, 137

Lagos 30, 44, 53, 185, 191, 207, 212,
    213, 235n
Lamb, R. M. 82n, 94
Language learning 32, 37, 88, 204
Lay ministry 38, 167-171, 175
Lee, Professor 204
Leighton, Archbishop 91
Letters to missionaries 27, 86, 87, 93-97,
    139-140, 141n, 177, 181n, 185-
    186, 194, 197, 198-200, 201-205,
    205n, 217-218, 235n
Libraries 186, 188
Licensing of a missionary 153-155, 158
Livingstone, David 22, 23, 52, 53
Loan societies 186, 187
London, Bishop of 28, 97, 116, 152, 153,
    157, 166, 173n, 211, 230
London, University of 33n
Long, J. 93, 181n, 198-199, 205n
Lucknow 123
Lutherans 115, 156

Macaulay, Life of Lord, by G. O. Trevel-
    yan 32
Macaulay, Zachary 54, 55, 56, 57, 140n
Mackenzie River 124
Macleane, J. 140n
Madagascar 40, 46, 48, 68, 124
Madras 26, 37, 39, 44, 45, 165
Madras, Bishop of 24, 120, 155, 172
Mahratta 171
Malayalam 171
Malligaum 123
Malta 115
Maltese 171
Mandingo 200, 201
Mangalore 203
Manitoba, Lake 162
Mansfield, Lord 54
Marriage 79-82
Marsden, Samuel 115
Marsh, W. 82n
Martyn, Henry 137
Masulipatam 122
Mauritius 123, 124
Maynooth 177
Mayor, R. 137
McHenry, G. 140n
Meerut 94
Melbourne, Bishop of 38, 173n, 175
Melbourne, Diocese of 228, 231
Memoir of Henry Venn, by William
    Knight 11, 48
Memorial to Henry Venn 49
The Mendi (Mende) 73
Mengé, J. P. 92, 94, 104n
Methodists 42, 168-170, 175, 227, 229,
    231
Metropolitan of India (see Wilson, Daniel)
Middleton, Bishop 166
Middle East 23
Millington, Thomas 141n
Milton, John 198
Missionaries 24, 25, 26, 27, 32, 33, 39, 43,
    48, 53, 59, 61, 62, 63, 64, 65, 66,
    67, 69, 70, 71, 72, 75, 76, 78, 79,
    81, 85-104, 115, 136-140, 144
Missionaries' Children's Home 37, 42, 43
Missionaries, Itinerant 64, 66, 89
Missionaries, Station 66, 88, 89, 94
Missionary Register 35
Missionary society 25, 27, 29, 31, 39, 40,
    41, 42, 43, 47, 53, 56, 60, 61, 65,
    67, 68, 69, 70, 71, 77, 78, 90,

105-141

The Missionary Impact on Modern Nigeria, 1842-1914, by E. A. Ayandele 33n

The missionary spirit 63, 64, 71, 72, 74, 91

Mohammedans (Muslims) 45, 79, 123, 163, 192, 218

Montreal, Bishop of 162

Mooltan (Multan) 123

More, Miss Hannah 56

Moule, H. 173n

Mules, J. 140n

Muncaster, Lord 57

Murchison, Sir G. 52

Musgrave, Archdeacon 104n

Native catechists, Ordination of 65, 66, 83n

Native church, Development of 16, 25, 26, 28, 40, 42, 44, 45, 48, 60, 61, 63, 66, 69, 70, 75, 78, 85, 204

Native church fund 49, 60, 66, 68, 70, 75

Native Episcopate 25, 29, 30, 39, 68, 70, 165, 167

Native ministry (Native pastorate) 26, 28, 30, 33n, 43, 60, 62, 64, 65, 67, 70, 75, 87, 89, 96, 119, 122, 125, 136, 162, 167, 189

Native missionaries 62, 66

Native teachers 62, 63, 64, 67, 68, 69, 87, 89, 115, 138, 160, 209, 211, 218

Nazareth 123

Neill, Stephen 31, 34n

New South Wales 115, 221, 222, 230, 231, 232

Newton, John 54, 113, 114

New Zealand 23, 40, 45, 53, 63, 96, 98, 115, 121, 124, 125, 126, 127, 155, 159, 165, 171, 213

Nigeria 25, 30

Niger Mission 29, 53, 123

Niger River 29, 53, 60, 184, 211

Ningpo 121, 124

North American Indians 171

North Pacific 124

North West America (*see* Canada)

Norwich, Bishop of 37, 173n

Nova Scotia 219, 220, 222

The Orb and the Cross, by A. R. Vidler 34n

Orthography 32, 34n, 37, 88, 127, 204

Osborne, J. T. 104n

Oude 123

Owen, J. 114, 140n

Oxford 198

Oxford, Bishop of 227

Pacific 151

Pakistan 25

Palamcotta 89

Palestine 123

Palmerston 17, 41, 215

Paris, University of 180

Parliament 32, 37, 42, 163, 170, 177, 194, 201, 208-212

Paul, Saint 19, 20, 27, 31, 33, 56, 74, 100, 108, 111, 144-146, 197

Pekin 124

Pelham, J. T. (Bishop of Norwich) 37, 173n

Peshawur 123, 215

Phillimore, Dr. 222, 223

Pierson, W. J. 140n

Polygamy 46, 52, 79-82

Pope, Alexander 198

Pope John XXIII 176

Port Lokkoh (Loko) 200

Porto Novo 213

Pratt, J. 37, 107-117

Prayer, 31, 46, 69, 71, 86, 87, 88, 93, 96, 97, 99, 102, 103, 122, 127, 131, 152, 176, 177, 218

Primrose, Miss 173n

Prince Rupert's Land 26, 37, 42

Printing, Printing press 57, 191

Protestants 23, 53, 90, 162, 176, 177, 180, 181n

Providence, Providential circumstances 41, 51, 54, 82n, 87, 90, 94, 95, 97, 106, 118

Provident societies 187

Punjab 20, 39, 127, 176, 181n, 215, 235n

Queens' College, Cambridge 13, 31, 97

Quiah 196

Ragland, T. G. 36, 64, 137

Recruits 24, 44, 138-140, 141n

Red River 124, 162

The "Regions Beyond" 22, 29, 60, 62, 85

Remains (Cecil, R.) 95

Renner, M. 57

Reuther, C. F. 94
Ritual Commission 48
Robbin, H. 191, 205n
Rocky Mountains 124
Romaine, William 113
The Roman Catholic Church 47, 129, 176
Roman Catholic Emancipation 175
Roman Catholics 162, 218
Rouse, Ruth 31, 34n
Russell, Lord John 160

Saint Ann's, Blackfriars 54
Saint Helena, 196
Saint Marylebone, Parish church of 173n
Saints in Politics – the "Clapham Sect"
    and the Growth of Freedom, by E. M.
    Howse 32, 33n, 34n
Salisbury, Diocese of 132-134
Salisbury Square 30, 129
Sandys, T. 198
Santals 123
Savings bank 186, 187
Schön, J. F. 60, 61, 205n
Scotland, Established Church of 222,
    225, 229, 231, 232-233
Scott, Thomas 114, 119
Sechuana 204
Secretariat of C.M.S. 38, 93, 130-131,
    140n
"Secularity" 105-106, 130
Self-extending church 26, 45, 51, 52, 64,
    67, 71, 74, 75, 76, 77, 118
Self-governing church 25, 26, 45, 51, 52,
    67, 68, 71, 74, 75, 118
Self-supporting church 26, 41, 43, 45, 51,
    52, 60, 64, 67, 71, 74, 75, 95, 118,
    122, 124, 125
Serious Call to a Devout and Holy Life, by
    William Law 17
Shaftesbury, Lord 22
Sharp, Granville 53, 54
The Sherbro 196
Shorting, Charles 128
Sierra Leone 25, 26, 32, 40, 41, 43, 45,
    52, 53, 54, 55, 56, 59, 60, 71-74,
    82n, 83n, 96, 115, 121, 123, 124
    125, 160, 173n, 186, 187, 189,
    190, 194, 196, 208-212, 230
Simeon, Charles 86, 114
Singhalese 171
Slave trade 40, 46, 52, 54, 55, 60, 183,
    194, 196, 208-213

Smith, Bishop George 37, 43
Smith, Isaac 191
Smyrna 123
Society for Promoting Christianity among
    the Jews 118
Society for the Propagation of the Gospel
    42, 112, 118, 135, 164, 167
Social History and Christian Mission, by
    Max Warren 33n, 235n
Social welfare 31, 32, 184-185, 186-189,
    210
South America 193
Squires 137
Stanley, Lord 39, 177
Stock, Eugene 11, 140n
Syra 123
Syria 176

Tamil 64, 171
Tasmania 221-222, 232
Telegu 123, 171
Thomas, J. 126
Thornton, Henry 18, 54, 56, 57
Timneh (Temne) 73
Tinnevelly 64, 120, 123, 125, 126
To Advance the Gospel, by Rufus Ander-
    son, edited by Pierce Beaver 11
Townsend, H. 191, 205n, 235n
The Tractarian Movement 21, 22
Travancore 123, 155
Trevelyan, G. O. 32
Tucker, J. 137
Turkey 123

Uganda 25
Umritsur (Amritsar) 123
Uniformity, Act of 1662 175, 225, 226
Union schemes 44, 46, 132-134
U.S.A. 23

Van Cooten, E. C. 171
Van Diemen's Land (see Tasmania)
The Vei 73
Venn, John 18, 33n, 35, 48, 57, 114
John Venn and the Clapham Sect, by
    Michael Hennell 33n
Vidler, A. R. 34n
The Voluntary Principle 24, 28, 29, 41,
    48, 105, 131-134, 140n, 143-173
Victoria (Hong Kong), Diocese of 37

Waiapu 125

Wales 225
Webster, James Bertin 33n
Weitbrecht, J. J. 36, 104n
Wesleyan Connexion (*see* Methodists)
West Africa 16, 21, 30, 48, 52, 53, 54, 60,
     78, 115, 123, 124, 160, 171, 184,
     205n, 209
West African Colonies (Henry Venn) 39,
     196, 205n
West African Native Bishopric Fund 39,
     45
West African Squadron 20, 38, 42, 185,
     208-212, 235n

West Indies 59, 78, 115, 121, 221
Whitefield, George 17, 113
Wilberforce, Archdeacon Samuel 42
Wilberforce, William 18, 22, 32, 54, 57
Wilkinson, M. 104n
Wilson, Daniel, Bishop of Calcutta
     18, 23, 37, 129, 158, 181n

Xavier, St. Francis 27, 35, 49, 85, 175,
     176, 178-181

York, Archbishop of 46, 140n
Yoruba 30, 63, 121, 123, 191, 204, 211